VALUE INVESTING *and* BEHAVIORAL FINANCE

Insights into Indian Stock Market Realities

VALUE INVESTING *and* BEHAVIORAL FINANCE

Insights into Indian Stock Market Realities

Parag Parikh
Chairman
Parag Parikh Financial Advisory Services Ltd., Mumbai

McGraw Hill Education (India) Private Limited

Published by McGraw Hill Education (India) Private Limited,
Anjana Complex, No:5/90A, Butt Road, St. Thomas Mount, Chennai – 600016,
Tamil Nadu, India.

33rd reprint 2025

ISBN-13: 978-0-07-007763-8
ISBN-10: 0-07-007763-0

34 35 36 37 38 SAU 29 28 27 26 25

Typeset at Bukprint India, Delhi 110 092, and,
Printed and bound in India at Saurabh Printers Pvt. Ltd., 67A-68, Ecotech Ext-I, Kasna, Greater Noida, Gautam Budh Nagar (U.P.), 201308

Cover Design: Kapil Gupta

Visit us at: www.mheducation.co.in
Toll free in India: **1800 103 5875**
Write to us at: support.india@mheducation.com
CIN: U80302TN2010PTC111532

To
My wife Geeta

Praise for
Value Investing and Behavioral Finance

"Emotions can get in the way of sound investing. This is a universal state of affairs that applies equally to India and America. Parikh's book will help you understand how vulnerable most investors are to psychological influences, and what they can do to protect their portfolios from the destructive effects of their own emotions. For Indian investors especially, it is a must read!"

Hersh Shefrin

Author of *Beyond Greed and Fear: Understanding Behavioral Finance and The Psychology of Investing*

"Parag Parikh has taken the best of the recent research in behavioral finance and has successfully applied its models to the Indian stock markets. I recommend this book to all Indian investors."

Sanjay Bakshi

Visiting Professor (Behavioral Finance and Business Valuation), Management Development Institute, Gurgaon

"If you are looking for stock tips to double your money in these difficult times, don't read this book. Read it if you want to create wealth in these difficult times and preserve it through the next upturn and downturn that are bound to follow. Parag distills his experience of three decades as one of India's foremost wealth managers into this book. He explains the subject like a wonderful teacher, grounding you in the basics and then helping you easily grasp concepts that some of today's wealth managers would do well to follow."

Senthil Chengalvarayan
President and Group Editorial Director,
Television 18 Business Media

"*Value Investing and Behavioral Finance* deals with the quirks of the mind, their impact on making decisions and the consequences of investment performance. Parag is spot on in urging investors to adopt a more empirically skeptical approach based on a clear understanding of one's own blind spots and biases. The insights from applied psychology in coming to terms with IPOs, index investing and spotting bubbles will save you a lot of pain and money. Every serious investor would do well to have a copy of this fine work on their bookshelves."

Sanjoy Bhattacharyya
Partner, Fortuna Capital

"Creating wealth from equity investing is not purely a number game. In fact, it is more of a mind game. Each one of us reacts to a financial situation differently. Unless an investor considers psychological angle to investing, wealth creation will always remain an illusion. This book throws light on the psychological aspects of equity investing. It is a must read for all investors."

Gaurav Mashruwala
Certified Financial Planner

"The wild gyrations of the stock market in the last 12 months have left investors with heavy losses. Many are bewildered and have lost faith in equity investments. Parag Parikh's timely book offers a pragmatic way of understanding market behavior and facilitating better investment decisions."

Ashok M. Advani
Chairman & Managing Director,
Blue Star Ltd.

"All the techniques required to play in the markets are explained by Parag Parikh. His analysis—spanning last three decades—and expert observations provide the reader with the much needed framework to help him carve his way to wealth by investing intelligently."

Harsh C. Mariwala
Chairman & Managing Director,
Marico Ltd.

"Parag Parikh delivers once again. If his first book, *Stocks to Riches* was a timely offering and a bestseller several times over, his second one, *Value Investing and Behavioral Finance* is critical. It is a guide on how to retain your cool in times of meltdown, your patience and your investments when everybody is losing all three with disastrous consequences. Parag does not claim to provide a magic bullet to shoot into the heart of the stock market. In fact, he confesses upfront that he is neither an economist nor an academician. But, what he does have is astute common sense, and three decades of experience in studying the market, money management and investor behavior. From this rare armoury, he has forged the essentials of success and failure in investing.

The result is a book that helps you understand your own motivations, which is the first step towards understanding investment, and then achieving mastery over the market. Simple without being simplistic, it tells you everything you wanted to know about managing your portfolio, but never thought you'd find someone to explain it all so clearly."

Bachi Karkaria
Consulting Editor,
The Times of India

"Parag Parikh has amply demonstrated by giving real-life situations how lack of understanding of universal principles of life and lack of self-awareness unleash greed and fear, spelling loom and doom as we are witnessing currently. His insights into behavioral finance serve as a lighthouse whose powerful beam illuminates, empowers, enlightens and guides investors to steer their equity portfolio ships safely and rationally to the shores of gains and profits. Further, this book shows that to be myopic and seek instant gratification is the sure recipe for disaster."

Sudit Parekh
Founder Partner,
Sudit K Parekh & Co.
Chartered Accountants

"Investing 101, with a focus on Indian markets."

Abhishek Dalmia
Director, Renaissance Group

"If one wishes to understand behavioral finance in investment decisions, he will need to spend considerable time and energy in doing so. This book can save a lot of time and effort, by helping one understand the multiple facets of an investor...The book is extremely informative... There are a lot of good pointers to the behavioral anomalies of investors and the crowd psychology that we would have never otherwise thought of or realized...the book is complete in the coverage of all areas of investor behavior and behavioral trends. The author's readiness to explain every aspect of the theme is also really helpful, which makes both reading and understanding easy...I will recommend it to anyone interested in the subject."

Y.M. Deosthalee
Chief Financial Officer & Member of the Board,
Larsen & Toubro Ltd.

PREFACE

Currently, book stores are flooded with books on the wisdom of investing. All of them talk about the virtues of value investing. Investors spend money and time to learn about the wisdom of investment success by reading books, attending lectures and seminars of investment gurus, joining internet chat sites, etc. Every effort is made to grasp the next best idea or the new way to achieve investment success.

However, investment success evades most of them. This is also true for professional money managers, equipped with high-flying academic qualifications and managing huge pools of money, but succumbing to investment blunders.

Is it not strange that in spite of knowing the tricks of the trade, and being smart, one yet fails? The answer is quite simple. The inability to delay gratification is the root of failure. This is one of the human traits that makes people lose patience. Investing is all about having the patience to hold on to your convictions. When you are unable to delay gratification, your greed is strong and it gets you in trouble in the financial markets.

I have studied the behavior of professional investors. When they go on their marketing trips, they talk about the virtues of value investing, long-term approach, preservation of capital, etc. However, when they are confronted with the real world of investing in the stock markets, they falter. They fail to 'walk the talk'. They fall into the *Integrity Trap*. Due to their inability to control their emotions, and the fear of being left out of the crowd, they lose their conviction and get carried away by crowd behavior. They are swayed between bouts of fear and greed leading to self-doubt.

I have applied the knowledge of investor psychology to studying investing follies. Everyone believes in capital preservation. But then why does everyone act against his/her belief? I find the books on behavioral finance theoretical. I have studied their effects in real-life situations and have explained these by taking examples of the Indian stock market and Indian companies. This, I am sure, will be a refreshing change from the usual coverage of leading MNCs like Coca Cola, IBM, Microsoft, etc. The research on Indian capital markets has been done more with a view to show the trends rather than add any academic value. I believe that knowledge is not important as it changes continuously, but what are important are the trends. We have collected data on the BSE Sensex from 1979 and there might be flaws in some of our calculations. There have been quite a lot of corporate events like mergers, acquisitions, de-listings, rights offers, split stocks and dividends, some of which could, perhaps, have escaped attention. Moreover, we had difficulties in sourcing data of the initial years from a single source and collected it from various sources. This could, in some way, affect our calculations; but definitely it will, in no way, affect the strength of our argument.

The book was completed in May 2008; hence all the data pertains to the period prior to May 2008. Moreover, a present and past tense disconnect may appear as the book was written over a period of two years. I am trying to convince the readers about where the returns and the opportunities lie in this chaotic investment world.

This book is all about identifying a good business managed by good people, paying the right price for the stock and having the patience to hold on to such investments for a long period of time. I have shown such investing and behavioral trends that affect investor decision-making and ultimately investor returns.

We understand the law of physics—for every action there is an equal and opposite reaction. However, this does not happen in the markets. From 2005 to 2007 the price per barrel of oil moved up from $40 to $100. It was not a good news. However, during the same period BSE Sensex moved up from around 6000 to 20000. And in 2008 the price of oil moved up by 30% to $130 and during the same time period BSE

Sensex came down from 21000 in January 2008 to less than 15000. What explains this behavior?

Stock markets are not a zero-sum game. Wealth is not transferred, it just goes up or down. Even if you do not do anything, your wealth fluctuates according to the ups and downs in stocks. Your inaction can also result in a reaction. Stock market behavior is not in tandem with rational human thinking.

This brings us to the fundamental question: why are stock markets difficult to understand? As we know, the shareholders of a company are the owners and have the authority to demand performance from the managers appointed to run the company. However, they don't act responsibly towards the well-being of the company they own. At the slightest hint of bad news they want to sell the shares they own. Can owners really behave against the interest of the assets they own? In stock markets the ownership relation is different. When a stock is listed, ownership changes within seconds as investors are allowed to enter and exit within seconds. Stock markets are made up of such transient investors who play havoc with stock prices. In the absence of any loyalty by the owners towards their companies, it is imperative that we understand them through their weaknesses which come in the form of pursuit of instant gratification, greed, fear, integrity gap, social mask, etc.

In my earlier book *Stocks to Riches: Insights on Investor Behaviour* (2005), I had predicted that I was writing it at the start of the biggest boom in the history of the Indian stock markets. The worst period for the stock markets seemed to have ended mid-2003 with dividend yield on stocks touching between 5 to 8%. Some good stocks were available at a price to book of one or less than one. The valuations were attractive, there was renewed optimism and the sentiment was bullish. There was good corporate news of rising profits. Lower interest rates were fueling the consumer boom. Cheap money was adding to the stock and the real estate boom. All the available information on the markets, companies, and economy was extremely positive. The foreign institutional investors had started showing interest in the markets and were pouring money into the Indian markets. It was no rocket science that my prediction came true. However, during the last year, I noticed that something was wrong. The seeds of excesses were being sown. Investors, politicians, academicians, market pundits, investment bankers, stock brokers, analysts, company managements, foreign institutional investors, mutual fund managers—all were overly optimistic. There was a strong belief that the market could go only one way and that was upwards. Making money in the market seemed so simple that people started believing that the only way to make money was to invest in stocks. One very disturbing trend was that we had asset inflation in the form of stocks, real estate and commodities going up but the consumer price index or inflation was under control. This was strange. I am not of the opinion that the India's growth story is over but the way the markets were discounting the future was a matter of concern. The stocks were going up too fast and a correction was due. In fact, in the second chapter, "Understanding Behavioral Trends", we have presented an interesting study, "Making Sense out of the Sensex". It is clear that the rise of Indian markets even in 2007 and early 2008 when the Sensex touched 21000 was backed by strong fundamentals. Although the element of speculation did play a role it was nowhere comparable to the hollow 1991–92 boom. In 1991–92 the total return on the sensex was 37.7% of which 6.6% was fundamental return and the remaining 31.1% was speculative return. However, in 2007–2008, the total return was 48.2% which comprised of 22.2% fundamental and 26% speculative. A correction was in the offing and it did happen. I have tried to explain the excesses of a bull market and the different types of behavioral biases and traits which prohibit people from thinking and acting rationally. If one is vigilant and has common sense, one can not only avoid the pitfalls but also see the opportunities all the way.

My firm, Parag Parikh Financial Advisory Services Ltd, has been doing extensive research in the field of behavioral finance. In fact, we apply these concepts in our investment decisions for stock broking activities, portfolio management services and advisory services. In fact, this has been one of our most distinguishing features. I am sure the findings of our research team will help one to be a wise and emotionally self-restrained investor.

I am neither an economist nor an academician. I am an investor first. I run a stock broking and a portfolio management firm as a profession rather than a business. This gives me the courage and excitement to do what is right rather than do the right thing. I am a keen learner and believe that learning is a never-ending process. My knowledge comes from my passion for the subject of investing and my extensive study of the works of scholars in various fields of investment, money management and behavioral finance. These include great thinkers and scholars like Amos Tversky, Daniel Kahneman, Richard Thaler, Hersh Shefrin, Robert Shiller, Benjamin Graham, Warren Buffett, Charlie Munger, Christopher Browne, Stephen Covey, Gustave le Bon, Max Bazzerman, Gary Belsky, Jeremy Siegel, David Dreman, Michael Mauboussin and Nassim Taleb, to name just a few, some of whom I have had the good fortune to interact with.

The vast potential of the subject of behavioral finance dawned on me when in 2006, I attended a course on Behavioral Corporate Finance by Hersh Shefrin at the Amsterdam Institute of Finance. Not only the lay investors but also the big organizations are prone to behavioral biases especially when subjected to the pulls and pressures of the stock markets.

Gathering knowledge from these great thinkers, I have developed my unique perspective on the activities in the Indian stock markets. Here is a brief summary of the chapters.

1 SUCCESS AND FAILURE

Listening to various emotionally and spiritually charged speeches on personal growth is my habit. The other day I happened to listen to Brian Tracy's collection on "The Psychology of Achievement". Our destiny is in our hands. If we understand the universal principles of life and live by them not only do we become successful but also realize our wildest dreams. Our success in life depends on our self-awareness. The more we understand ourselves the more we are able to achieve personal growth. All the problems in life and with money start due to the basic human tendency for instant gratification. This again is very true of the stock markets. I found the learning so appropriate that I decided to include the same in the first chapter as it lays the basis for preparing the reader to better understand the concept of behavioral finance.

2 UNDERSTANDING BEHAVIORAL TRENDS

Equities are considered inherently riskier than investments in bonds. What makes equity investing risky? Is it because of the inconsistent performance of businesses behind the stocks or is it because of the behavior of the market participants, who as a result of greed and fear get excessively optimistic and pessimistic about the future resulting in bull and bear phases? In this chapter we have tried to answer these questions using a conclusive study done on Sensex which highlights that it is not the inconsistent performance of companies constituting Sensex but the follies of crowd behavior which make investing risky. Understanding the behavior of stock market participants is central to designing a successful investment strategy. It would be fit to mention Daniel Kahneman and Amos Tversky, the proponents of the Prospect Theory and the winners of Nobel prize for their research in behavioral finance. Their work has been of immense help to me.

3 BEHAVIORAL OBSTACLES TO VALUE INVESTING

In 2001, I attended a course, "Investment Decisions and Behavioral Finance", at the Kennedy School of Government at the Harvard Business School. I was impressed by a talk by Christopher Browne on value investing and behavioral finance. Again, his speech on the same at the Columbia Business School on 15 November 2000 was an eye opener for me. This instilled in me the courage to expand my knowledge in this burgeoning field. I was excited by the opportunities the markets would offer if one was able to control one's emotions. Which investment style has historically outperformed other styles? What are the traits that distinguish successful investors from others? What role does emotional discipline play in successfully implementing an investment strategy? What are the behavioral traits that act as impediments in achieving investing success? These are the questions that have been answered in this chapter. Just as it helps to understand the rules of any game to become victorious, it helps to understand the characteristic traits that make a successful investor. Drawing upon the wisdom of Christopher Browne on value investing and behavioral finance I have tried to explain the obstacles faced by value investors.

4 CONTRARIAN INVESTING

Homo sapiens have evolved in groups. As a consequence, sticking our necks out and taking a solitary view of things does not come naturally to us. However, bargain issues are a result of negative perception of a stock or a sector and the ability to take a stand that runs contrary to that held by the crowd is an indispensable tool for any investor. One must have the courage to stand by one's conviction irrespective of the noise around. In this chapter, the impediments faced by human beings in developing contrarian thinking are discussed in detail. The results that can be expected from following a contrarian approach are also highlighted using a study titled "Conventional and Contrarian Portfolio" which shows the superior results expected from a contrarian investor. The writings of the renowned contrarian investors, David Dreman, and Michael Mauboussin, have been central to developing my understanding of contrarian investing in this chapter.

5 GROWTH TRAP

In 1949, Benjamin Graham, the dean of value investors, observed in his work "*Intelligent Investor*" that the obvious prospects of growth do not necessarily translate into obvious profits for investors. In this chapter, using an extensive study covering the stock performance from 1979 to 2005, we highlight that growth trap, i.e., the act of chasing growth stcoks, results in sub-optimal returns. The lessons from the study hold special significance in achieving success as an investor in the long run. My inspiration of working on this chapter came from reading the book titled *Future for Investors* by Professor Jeremy Siegel. He has brought out the concept of the growth trap with examples of the companies in the United States. I have applied the same knowledge to support the growth trap theory with examples of Indian companies.

6 COMMODITY INVESTING

Investing can be defined as the act of acquiring a company, which is run by capable managers, enjoys a competitive advantage in its area of operation, has favorable prospects, and more importantly, is available at an attractive price. Under that definition, commodity stocks would not qualify as potential candidates for investment. However, the equation changes when stock prices are excessively beaten down and the prospects of revival in the underlying commodity can be reasonably expected. In this case, what is the right way to go about investing in commodity manufacturing companies? This is the question that is the subject matter of this chapter. Our studies support a counter-intuitive method that seems to work better than the conventional approach used by the vast majority of investors. I owe many thanks to Benjamin Graham for it was his discussion on this topic in *Security Analysis* that helped me broaden my perspective on this topic.

7 PUBLIC SECTOR UNITS

Can Public Sector Units have the autonomy to look after the interests of all stakeholders and create value for shareholders? Should an equity investor look for potential bargains in this space or should he overlook this area? What lessons does the historical performance of PSUs since the liberalization in 1991 hold? In this chapter, these are the questions that have been answered. In this age of globalization it is assumed that government-controlled corporations would cease to exist in a competitive environment. But, India has shown that it is not the case. The public sector units, which were the product of a controlled economy, have been able to thrive in the liberalized environment with considerable success, thanks to the resilience and hard-working nature of the Indian work force. The slow pace of reforms with a human face has enabled the PSUs to meet the challenges of the competitive market. It's only up to the politicians to allow them to bloom and grow. How have their investors fared? What behavioral anomalies played a role in throwing up opportunities? Those who followed the contrarian approach and thought long term have done exceedingly well.

8 SECTOR INVESTING

A common strategy employed by a vast majority of investment professionals is to choose a sector, whose market perception is favorable, and pick up the leading players from that sector as potential bargain stocks. Though the strategy seems deceptively simple, the fact that everybody follows the same strategy and the expectations of their growth are discounted in the stock prices makes this approach questionable. In this chapter, the performance of major sectoral indices since their constitution is studied. Human behavior plays an important part in a sector being a fancy or it being ignored. Sector bubbles are formed when the investors get very excited about the fortunes of a sector due to the change in the economic conditions and government policies. A study of the sectors in the Indian market in the last decade throws light on irrational investor expectations which give rise to sector bubbles. It is during such bubbles that managements cash in on by bringing IPOs in the market at ridiculous valuations. Investor greed becomes their graveyard when the sector fancy recedes. The last five years make an interesting study on such sectors. It's like a game of musical chairs. Sector fancy changes with the changes in investor sentiments.

9 INITIAL PUBLIC OFFERINGS

Initial Public Offerings (IPOs) help corporations approach potential investors for capital to fund their expansion plans. However, for an investor, does it make sense to subscribe to the deluge of offerings, which come up during bull markets? Is the promoter whose stake is to be diluted likely to offer the new shares at a discount? What kind of role do the investment bankers, who undertake the book building process, play in the IPO process? What has been the historical performance of IPOs during the last two decades? And what important lessons do they hold for investors? How investor greed is exploited? In this chapter, these are the questions that have been answered and their understanding is critical. IPO investing is not for a value or a contrarian investor. Values are found in bear markets and IPOs are a product of bull markets. IPOs and the craze for them among investors reinforce the fact that greed plays a dominant role in the markets. The company coming out with an IPO appoints an investment banker to sell the issue at the highest possible price. It pays a fee to the investment banker. Investors apply for IPOs based on the information and research provided by the investor bankers. We have created financial markets where such insanity works.

10 INDEX INVESTING

What is Index Investing? What are Index Funds? What are the characteristics that guarantee a place in the Index? Why are Index funds popular? Do these characteristics make sense from the perspective of an investor? Is the rationale for replacing index stocks with reference to their market capitalization correct? Does the advantage of low cost override the superiority of carefully applied investment strategy? How have the stocks that have been removed from the Index to be replaced by upcoming companies performed? What is de-indexing? These are the questions that have been addressed in this chapter. Research on the Indian indices highlights some important drawbacks of passive investing. It may be the most popular thing to do, but definitely it is not the right thing to do, thanks to PPFAS research for the research inputs.

11 BUBBLE TRAP

My previous book *Stocks to Riches: Insight on Investor Behaviour* had a chapter devoted to how a bubble was formed and ultimately how it would burst and how investor sentiments and behavior was responsible for the same. In this book I have applied the knowledge to the Indian stock markets to identify bubbles which were about to burst.

Crowd psychology, when subject to excessive fear and greed result in bull and bear phases from time to time. The transition from one phase to another is not a smooth one, but one which happens all too suddenly resulting in investors feeling helpless. An understanding of how favorable times result in getting herds of investors getting attracted to the equity markets help to take stocks to dizzy valuations. Excesses are thus committed, leading to mass folly, which eventually leads to bubbles. As a bystander it is easy to spot a bubble and if one understands how it is formed one can not only avoid getting trapped but can also benefit from it. A study on the various bubble formations in the Indian markets would add to the investor understanding of the vagaries of the markets. This chapter is a tribute to Gustave Le Bonn, for his excellent insights into the crowd behavior in his book *The Crowd* and Charles Mackay for his *Extraordinary Popular Delusions*. Both these books have numerous lessons for any thoughtful investor and can help one save a fortune by not getting influenced by the crowd psychology.

12 INVESTOR BEHAVIOR BASED FINANCE

In 2002, I came across an article in the Harvard Business Review titled "Taking the Mystery out of Investor Behavior" by Kevin P Coyne and Jonathan W Witter. This made me ask: "investors do research on companies but do companies research their investors?" This laid the basis for an interesting concept to be developed. Being in the stock broking profession it was my duty to understand my clients who happened to be fund managers with mutual funds or financial institutions. PPFAS research team started studying investor behavior and set in motion a new service offering "Investor Behavior Based Finance" for corporate clients. This chapter explains how important for a corporate client it is to study investor behavior. These same investors happen to be its owners but, being transient investors their behavior is guided by greed and fear. They behave more like mercenaries on a mission to make money. Investor behavior based finance is an idea whose time has come. Some may question its viability, as it is a difficult thing to do. My answer is simple: it is as simple or as difficult as trying to understand employee or customer behavior. There exist huge industries in the form of consumer market research, human relations development and placement agencies doing the same. I am sure the readers will get new insights from the chapter.

Currently, the world economy is going through tough times. The stock markets have had a very good bull phase starting in 2003. However, now the oil prices and inflation are the biggest challenges facing the world. People have been accustomed to making easy money from the stock markets. The challenge ahead is to have the courage to be a value investor and, of course with it, the patience to hold on to investments. This calls for not only a strong mind but a strong heart to enable one not to be swayed away by emotions. They will be much stronger with the turbulent times ahead. Self-belief and conviction will sail you through. Bull and bear markets always follow each other. It's your ability to always keep learning that will help you.

PARAG PARIKH

ACKNOWLEDGEMENTS

This book has been conceived and shaped with the contribution of many people. I would like to acknowledge the various roles they have played in my life and in shaping the book:

- Arpit Ranka, research analyst in the field of value investing at Parag Parikh Financial Advisory Services Ltd. He has devoted more wee hours to this book sniffing through the vast databases of numbers and events than he cares to remember. It was his passion and toils that enabled me to offer interesting insights in this work.
- My late father Shirish Parikh who gave me the wisdom of following the common sensical approaches to investing.
- Dr. Shantanu Nagarkatti who gave me the foresight to pursue learning in the upcoming field of behavioral finance a decade back.
- Mr. Chandrakant Sampat who taught me how to distinguish right from the wrong and ingrained the principles of value investing in me in the beginning of my career in the stock markets.
- Rajeev Thakkar, a special person who played a special role in providing both intellectual and emotional support for this task.
- R. Chandra Sekhar of McGraw-Hill Education (India) who gave me the encouragement and confidence to venture into the challenging field of writing.
- The publishing team at McGraw-Hill Education (India) for its support and encouragement.
- The extraordinary team of PPFAS led by Rajeev Thakkar, which was always by my side, offering a helping hand during the various stages of the writing of the book.

- Nirjhar Handa and Melwin Mehta for their valuable professional contribution and their efforts and time spent in going through the first draft and coming up with useful suggestions and insights.
- My assistant Hiroo Thadani for her administrative support and managing heaps of data that would lie cluttered on the desk.
- The Bombay Stock Exchange Library, CMIE, Economic Times Intelligence Unit, Bloomberg and PPFAS research for providing valuable data.
- My mother Tarunika, wife Geeta, sons Neil and Sahil and daughter-in-law Sitanshi who together have been an enduring source of light, learning, joy, inspiration and unfailing support in all stages of the project.
- To various people who have, in some way or the other, helped me in my endeavor to write this book. It is not possible to name all of them, but I am indebted to them for their contribution.

And above all, I thank the Almighty without whose will and blessings nothing can happen. I thank him for having chosen me for this project.

Parag Parikh

CONTENTS

ONE

1

SUCCESS AND FAILURE

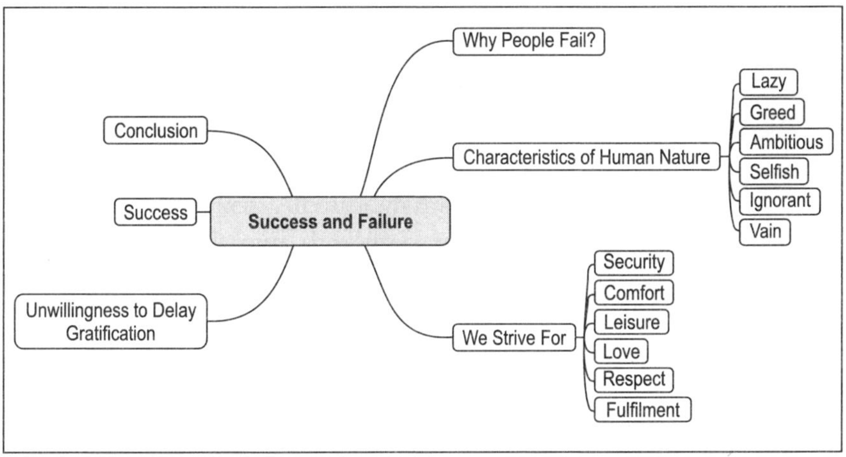

1.1 Why People Fail

1.2 Characteristics of Human Nature

1.3 We Strive For

1.4 Unwillingness to Delay Gratification

1.5 Success

1.6 Conclusion

1.1 WHY PEOPLE FAIL

Why people fail? This was the subject of an interesting talk by Brian Tracy, one of the best motivational speakers. I would like to share with you his understanding of human nature, which sets the basis for this book, blending value investing and behavioral finance.

Why is it that so many people fail in life? There is so much more information available today on how to be successful than ever before. Self-improvement books are amongst the best sellers in bookstores, millions have read them but the vast majority of people live their lives far below their potential, achieving far less than their capacities permit.

Failure is as predictable as success because it is the strength of character, which separates the winner from the loser.

Economists say that the inability to delay gratification is the primary reason for economic failure in life. People fail because in life they do what is fun and easy rather than what is hard and necessary. They do what is tension-relieving rather than goal-achieving.

Failure is as predictable as success because it is the strength of character, which separates the winner from the loser.

Success and failure are more the results of habit. Ninety percent of what we do is dictated by habits. We eat the same food, work in the same way, associate with the same people, and act the same way when things happen to us over and over. When a habit is formed, we become comfortable with it, and then we strive to remain consistent with what is familiar, even if our habits are leading to failure.

We are always striving to be consistent with what we have done and said in the past. Thus, we resist change of any kind. Psychologists call this tendency to become comfortable as getting into the comfort zone. Even if this comfort zone is keeping us at a low level of performance, we prefer to stay in it rather than change.

Sow a thought and you reap an act, sow an act and you reap a habit, sow a habit and you reap a character, sow a character and you reap a destiny. All changes in our life starts with changing our thoughts and actions so that we form habits that sow the seeds of our success and make those habits our masters.

All understanding of human nature begins with understanding the way we are, and it begins with an honest understanding of ourselves. The key is self-knowledge and self-awareness.

1.2 CHARACTERISTICS OF HUMAN NATURE

Let us look at some of the characteristics of human nature based on our study of human action. Study of human action is the study of what people do, what people say or what people intend. It simply studies their actions, and it is only in studying the actions of people that we see what it is that they see or think or mean or intend.

1.2.1 Laziness

When we first study human action, we find that all human beings value leisure. We like to take it easy, and so we are always trying to shorten the time needed to perform any task. We always seek the easiest way to do anything. In fact, we are structured mentally in such a way that we cannot consciously choose a more difficult way to accomplish something if we can choose an easier way. Given a choice between an easier way and a harder way, we will always choose the easier option because the sooner we get the job done the sooner we can enjoy.

> **The inability to delay gratification is the primary reason for economic failure in life.**

So, in a sense we are all lazy. This is neither good nor bad. It is only what we do as a result of this laziness that is good or bad. All human progress comes from people seeking faster and easier ways to get the things we want. Thus, in certain sense, laziness is a motivator of human progress.

1.2.2 Greedy

The second characteristic of human nature is that we each try to get the very most with the very least expenditure of money or effort. Given a choice between more or less, we strive to maximize what we get. If we are offered a choice to work for Rs.500 an hour or Rs.700 an hour, we will choose the Rs.700 an hour option. When offered a choice between a large piece of cake or a smaller one at the same price, we will choose for the larger one. The study of the economics of all human actions, and the study of economics itself is the study of allocation of resources to get the greatest possible output per unit of input. This is rational, sensible and appropriate human behavior.

In this sense, we are all greedy. This is again neither good nor bad. We are greedy, we are never satisfied, and we are continuously striving for more and more. We are never ever really contented.

1.2.3 Ambition

> **Sow a thought and you reap an act, sow an act and you reap a habit, sow a habit and you reap a character, sow a character and you reap a destiny.**

Each of us is always striving to improve the quality of our lives. All human actions are motivated by a desire for improvement in our condition. In fact, we cannot consciously act to worsen our situation. Even a person who jumps off a building to commit suicide believes that he would be better off by putting an end to his life than by being alive. We may not always succeed, but every action that we take is an attempt to be better off than we would be without the action.

In this sense then, every human being is ambitious. We may be ambitious for different things or may have more or less opportunities to realize our ambitions but, we are all ambitious.

1.2.4 Self-Interest

The fourth characteristic is that each person thinks, feels, acts and experiences happiness or sorrow, by and for himself/herself. Therefore, we primarily act from our point of view.

In other words, we are all selfish, centered on ourselves living inside out. Everything we do, even acts of charity, we do because in our personal opinion at that moment it is the best thing for us. Selfishness and self-centeredness render us with a sense of survival.

1.2.5 Ignorance

Our fifth characteristic is that we all act on the basis of incomplete information because no one in the world can possibly know everything there is to know about one subject.

In this sense, we are all ignorant. No matter how much we learn we must still act with some uncertainty. Some ignorance of the facts often with great ignorance or sometimes with complete ignorance.

1.2.6 Vanity

Lastly, as human beings we have an ego. We always think very highly of ourselves. We consider ourselves superior to others in many ways in terms of intelligence, personality, appearance, wealth and so on.

In other words, we are all vain. This is neither good nor bad, it's just human nature. The cosmetic industry, the fashion industry, and the furnishing industry all appeal to our vanity and certainly not to our basic needs.

1.3 WE STRIVE FOR

So, we have a basic human nature that, by definition, causes many of us to be lazy, greedy, ambitious, selfish, ignorant and vain. And, we know that giving in to the worst side of this nature is the reason for so much unhappiness in the world. It's no wonder that there are so many problems in the world where we have over six billion lazy, greedy, ambitious, selfish, ignorant and vain people running around trying to make a living. And now these same people also want the same things in the following order of priority but with different degrees of intensity: security, comfort, leisure, love, respect, and fulfilment.

1.3.1 Security

Security is our basic need. The survival instinct. Security of life and health. Physical security, economic security, emotional security etc. We value security very highly. Any threat to our security in any area brings forth our instinct to protect and defend. Lack of security makes us angry, fearful and defensive.

1.3.2 Comfort

The second thing we want after we have achieved our security is comfort, especially physical comfort. We pay an enormous amount and work very hard to gain the comforts that we desire.

1.3.3 Leisure

After security and comfort, the third thing we want is to relax and take time off work. We need leisure. Leisure is a valued good and we work very hard and pay duly for it. Our holidays are leisure, Golf is leisure, and theatre is leisure. Leisure activities in our society consume hundreds of crores of rupees. This is due to the fact that, by definition, we are all lazy, and we all like leisure, and are prepared to pay very highly for it.

1.3.4 Love

The fourth in priority is love. We seek the affection and the love of others. This is something we desire so intently that we will even die for it. Each of us needs to be loved to feel fully human, and we strive for love all our lives.

1.3.5 Respect

The fifth thing that we all seek is respect. We need to be recognized and respected by others outside our family group. Because we are basically vain, we seek the praise and appreciation of other people. We will make great efforts to earn and keep the goodwill and respect of others.

1.3.6 Fulfillment

And finally, the sixth thing that we want is fulfillment. Each of us has a deep craving for meaning and purpose in life. This is the deepest of all subconscious cravings. We want to feel that we are fulfilling our potential and becoming everything that we are capable of becoming.

1.4 UNWILLINGNESS TO DELAY GRATIFICATION

So, the human race is made up of people—you and I— who are basically lazy, greedy, ambitious, selfish, ignorant and vain. All of them are striving for the same things: security, comfort, leisure, love, respect and fulfillment.

And here is the key point. The basic law of human nature is that people always tend to seek the fastest and the easiest way to get the things they want. And usually to get the things they want right now.

Brian Tracy calls this the "Expediency Factor" or the "E" factor, which explains why people succeed and why they fail.

Why do families, corporations, organizations, businesses and individuals and even nations succeed and fail? Because of their unwillingness to delay gratification, the vast majority of people act immediately to get the things they want at that moment. The fastest and the easiest way. Even if the long term consequences of the actions will be under-achievement and failure.

The following are a few examples of people going for short-term gain and ending up with long-term pain.

1. Students cram a month before the exams. They pass the exams, but have they learnt anything? Long-term career suffers.
2. A young man drops out of college, takes a job to buy a car to impress the girls. That's the expedient thing to do. The long-term price is a lifetime of low-paying jobs. Short-term gain for long-term pain.
3. Labor unions strike for higher than market wages at the long-term price of permanently crippling the industry and causing permanent unemployment. A perfect example is the textile strike in Mumbai which has closed the mills and rendered millions unemployed.
4. Another example is that of criminals. They engage in robberies, burglaries and theft to get immediate funds at the price of a ruined life and social stigma in society.
5. Politicians dole out largesse to gain votes and popularity, especially before the approaching elections. They achieve short-term gain at the cost of long-term consequences for the country. The farmer loan waiver scheme is an example.
6. Employees do only what is expected out of the pay checks they receive. They only do what they have to do. The other time is spent on socializing and leisure. No effort is made to learn new skills or make themselves more beneficial to the organizations they work for. The long-term price is failure in life.
7. Men and women everywhere do what is fun and easy rather than what is hard and necessary at the long-term price of never fulfilling their unique potential.

The pull of the "E" factor is very strong. It causes the vast majority of men and women to indulge themselves at whim, to ignore the secondary long-term consequences of their actions, and by refusing to delay gratification, to engage in short-term gain for long-term pain, they condemn themselves to lives of frustration and disappointment.

The "E" factor explains most of the failures in our lives. Only those rare few men and women—less than five percent in each generation—who consciously master them and resist the gravitational pull of the "E" factor ever really succeed in the long run.

1.5 SUCCESS

The one human quality that must be developed for success is self-discipline—the will-power to force yourself to do what you know you should do, when you should do it, whether you like it or not, whether you feel like it or not.

> **Investing is simple, but the industry has made it complicated. In its quest for instant gratification, it has woven a web of complexity to confuse the investor.**

Napoleon Hill, the author of *Think and Grow Rich*, after a lifetime of studying some of the most successful men and women, came to the conclusion that the ability to exert self-discipline on oneself is the key to riches.

Successful people are simply those who make a habit of doing what unsuccessful people don't like to do. And what are the things that unsuccessful people don't like to do? They are the same things that successful people do not like to do. But, successful people do them because they know that these are the price of success.

Every act of self-discipline strengthens the habit of self-discipline, just as every act of expediency or instant gratification strengthens the tendency to act expediently. It has been proven that hard work, persistence and focus on clear specific goals are the keys to success.

The strength of character you have is in direct proportion to your ability to resist expediency. In fact, the strength of character is simply the ability to resist acting in a lazy, greedy, ambitious, selfish, ignorant and vain way.

The key to success in life is to resolve to do what you know you should do, what other successful self-disciplined people do, and to do it when you should do it, whether you feel like it or not.

True self-esteem, the foundational quality of your success, comes from mastering yourself, resisting the temptation to take the fastest and the easiest way, and sticking to what you know to be right until you win through.

This is the psychology, the mindset of success. Self-esteem requires self-discipline and self-discipline builds self-esteem.

1.6 CONCLUSION

There are certain universal principles that do not change irrespective of the circumstances, technological changes, geographical boundaries, demographic changes, etc. One such universal principle is the "Law of the Farm". You cannot sow a seed today and reap tomorrow. It takes time for the seed to grow into a tree. It has to go through different seasons. There is no way that we can have an instant tree growing. Nature does not help us with instant gratification.

If our life is tuned with nature, it is but natural that we follow the laws of nature. Success in our life comes with our ability to understand that there are no short-cuts in life. If one goes for such short-cuts, one is bound to fail.

So is the case with investments. You just cannot hope to make a fast buck through investing. Today, most people are trying to invest in the hope of making fortunes.

Look at the successful investors around you. They are successful because they could delay gratification and understood the law of the farm. Successful investors like Warren Buffett, Charlie Munger, Peter Lynch, to name a few, owe their success to their ability to avoid the pull of the "E" Factor.

This understanding of human nature forms the basis for the different facets of this book and will help the investor to understand the simplicity of investing. Investing is simple, but the industry has made it complicated. In its quest for instant gratification, it has woven a web of complexity to confuse the investor; the same person on whom the industry is dependant for its livelihood.

We human beings are more concerned about concentrating on improving our intellect, and hence, concentrate on developing the Intelligence Quotient (IQ). However, the most important balancing mechanism in us is the Emotional Quotient (EQ). We are human beings having a mind as well as a heart. The mind controls our intellect and the heart controls our emotions. A proper understanding and the balance of the two lead to a successful life and lead us to a more fruitful, happy existence.

Daniel Goleman in his book "*Emotional Intelligence*" brings out this concept of Emotional Quotient (EQ) very convincingly.

Parents want their kids to study in the best possible schools. The motive behind such action is the belief that the surroundings, classmates and teachers would help their kids realize their true potential, which in turn would help the kid to achieve great success when he grows up. The potential is often measured as scoring high on tests and recording high intelligent quotients (IQs). But many a times, we fail to understand if IQ alone guarantees success or is there something else. Just take a look around you and you will notice that there are numerous people who are not really smart but are doing very well in terms achieving financial well-being and, more importantly, in achieving happiness as well. On the other hand, there are also numerous people who in spite of being brilliant in terms of IQ pan out low in the race of life, end up getting stuck up on the corporate ladder and fail to achieve a constant dose of happiness and contentment. This anomaly is better understood by understanding what scientists call 'EQ'.

What is Emotional Quotient? Just as IQ is used to define the competence in terms of cognitive abilities, EQ relates to the mental composure of a person. A person who has the ability to think clearly through the hurdles faced in life and accept failures without letting them de-motivate him from moving ahead in life is well-placed to achieve success in life. Schools fail to develop this ability in the kids. But, it can be cultivated by introspecting on our own behavior and of those around us and observing how understanding and controlling emotions alone can help us realize our true potential.

This book is designed in such a way that it will throw light on various methods of developing one's EQ as a person and as an investor.

TWO 2

UNDERSTANDING BEHAVIORAL TRENDS

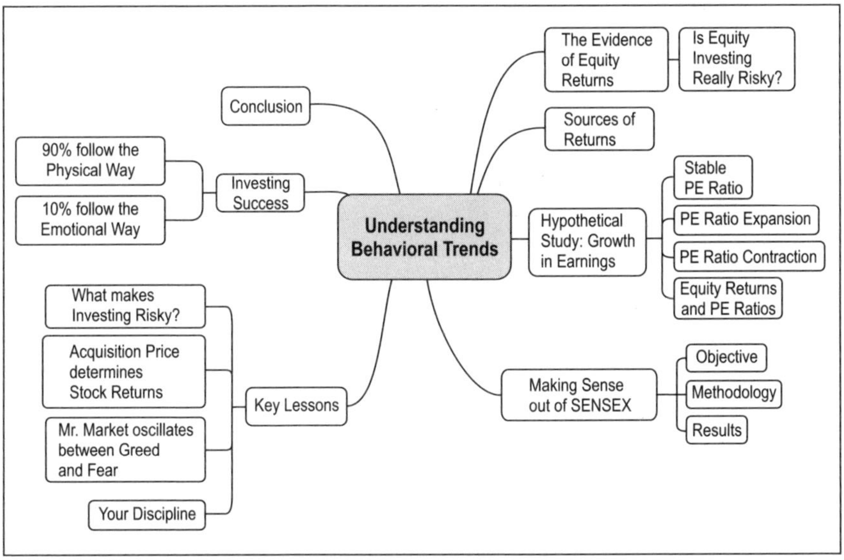

2.1 THE EVIDENCE ON EQUITY RETURNS

Normally our minds are tuned with the law of Physics: For every action there is an equal and opposite reaction. Hence, we are always under the impression that higher the returns, higher the risks undertaken. Thus, we come to our own conclusion that equity investments are risky by their very nature while fixed income instruments are safe investments. Equity investments appear risky due to the volatility in their prices, while fixed income securities appear safe as their prices do not fluctuate. In reality, the factor of inflation makes the fixed income securities much riskier. It can eat into your fixed returns. In contrast, equities are a good hedge against inflation. The following chart shows the returns on equities as well as returns from a fixed income instrument Public Provident Fund from 1979 to 2007.

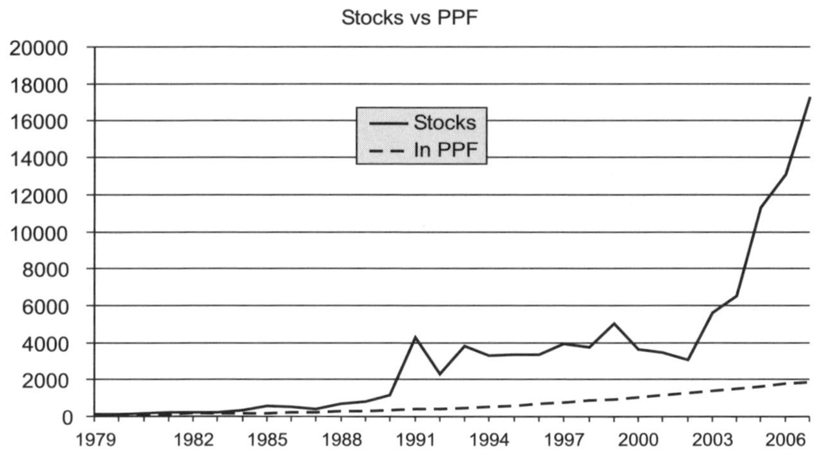

Fig. 2.1 Returns on Equities vs. PPF (1979–2007)

Equities have returned 19.67% per annum over these years while the returns on PPF have been just over 10.4% per annum. In economies where rising inflation is a reality we all have to live with, fixed income securities score very poorly. Equities as an asset class have performed exceedingly well. If one had bought the Sensex in 1979 and stayed invested, one would have made immense wealth. That is the power of equity investing.

However we observe that investors find the equity asset class dangerous due to its wild fluctuations and many people shun equities as there are various examples of investors and corporations having gone bankrupt in equity investing.

Isn't it a paradox that equity investments have done so well, but the investors have done poorly? Why is it that we have so many "rags to riches" and "riches to rags" stories in equity investing? Why are the stock markets known as glorified casinos?

The answer lies in understanding investor behavior and its effect on stock prices.

2.1.1 Is Equity Investing Really Risky?

Investing in equity is considered inherently riskier than investments in bonds. In spite of widespread acknowledgement about this risk-reward relationship of bonds and equity, little time has been spent on understanding what makes equities riskier than bonds. Has it got to do with the inconsistent performance of the companies behind the stocks? Or, has it got to do with the way the equities are approached and appraised by broader market participants, who are prone to fear and greed, leading to wide swings in returns for investors?

> **It is the behavioral traits of the investor in particular and the crowd behavior of the markets in general which makes equity investing appear a risky proposition.**

Finding an answer to the above questions would not only help us put things in perspective but would also help us decide if it would really be prudent on our part to take the route of equities while deploying our savings, with the aim of generating better returns. Alternatively, we would conclude that the risk associated with equities cannot be reduced by an investor, under any circumstances, and hence, s/he should shift his/her savings towards fixed income generating securities, i.e., bonds. Let us try and find the answer to the questions by discussing the various sources of equity returns.

2.2 SOURCES OF RETURNS

Two Sources of Equity Returns:

Unlike bonds, wherein the returns are dependent on only one source under normal circumstances, which in itself is known beforehand, i.e., interest income, the returns from equities are dependent on two sources:

(i) Fundamental

(ii) Speculative

Understanding the behavior of the stock markets is the most difficult because markets are made on the basis of varied opinions expressed by their participants.

The fundamental element concerns the earnings behind the enterprise along with the dividend paid out during the holding period.

The speculative element concerns the changes in the appraisal of the current performance and prospective profitability by the market participants, as a group, having a bearing on PE expansion or contraction, thereby increasing or decreasing the total shareholder return. The speculative element can be simply calculated by the earnings multiplied by change in PE ratio and that number divided by the price paid, expressed as a percentage.

This speculative element is the product of the general sentiment prevailing and the presence of greed and fear amongst the investors. This is subject to fast changes and this is what makes the markets volatile and unpredictable and, of course, interesting.

Before we move ahead and discuss this framework in the context of the performance of the SENSEX during the last 16 years, it would be helpful to go through the following simple hypothetical example of situations arising in the real world.

2.3 HYPOTHETICAL STUDY: GROWTH IN EARNINGS

How 20% Growth in Earnings Can Lead to a Weird Set of Performances:

Let us imagine that there is a company by the name ABC Ltd which has earnings per share of Rs.10 and is quoting at a PE ratio of 20, resulting in a stock price of Rs.200. Fast forward one year and imagine that ABC Ltd grew its earnings by 20%, resulting in earnings per share of Rs.12. In essence, with the business growing at 20%, what is the type of result that we can expect ABC Ltd to have generated for its shareholders?

In the present example, the 20% growth in earnings constitutes the fundamental source of shareholder return. But, the overall result will also be a function of sentiment prevailing and the behavior of investors guided by their emotions of greed and fear. We discuss below three distinctive scenarios.

> **In stock markets analysis does not work, but the jobs of the analysts are always secured.**

2.3.1 Stable PE Ratio

Scenario 1 – Stable PE Ratio

Under this scenario, let us assume that the earnings would be appraised at the same multiple of 20. This would result in the stock price rising to Rs.240 [earning per share of Rs 12 multiplied by PE multiple of 20]. In the absence of any speculative element having any impact on the earnings, the total returns generated by the investor from ABC Ltd would be indicative of the fundamental aspect of the business alone and nothing else.

Table 2.1 Stable PE Ratio

Scenario 1	
Fundamental	20%
Speculative	-
Total Return	**20%**

Over very long periods of time, the stock price has the tendency to reflect the true economics of the business. But, over shorter periods of time, the market has a tendency to see only favorable factors affecting business, and resulting in high speculative interest, just as at other times, they have a tendency to focus only on the negative variables affecting the business and resulting in no speculative interest. Under such gyrations, the investor who enters such a business during rough patch for the business or stock markets in general, resulting in low PE ratios, will not only reap the benefits of fundamental growth in earnings, but also benefit from the return of speculative interest resulting in re-rating of the PEs upwards.

2.3.2 PE Ratio Expansion

Under this scenario, let us assume that the earnings would be appraised at a multiple of 25. This increase in high speculative interest could be due to various reasons such as, a change in sentiments, expected better fortunes of the sector or the company, or optimistic outlook of investors. This results in the overall expansion of market valuations with a commensurate impact on PE multiples of companies across the board.

Investment success comes from following the emotionally difficult path. Do not get carried away by market sentiments.

This would result in the stock price rising to Rs.300 [earning per share of Rs 12 multiplied by PE multiple of 25] . The presence of a speculative element is significant as the total return surpasses the returns due to fundamental change in the business behind the stock.

Table 2.2 PE Ratio Expansion

Scenario 2	
Fundamental	20%
Speculative[1]	30%
Total Return	**50%**

Note:

(1)

$$\frac{((EPS\ at\ the\ end\ of\ the\ Year) * (change\ in\ PE\ ratio))}{Price\ Paid}$$

In the present example, it is ((12)*(+5))/200 = Rs.60 (or) 30%.

2.3.3 PE Ratio Contraction

In this scenario, let us assume that the earnings would be appraised at a multiple of 15. The decrease in speculative interest towards the stock could result when the sector loses favor or simply the market participants grow pessimistic about the future prospects of the business.

This would result in the stock price falling to Rs.180 [earning per share of Rs 12 multiplied by PE multiple of 15]. In spite of the exceptional fundamental return of 20% generated for shareholders, the negative speculative element impacted the earnings appraisal in such a way that the total return generated for the shareholders was – 10%.

Table 2.3 PE Ratio Construction

Scenario 3	
Fundamental	20%
Speculative[1]	–30%
Total Return	**–10%**

Note:

(1)

$$\frac{((EPS\ at\ the\ end\ of\ the\ year) * (change\ in\ PE\ ratio))}{Price\ Paid}$$

In the present case, it is [(12)*(–5)]/[200] = – 30%

2.3.4 Equity Returns and PE

Role of PE Expansion and Contraction in Equity Returns:

The above hypothetical examples drive home the importance of the PE ratio's contraction or expansion to the quality of returns generated by the investors. Understanding this relationship between stock returns and PE ratios helps one to identify opportunities which not only offer reasonable prospects of growth, on the fundamental aspect, but also where a positive re-appraisal of the earnings in the form of expansion of PE ratios is possible. In essence, the price paid, and not just the prospects alone, should determine the quality of returns.

> The most successful investment money managers like Warren Buffett, Charlie Munger, Peter Lynch owe their success not only to their intellectual ability but also to their discipline and emotional control.

Such opportunities come when investors extrapolate too much into the future on the announcement of a bad quarter earnings, a reversal in the economic fundamentals or some act of God. The reversal of a bull market trend also ignites fear in the minds of investors and makes their behavior irrational. Mispriced opportunities thus arise, and the wise investor considers such opportunities as a good value proposition. When the bull markets return, such irrational investors will be willing to pay much more than the fundamentals suggest. The wise investor or a value investor is thus blessed with the exit option. This is how the returns multiply for a value investor due to irrational investor behavior.

2.4 MAKING SENSE OUT OF SENSEX

It will be interesting to study the returns generated by the BSE Sensex for the last 16 years. These historic results are very important as they help us draw some very important lessons.

2.4.1 Objective

The objective is to try and dissect the performance of the Sensex into two components, fundamental and speculative. The fundamental component reflects the trend in the earnings behind the corporations comprising the Sensex and its impact on investment returns. Speculative component reflects the impact of change in appraisal of earnings, which is change in PE ratios, due to investor optimism or pessimism and how this impacts investor returns.

2.4.2 Methodology

The method will become clear once we discuss a year's record in detail below.

Dec. 1991 to Dec. 1992:

> **Equanimity in times of market noise will help one to be a successful investor.**

If one would have bought the Sensex on the last trading day of 1991 at 1,909, one's capital would have grown by 37.7% at the end of 1992, as the Sensex closed at 2,615. What led to the 37.7% return for the Sensex? Was it the superior performance of the businesses constituting the Sensex? (Or) was it something else? The following table summarizes the components of the returns:

Table 2.4 Returns from the Sensex (1991–92)

Date	Sensex	PE Ratio	Total Return[1]	Fundamental Return[2]		Speculative Return[3]	Div. Yield
				EPS	Return		
Dec-91	1,909	24.5	–	78	–	–	
Dec-92	2,615	31.7	37.7%	82.5	5.8%	31.1%	0.8%

(1) **Total Return** = (Fundamental Return) + (Speculative Return) + (Dividend Yield)

(2) **Fundamental Return:**

The earning per share, for the Sensex, was Rs.78 when it was trading at 1,909 at the end of 1991. This discounts the earning at 24.5. Fast-forward one year to the end of 1992, the EPS was Rs.82.5. Presuming that at the end of 1992, the Sensex was discounting the earnings at the same multiple of 24.5; the Sensex would have been trading at 2021. This would have delivered a return of 5.8%.

Table 2.5 Analysis of Fundamental Return

	1991	1992
Sensex EPS	78	82.5
Sensex PE	24.5	24.5
Est. Sensex	1909	2021
Total Return	**5.8%**	

This 5.8% represents the contribution of *fundamental* change in the total return for the Sensex.

(3) **Speculative Return:**

But the PE ratios are subject to change as the expectations and sentiments of investors change. In the present example, the PE ratio at the end of 1992 was not 24.5 but 31.7. The impact this change in PE ratio has on investor return is speculative in nature because this change, in part, is subject to fear and greed of the market participants from time to time and not predictable over a one-year period.

Accordingly, the impact of change in PE ratio on the overall return for the shareholder in 1992 can be calculated using the following formula:

$$\frac{((\text{EPS at the end of 1992}) * (\text{change in PE ratio}))}{\text{Price Paid}}$$

That is,

$$((82.5)*(7.2)) / 1909 = 31.1\%$$

Thus, it can be seen that the total return of 37.7% for the Sensex during the 1991–92 period was a combination of fundamental change to the extent of 5.8%, on the back of increase in earnings, plus 0.8% dividend payable during that period. The remaining 31.1% was the result of change in the market's view about stocks in general.

Moreover, in 1992 there was a case of positive change in PE ratio, i.e., expansion of PE ratio. On the other hand, if there is a contraction of PE ratio, then the impact on total return for the Sensex is negative. This is reflected in the 'Speculative Return' column with a positive speculative return indicating 'PE Expansion' and negative speculative return indicating 'PE Contraction.'

2.4.3 Results

Based on the methodology described above, we have analyzed the return for the Sensex as a whole into fundamental and speculative sources for the last 16 years from 1992 to 2007 as shown in the table below.

Table 2.6 Returns from the Sensex (1991–2007)

Date	Sensex	PE Ratio	Total Return[1]	Fundamental Return[2]		Speculative Return[3]	Div. Yield
				EPS	Return		
Dec-91	1,909	24.5		78	–	–	–
Dec-92	2,615	31.7	**37.7%**	82.5	5.8%	31.1%	0.8%
Dec-93	3,346	40	**28.9%**	83.6	1.3%	26.6%	1.0%
Dec-94	3,927	34.5	**18.1%**	113.8	36.1%	–18.7%	0.7%
Dec-95	3,110	16	**(–19.7%)**	194.2	70.7%	–91.5%	1.1%
Dec-96	3,085	12.2	**0.7%**	252.6	30.1%	–30.9%	1.5%
Dec-97	3,659	13.5	**20.1%**	270.8	7.2%	11.4%	1.5%
Dec-98	3,055	12.1	**(-14.7%)**	252.4	–6.8%	–9.7%	1.8%
Dec-99	5,006	21.7	**65.1%**	230.5	–8.7%	72.4%	1.4%

(Contd.)

Date	Sensex	PE Ratio	Total Return[1]	Fundamental Return[2]		Speculative Return[3]	Div. Yield
				EPS	Return		
Dec-00	3,972	20.3	**(–19.5%)**	195.6	–15.1%	–5.5%	1.1%
Dec-01	3,262	15.7	**(–16.1%)**	207.6	6.1%	–24.0%	1.8%
Dec-02	3,377	14.6	**5.6%**	231.1	11.3%	–7.8%	2.1%
Dec-03	5,839	18.9	**75.0%**	308.7	33.6%	39.3%	2.1%
Dec-04	6,603	17.1	**15.1%**	386	25.0%	–11.9%	2.0%
Dec-05	9,398	18.6	**43.8%**	505	30.8%	11.5%	1.5%
Dec-06	13,787	22.8	**48.0%**	604.5	19.7%	27.0%	1.3%
Dec-07	20,287	27.7	**48.2%**	732.2	21.1%	26.0%	1.1%

Notes:

(1) **Total Return = (Fundamental Return) + (Speculative Return) + (Dividend Yield)**

(2) **Fundamental Return = Percentage change in Earning per Share, year on year.**

(3) **Speculative Return:**

$$\frac{((\text{EPS at the end of the Year}) * (\text{change in PE ratio}))}{\text{Price Paid}}$$

1991 saw the liberalization of the Indian economy, which was greeted with enthusiasm by the stock markets, and we had the Harshad Mehta boom. There was no change in the fundamental returns of the companies but the sentiment had changed, leading to widespread optimism. This is reflected in the above table when one sees that speculative return in 1992 was 31.1% as against a measly fundamental return of just 5.8%. This fundamental return dipped to just 1.3%, but the speculative interest was 26.6%.

However, from 1994 to 1996 the fundamental return started going up but the speculative returns were highly negative, signifying irrational investor behavior.

Again, during the tech boom in 1999/2000 we notice a high level of speculative activity but a decrease in fundamental returns. However, this was only in the technology sector, and lasted for just a couple of years.

From 1994 to 2003, we had a prolonged bear market where in spite of a rise in fundamental returns, the lack of investor interest and pessimism is evident with high negative speculative returns barring a stray couple of years.

From 2003 onwards, the sentiment started improving as good corporate results started flowing in. The fundamental returns began improving and so did the speculative returns. The bullish conditions were back and investor interest in stocks started soaring. Along with this the growth in GDP, increased Foreign Institutional Investor(FII) interest, the commodities boom and a host of other positive news as well as reforms of the economy took the index up from 2,800 in 2003 to 21,000 in January 2008. Such high speculative returns were backed by fundamental returns also and the ratio of speculative to fundamental returns in 2005 – 2007 is quite balanced and not as skewed as we saw in 1992/1993.

The above study clearly depicts how investor behavior affects stock prices. If one understands this, one will be able to benefit by making rational investment decisions and at the same time benefit from other's irrationality.

2.5 KEY LESSONS

2.5.1 What Makes Investing Risky?

A look at the above study highlights that during the 16 year period under consideration, corporate earnings have shown a steady growth, resulting in a compounded rate of return of around 16%, as reflected in the earnings per share. During this period, the earnings have experienced a decline only during the 3 years from 1998 to 2000, which is explained by the fact that many good profitable companies comprising the Sensex were replaced by low profit-making, information technology companies just because the IT sector happened to be a "fancy" sector. Investors were willing to pay excessively high multiples for such stocks in the hope of good profits coming in the future.

Even this drop in earnings, can be considered as an aberration. It can thus be concluded that earnings in general have been consistent, reliable and good during the last 16 years. This fact is reflected in the compounded return of 18% delivered by the Sensex during the same period.

The yearly return from the Sensex was, however, anything but consistent due to irrational investor behavior. This highlights an important factor pertaining to equity investing. The returns not only depend on the earnings of the corporations constituting the Sensex but also on the changes in the PE ratios.

2.5.2 Acquisition Price Determines Stock Returns

The change in PE ratios over a period of time signifies the change in sentiments of the investors. These changes could be due to several factors like the change in business environment, change in the fortunes of a company, changes in sectoral performance, macroeconomic factors, government deregulation and overall optimism or pessimism.

These factors can bring in great opportunities for an investor waiting for such behavioral mispricing. This is amply evident if we look at the stellar performance of companies from 1995 to 1997 and the returns on the Sensex. These three years presented immense opportunities as tremendous amount of pessimism prevailed in the markets. The negative speculative element virtually threw up great bargains.

Table 2.7 Returns from Sensex (1994–97)

Date	Sensex	PE Ratio	Total Return	Fundamental Return		Speculative Return	Div. Yield
				EPS	Return		
Dec-94	3,927	34.5	–	113.8	–	–	–
Dec-95	3,110	16	**(–19.7%)**	194.2	70.7%	–91.5%	1.1%
Dec-96	3,085	12.2	**0.7%**	252.6	30.1%	–30.9%	1.5%
Dec-97	3,659	13.5	**20.1%**	270.8	7.2%	11.4%	1.5%

During this period, the corporate earnings grew from Rs.113.8 at the end of 1994 to Rs.270.8 at the end of 1997 translating into a 33.6% CAGR for earnings. However, the Sensex dropped from 3,927 at the end of 1994 to 3,659 at the end of 1997 resulting in a negative –6.8% return. As we add the dividends received during this period amounting to 4.1%, we get a negative –2.7 return from the Sensex.

What explains this anomaly of 33.6% CAGR for earnings translating into –2.7% return for shareholders?

During the year 1994 excessive optimism prevailed and investors were willing to pay high valuations, which are reflected in the high PE of

34.5. However, this high PE prohibited the fundamental performance from being translated in to commensurate returns for the shareholders.

During the years 1995/6/7 investors benefited immensely as the prices they paid were much below the fundamental values due to excessive pessimism.

It is the acquisition price that determines stock returns.

2.5.3 Mr. Market Oscillates between Greed and Fear

The above anomaly was not a oneoff case. It repeats as the markets sway between optimism and pessimism.

Markets are made up of emotional people whose decisions are based upon the prevailing sentiments in the environment. At times they display greed and at other times this greed is displaced by fear. Bouts of greed and fear make the stock prices volatile and investors get trapped in such volatility to lose fortunes.

During the period 2001 to 2002, the corporate earnings grew at 8.8% CAGR (Compound Annual Growth Rate) from Rs.195.6 at the end of 2000 to Rs. 231.1 at the end of 2002, but the Sensex delivered a negative –14.9% return to the investors. It slipped from 3,972 at the end of 2000 to 3,377 in 2002. As we add the dividends received during this period amounting to 3.9%, we get a negative –11% return from the Sensex.

Table 2.8 Returns form the Sensex (2000–02)

Date	Sensex	PE Ratio	Total Return	Fundamental Return		Specu-lative Return	Div Yield
				EPS	Return		
Dec-00	3,972	20.3	–	195.6	–	–	–
Dec-01	3,262	15.7	(–16.1%)	207.6	6.1%	–24.0%	1.8%
Dec-02	3,377	14.6	5.6%	231.1	11.3%	–7.8%	2.1%

Corporate performance and shareholders performance can be diagonally opposite. It is the behavioral traits of the investor in particular and the crowd behavior of the markets in general which makes equity investing appear a risky proposition.

Being aware and keeping one's emotions under control and at the same time understanding others' behavioral anomalies enables a wise investor to identify bargains.

2.5.4 Your Discipline

It is not the fundamental performance alone which determines the returns, but also the price one pays for those set of fundamentals. Paying 25 times recent earnings for a business and then expecting it to grow at 25% over the next few years, can expose you to disappointments on two fronts. Firstly, if and when earnings turn out to be below expectations, say below 25%, and secondly, losing on the speculative return front, that is, change in the PEs.

Being disciplined in your investment approach is very important. You don't get opportunities everyday and one must be prepared and ready with the money when opportunities come. It so happens that investors tend to chase stocks when they get tips and they are so much stuck up with expensive stocks that when the markets tank and opportunities arise they don't have the money.

Real discipline and courage is: you buy when you emotionally do not feel like buying, and sell when your heart says no but the mind and the logic say yes.

2.6 SUCCESSFUL INVESTING

Why is Successful Investing so Difficult?

The most difficult part is understanding the behavior of the stock markets. Why is that so? Because markets are made on the basis of varied opinions expressed by their participants. These opinions are subject to change with the changes in the sentiments of these emotional people. It's the crowd behavior that dominates the decision-making and is responsible for the sudden changes in the sentiments.

Take for instance the "black Monday" in May 2004 when the markets lost around 700 points as the election results brought the Congress to power. What precipitated this huge fall? Had anything gone drastically wrong with the performance of the companies whose stock prices crashed? Definitely no. But the sentiment changed. BJP going out of power was a big change and normally we do not like changes. Hence, there was gloom all around and people started dumping stocks as though there was going to be no future. The markets started crashing on reflexivity as each one wanted to get out faster than his neighbour. Herd mentality was at work and no rational thinking would work.

Or take the case of the Technology boom in 1999–2000. Profits did not matter and people were willing to pay ridiculous valuations for technology stocks on the basis of eyeballs and future dreams. We saw small internet start-ups gobbling up decades-old companies. AOL acquired Time Warner. The sentiment towards Technology was very bullish and when this sentiment changed the prices of these stocks came crashing down, leading to investors losing fortunes. Investors stopped being irrational and this led to some sanity in stock prices.

A similar situation arose in January 2008 when the market touched a dizzy height of 21,000 ignoring all the global negatives of US subprime crisis, asset inflation, falling US dollar, income inequalities, rising inflationary pressures due to rising oil prices etc. However, all of a sudden within two months the market was down to 16,000 as investor sentiment changed drastically.

What happened to all the analysts and their analysis? In stock markets analysis does not work, but the jobs of the analysts are always secured.

Imagine yourself being emotionally strong and you bought when the others were panicky. You didn't require any analysts or their analysis. You used your emotional intelligence. You would end up making a huge fortune. But, this seems easy only in hindsight. At that point of time to go against the crowd is the most difficult but the most sensible thing to do.

It is evidently clear that the stock prices do not reflect only the fundamental value of a company but also the speculative value, that is, the built-in expectation of the investors. These may be highly optimistic or highly pessimistic. Thus it becomes important to understand what is the right way to invest. Understanding what the majority of the investors do should guide us on what not to do. Going against the crowd is the way to earn high investment returns.

2.6.1 Ninety Percent Follow the Physical Way

Investment success eludes you when you do what 90% of the people are doing. Follow the physically difficult path. They come to the office early and stay late. They do not know what their children are doing as they don't have time for them. They choose work over the family. They read a large number of reports very rapidly. They carry all the newspapers with them so that they can read them whenever time permits them. Their talk revolves on finding the next best investment opportunity to make money. They go for company visits and plant visits. They talk to the management to know more about their companies. They are in touch with a number of brokers as they believe that the more brokers they talk to, the more efficient they will be in making money in the stock markets. They love to have more and more information as it gives them a feeling of being well-connected and better informed. They love to be in an information-overload mode. They thrive on confusion. They are continuously monitoring stock price movements. At office they are in front of the terminals and watching the stock price movements. At office they try to catch the CNBC news and at home they are again excited about the NASDAQ movements. They carry huge reports home at night, determined to read them before the next day. When they are mobile they are busy on the mobile phones. They love to hear market gossip and are always excited on hearing rumors. They tend to make decisions based on gossip, rumors, and news. News regarding political development, monsoon forecasts, inflation figures, change in minister's portfolios, and GDP growth plays an important role in their lives. They tend to always look at opportunities to time the markets on such news. In every way they put tremendous amount of physical energy and effort to try to beat the market by outworking the competition. But they don't realize that this is the most mediocre thing to do, since 90% of the investors are also doing the same thing.

Unfortunately, professional and qualified investors also come into this category. One reason is that they are as prone to behavioral biases as any other layman and secondly due to their organizational compulsions which lay more stress on short-term performance rather than long-term one.

The physically difficult way is more about trying to time the markets, finding the direction of the markets and getting as much information as possible to make investment decisions. Trying to do so many things only results in information overload. This clouds the mind and distorts thinking. Good opportunities come once in a while and you spot them only when you are cool and thus have the time to think. The physically difficult way assumes that there are a lot of opportunities there and you have to be digging hard to be successful at investing. The current volatility in the markets is the result of too many people trying to invest following the physically difficult way. Life is simple. We make it complicated.

2.6.2 Ten Percent Follow the Emotional Way

Investment success comes from following the emotionally difficult path. When your friends tell you about a great investment opportunity, which could be a ten-bagger, and they feel that it is a great time to buy or an opportunity will be lost: don't buy. When your favorite TV channel everyday has analysts talking about great investment opportunities don't buy. When your broker calls you up and asks you to buy a great ten-bagger don't take the bait. When the newspapers talk about the stock markets offering great investment opportunities, please be wary of such news. When your neighbours talk to you about how the stock markets have made them rich in the last couple of months, avoid the temptation of buying. When you hear stories of how people have created great wealth in the stock markets in a short span, don't make the mistake of following them. When your banker starts offering you credit facility against your shares to buy more shares do not jump on such deals to buy more shares. Be absolutely uninterested.

When they tell you that the market is going to crash and the stock prices will nose dive; don't sell. When the analysts on the TV show talk about selling, stocks don't sell. When newspapers start reporting the setting of a bear phase and ask you to liquidate your portfolio, don't sell. When your neighbours are busy exiting the stock markets, don't follow them. When your broker asks you to sell as he sees bad times ahead, do not listen to his advice and sell. When you hear only gloomy news around you and find that people are exiting the stock markets, don't exit.

Be absolutely disinterested. Here you do not require any intellectual effort or any physical effort, but for most people emotional discipline is the most difficult. Do not get carried away by market sentiments. They only help you to make blunders. Try to control your emotions. Try not to follow the herd. Believe in yourself and the investment policy you have committed yourself to. On the contrary, it would pay to go against the popular opinion. When others are greedy be fearful and when others are fearful be greedy.

The emotionally difficult path lays stress on the virtue of patience as it considers the long-term approach to investments. Stress is on the cash flow approach to investments. Patience focuses an investor's attention on the goal of compounding money over a long period. Compounding can be magic even when the compounding rate is modest. To give an example: if one were to compound money at a modest rate of 7% the money would double at the end of 10 years and it would be 16 times at the end of 40 years. Patience also helps one to control the transaction costs. The more you churn your portfolio the more you pay the broker in terms of brokerage and of course the government has its share of the revenue on the capital gains you make. Then you also have costs like depositary charges, transaction tax and service tax. All these costs could be avoided if one has patience.

The emotionally difficult path requires an understanding of how our emotions guide our decision-making especially when we are dealing with money.

The most successful investment money managers like Warren Buffett, Charlie Munger, Peter Lynch —to name a few —owe their success not only to their intellectual ability but also to their discipline and emotional control.

2.7 CONCLUSION

In any given year, one might turn out to be a winner or a loser, because of the changes in speculative interest driving the markets, but it is the long run which separates a true investor from a speculator. Just as an investor would try and be subdued during periods of optimism because his fixation is not only on the recent twelve months' profit and next year's expectation but on the long-term trend of the earnings and profitability of the enterprises, a speculator will be fixated on the recent earnings and growth projections and be ready to pay a high premium for the current set of earnings, leaving him in a position where he might not be able to reap the profits of even a fundamentally superior performance just because he paid many times over the recent earnings leaving the prospective earnings to catch up a lot of ground in terms of growth rates and profitability ratios.

On the other hand, a true investor would wait for the period of optimism to subside and choose from opportunities, wherein the future is not favorably discounted into the price, leaving the stock price to catch up with the business fundamentals by means of PE expansion. All the while he would also look for companies where the fundamentals might continue to flourish just as well-creating a double-whammy for him. For one, increase in earnings which will contribute to fundamental returns and two, positive speculative interest towards the stock or sectors, over time, resulting in expansion of earnings from low PE to moderate or high PE ratios and superior returns.

The fact that equity as an asset class has given handsome returns but investors have fared poorly only points out the fickle-minded behavior of investors. We need to understand that we are human beings having a heart and a mind. We need to take decisions from our mind. If we use the mind then we know if a stock is expensive or not, whether we are paying for its fundamental value or not, the amount of speculative interest and its reflection in the price, the value you are getting as regards the price you are paying and the general sentiment of the markets, whether bullish or bearish.

However, when you use the heart you tend to go with the herd and do what they are doing. If everyone is buying, you start buying and thus buy expensive. Similarly, if everyone is selling you sell and thus sell cheap. You get moved by the market emotions as you become a part of the crowd and do foolish things, which harm your financial interests. You chase stocks as you become greedy when others are greedy and end up buying stocks at high prices. In reality you must be greedy when others are fearful so you can buy stocks at good valuations.

Being emotional beings, we tend to make decisions out of our heart and these may not be in our best financial interest. This emotional behavior becomes very evident in the stock markets as we sway between our basic emotions of greed and fear. With stock markets being volatile in nature and the end results being all about making or losing money, our emotions become volcanic. Money ignites our greed and fear. The challenge for an investor to be successful is to control ones emotions and not be swayed by emotional outbursts. Equanimity in times of market noise will help one to be a successful investor.

THREE 3

BEHAVIORAL OBSTACLES TO VALUE INVESTING

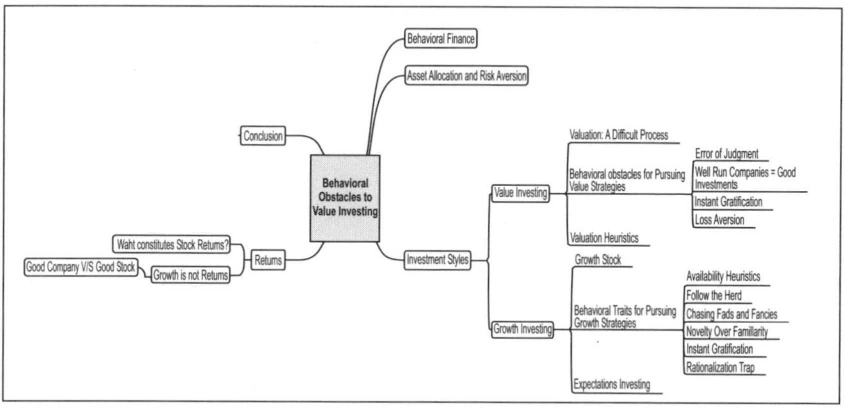

3.1 BEHAVIORAL FINANCE

What is Behavioral Finance?

Behavioral finance is an emerging field that combines the understanding of behavioral and cognitive psychology with financial decision-making processes. The traditional economic theory we understand talks about efficient markets and people making rational decisions to maximize profits. However, this new emerging school of behavioral economists argues that markets are not efficient, especially in the short run, and people do not make rational decisions to maximize profits. Human beings are susceptible to numerous behavioral anomalies, which become counter-productive to the wealth-maximization principle leading to irrational behavior.

What has Behavioral Finance got to do with Investing?

Just reflecting on our own investment decisions and the mistakes made in the past would highlight the essence of behavioral finance. Most common of these mistakes involve selling winners too soon and holding onto losers, buying expensive stocks, getting anxious on seeing our investments quote at a discount to our purchase price translating into quotational losses, buying when others are buying and selling because others are selling. These examples of investor behavior are not to be taken lightly. Just as any game involves overcoming the opponents; the game of investing involves dealing successfully with one's own emotional indiscipline to come out victorious. It is not that the great investors do not suffer from these behavioral anomalies; it is just that they understand the importance of emotions while investing and train themselves out of acting emotionally. As the legendary investor, Warren Buffett has observed, "It is only when you combine sound intellect with emotional discipline that you get rational behavior."

An understanding of how our emotions result in irrational behavior is indispensable for any investor. The study of behavioral anomalies helps an investor accomplish just that task.

My experience in the stock markets for the last 30 years has taught me one very important lesson. Intelligence and brilliance carries the day, but it is the wisdom that endures. This wisdom is a product of various factors:

1. Learning from one's own experiences and mistakes.
2. Using common sense.
3. Wisdom gained from the literature of past successful investors like Benjamin Graham, Warren Buffett, Peter Lynch, to name a few.
4. One's ability to control one's emotions and understand the emotions of others.
5. Discipline and ability to stay in the course in spite of all the temptations.

We live in a world where everything is a business and that includes education. Business schools are busy promoting academic studies in the field of investment and money management, and a lot of academic work has been done giving birth to new financial paradigms. Students of major business schools are taught about the Modern Portfolio Theory, the Efficient Market Theory and Beta coefficient. In my humble opinion this is garbage in and garbage out. These qualifications are good to help you get good jobs in large faceless organizations but they are a big zero when it comes to investments in the real world. However, these business schools send these overconfident students armed with knowledge and a degree, which is worthless in the real world of investments.

In recent years, two schools of thought have emerged as regards investments. The first is highly empirical and is based on academic studies that show that stocks have outperformed bonds, and that value outperforms both growth and the popular stock market indices over long periods of time.

We did a study of the BSE Sensex stock returns from 1979 to find a healthy return of 19.67% compounded as against the Public Provident Fund (substitute for bonds) return of around 10.40% (Fig. 3.1).

Stocks do outperform safe fixed income securities like bonds, but value outperforms both bonds and the popular indices. Value investing definitely provides superior returns compared to all other investment styles.

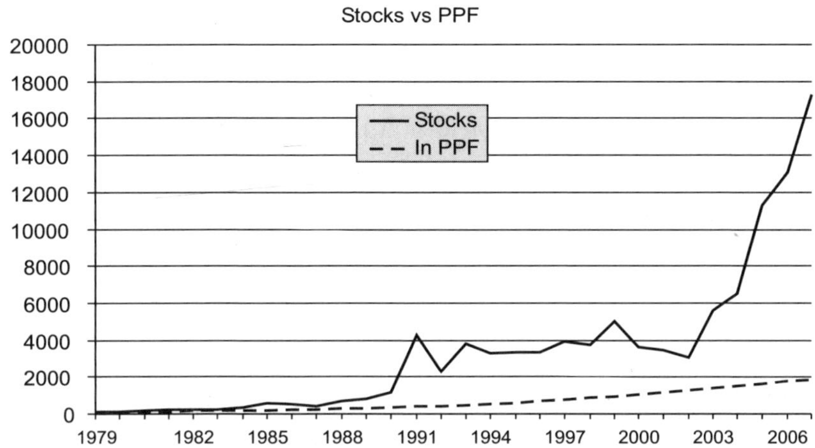

Fig. 3.1 Returns from the Stocks vs PPF (1979–2006)

If value investing works, then why do a majority of individual and professional investors ignore the empirical evidence and follow different investment strategies? Considerable study is being done in this field, which is dominated by some of the leading behavioral psychologists. Behavioral finance is emerging as a favorite topic at conferences.

Value investing definitely provides superior returns compared to all other investment styles.

Value investing strategies and an understanding of the basics of behavioral finance form the basic pillars for a successful long-term investor.

3.2 ASSET ALLOCATION AND RISK AVERSION

Why do money managers not take time to develop a valid set of investment principles? This is the topic addressed by behavioralists to understand the rationality of human actions.

In fact, asset allocation is the first step an investor should take before even choosing how to invest. The ability to understand the risk-reward ratio discounted in various asset classes is critical in designing an asset allocation strategy. Fixation only on risk, without considering rewards is a result of risk-averse behavior exhibited by vast majority of people leading to over-exposure to bonds.

We have seen, however, that equities have outperformed the secured fixed income securities by 9.2%. This equity return premium would more than compensate for the risk associated with equities. However, investor preference for high yield bonds only shows that the investors are risk averse.

The three integral sources of value are assets, earnings and growth.

Lately, financial planning has become a fashion, and the best way to be self-employed is to pass an exam in financial planning and get a degree and become a financial planner. Moreover, organizations consider financial planning as another service from their basket of offerings.

Financial planning is all about asset allocation. When I glance through the financial plans of my clients prepared by their financial planners, I am amused at the fact that most follow a fixed pattern of x% in fixed-income securities and y% in equities irrespective of the clients' needs and the financial positions. Of course, insurance also has a sizable component to cover the sense of safety. Moreover, if a very illustrious plan with different investment proposals is not presented there is a likelihood of losing the account.

The point I wish to make is that when equity returns have been so phenomenal, why are money managers and financial planners reluctant to go for equities.

The answer is again risk aversion. It is worth noticing, moreover, that a bond can turn out to be a risky investment, in an inflationary enviornement, and equities can turn out to be a safe-haven, if wisely chosen and held onto with patience.

3.3 INVESTMENT STYLES

The vast majority of money managers are categorized as either value managers or growth managers. Most of the money management firms believe in providing an asset allocation approach, and hence it is important for them to provide different styles of investing. It also works as a hedge for their business.

Too few managers take the pain and the trouble to analyze the fundamental characteristics of portfolios that produce long-term beating results and develop a set of investment principles and strategies based on such studies. This requires hard work and a lot of patience. This is value investing. Even the few who do follow value investing ultimately lose the conviction to stay in the course and get swayed by the noise of the markets.

Most managers are enamored of the glamour of the markets and the lure of a quick buck. No hard work and wait. They chase the fancies of the market in the name of growth stock and term themselves as growth investors. Since they do not do any homework and if asked about the wisdom of paying an awfully high price for a stock, they justify the action by saying that it is a growth stock.

> **People tend to take more risks simply to avoid acknowledging a certain loss and avoid taking extra risk even if it entails a higher profit potential.**

The stock markets judge these fund managers on a daily basis at the close of the market hours. In such a situation, more action and activity is demanded. Preference is for growth stock investing over value investing.

Process versus Outcome:

In the stock markets, a small percentage of people end up being successful in the long run whereas a majority of the people, in spite of being successful in the short run, end up losing money in the long run. It is only natural that people end up copying the tactics of the unsuccessful more often than these deserve to be followed. The reason is that people follow the outcome rather than the process.

The confirmation that Ramesh has made a fortune last Friday by buying stocks before noon and selling at 3pm is enough to convince a majority of the people that it is the right path. We must understand that chance plays a crucial role in the determination of an outcome in a singular event. But, in a sequence of events the role of chance diminishes and it is the process that plays the crucial role.

In the technology boom if one had tried to understand the basics of the valuation of the IT companies, one would have concluded that eye balls do not matter but profits do. However, in the name of growth everyone was chasing technology stocks at any price. The ensuing disaster is well known.

3.3.1 Value Investing

"Price is what you pay, Value is what you get." Benjamin Graham

What is Value Investing? The price of a stock is dependent on the expectations of the people in the market. In bullish times people are willing to pay a higher price to own a piece of the company and in bearish times they are willing to pay much less. That is the reason value investors buy stocks during bearish times as the expectations of investors are running low. Or, alternatively, during bullish times they are looking at good neglected stocks, which are out of favor with the investors.

Growth stock investing is based on hunches, dreams, illusions or popular opinion. They are better termed as 'dream stocks'.

When one buys a stock, one is buying a business. It is necessary to understand that the business is good and sustainable. Its earnings stream is also predictable. The price the investor pays for this business is important. A value investor will buy this business at a much lower value than the fundamentals justify.

There are many different ways of valuing a business. A prudent value investor would apply different modes of valuations depending on the businesses and do the hard work of looking into the future. He would buy when he believes that the price he is paying is much less than the current valuation of the company.

The value investing process requires the hard work of estimating future cash inflows and outflows, discounting them at an appropriate rate that can be expected to occur during the remaining life of the asset. This requires a good understanding of both the business and the environment to make the current assumptions.

Unfortunately, we live in a world where quick fixes are the order of the day and no one has the time to go through the hard work.

One major distinction on value one should bear in mind is between "value in use" and "value in exchange". Water has good value in use while gold has good value in exchange. This is the trap where investors bought technology stocks only to lose fortunes. Software was useful, but did not command much value in exchange.

Valuation: A Difficult Process

The process of valuation is easy to explain, but its efficient implementation is hard, as it requires making predictions about the future cash inflows and outflows for any given business. Moreover, the assumptions on the future of the business cycle and its sustainability are hard to come by. The three integral sources of value are assets, earnings and growth.

Even if one were prepared to do the hard work of valuation, one would require a lot of courage to stay the course. Along with the hard work, patience and discipline are integral attributes of a value investor.

Behavioral Obstacles for Pursuing Value Strategies

Error of Judgment

> Herd behavior is one of the reasons that growth stocks go up very fast and attract investor attraction. They also fall very fast as the herd comes to sell.

"Putting excessive weight on recent past history, as opposed to a rational prior, is a common judgment error in psychological experiments and not just the stock markets."

Lakonishak, Schleifer and Vishney in their paper titled "Contrarian Investment, Extrapolation and Risk" (1994), have made an analysis of why more investors do not pursue value strategies. One reason is that they may not be aware of the data despite evidence going back to the work of Graham and Dodd (1934) or that much of the evidence is refuted by the conclusions offered by consultants that value and growth perform equally over time. The authors further conjecture that the superior performance of value strategies versus what they call "glamor" or growth strategies is the preference for glamor strategies by both individual and institutional investors based on their disposition to extrapolate recent past performance with future performance.

Well-run Companies = Good Investments

Institutional investors are smart, but inspite of that why are they prone to judgement bias and invest in good well-known companies? Common sense would say that institutional investors prefer better companies, as they are prudent investments. But the catch lies in the competition. He is more concerned about doing things right than doing the right thing. He wants to go with the herd. If a fund manager bought an obscure company and if it performed badly he is likely to lose his job. However, if he bought a blue chip like Hindustan Lever and if it did badly, it did not matter much as everyone owned Hindustan Lever. The fact that investment risk is less a function of the individual company than the price of its stock is not recognized by investors.

Instant Gratification

The allure of immediate gratification plays an important part in investors' stock preferences. Value stocks require patience and take longer to work out than investors who are seeking more immediate, abnormal returns are willing to wait. This behavioral trait explains the popularity of momentum investment strategies.

Value buying is more of a philosophy of buying what is out of favor. From 2001 to 2003, the stocks were out of favor and many value stocks were available. Today, oil and refining sectors are very hot and hence the stock prices are also at fancy valuations. However, two stocks BPCL and HPCL are available cheap. They are not the flavor of the markets as their profitability is affected due to government control on their selling prices. However, the government is issuing oil bonds to compensate for the losses. It's a question of time for the anomaly to be corrected. These stocks could excite a value investor in this sector.

However, money managers will refrain from buying such stocks. Sticking their neck out could lead to short-term underperformance and perhaps a loss of bonus or even a job. It is this fear and the general market trend that makes value investors a scarce species.

Adhering to value principles is a difficult task. You are derided for not adapting to a changing world and failing to understand the new paradigms. During the technology boom how many times we heard of the advent of the new economy? The old rules of investing were of no relevance. Eyeballs and not profits were the valuation parameters of internet companies.

Common sense says that a business strategy that cannot produce a profit means that the business is worth zero.

Loss Aversion

The famous psychologists, Daniel Kahneman and Amos Tversky, who are sometimes referred to as fathers of behavioral finance, postulated the prospect theory, which explains that people tend to take more risks simply to avoid acknowledging a certain loss and avoid taking extra risk even if it entails a higher profit potential.

As an investor, each one of us experiences this to varying magnitude. Say one buys a stock and after a year it is trading at half the value. Going ahead, the fortunes of the company do not seem to be bright either. What are the chances of one to sell and booking the loss? Very few. Most of us have been in this position and we believe that it is better to hold on till the price appreciates. Or we even buy more on the pretext of averaging the cost of purchase. This is due to loss aversion. The pain of a loss is three times more than an equal amount of pleasure. Hence we are not able to acknowledge loss when we have one. This same anomaly also makes us sell the winners very fast. Hence we always end up holding the losers and selling the winners.

To successfully implement a value strategy, one has to learn to deal with such impulses because the volatility in markets can test one more often than one can bear to handle.

Valuation Heuristics

"*Heuristics are simple efficient rules of the thumb which have been proposed to explain how people make decisions, come to judgments and solve problems, typically when facing complex problems or incomplete information. These rules work well under most circumstances, but in certain cases lead to systematic cognitive biases*" - Daniel Kahneman

Heuristics are the short cut the brain takes when processing information. It does not process full information. This leads to cognitive biases.

Discounted cash flow analysis is the appropriate way of valuing a company. However this requires a lot of hard work in understanding the business dynamics and making the relevant assumptions to come to a fair valuation.

The stock markets move very fast and the lure of making a fast buck before the neighbor does is so great that short cuts or the rules of the thumb have become the innovations of the valuation game. These are so widely used that they have become the benchmark for the industry.

Some of the valuation heuristics are as follows:

1. Price/Earnings Heuristic:

PE ratios are the most commonly used valuation metric. Almost all the analyst reports circulating take note of it either on trailing earnings performance or historic performance. One noticeable misconception is that a low PE stock is a cheap stock and a high PE stock is an expensive stock. However, along with that one has also to look at other important factors such as return on equity and future growth expectations. The perception gap also plays an important role in the valuations of companies.

2. Price/Book Value Heuristics:

Another common misconception is that low P/BV ratio represents cheap stock. However it is important to look at other variables rather than follow this blindly. For example, a business whose assets earn around 6% on its equity and is also expected to do so in the future with interest rates at 10%, deserves to sell at a discount to the book value and in no way can be called a cheap stock. Alternatively, a business earning 24% return on equity and expected to do so in the future with interest rates around10% deserves to sell at a premium to its book value. Moreover, a business selling at close to its book value, with the business expected to maintain its return on equity and grow in the future would beat many other investment opportunities in businesses selling at lower P/BV ratios.

3. Price/Sales Heuristics:

Generally, price/sales ratios are used to compare investment opportunities within the same industry. But, this is not accorded its proper weight when one does not take into account the fact that two businesses generating different returns on capital employed and expected to perform differently in future, deserve to quote at different multiples to sales. Capital structure also influences the multiples assigned to the ratios. This is very important when one looks at commodity stocks.

Although these valuation ratios are widely used and quoted extensively, they are based on incomplete information and thus do not serve to give the right answers.

3.3.2 Growth Investing

Growth stock investing is more of a philosophy of buying what is popular. During the technology boom internet retailing stocks were glamorous. The stock market loved them. Hence, one paid a heavy price to own them.

When one cannot justify the high valuation of a stock one would argue that it is a growth stock and hence expensive.

For any stock to be a growth stock it has first to be a value stock. Value and growth are inseparable.

Many investors and managers alike don't understand the true impact of growth on the value of the company. Compensation packages linked to profitability increases indicate the magnitude of the widespread misconception that growth, irrespective of the amount of capital required, creates wealth for the shareholders.

A good example in the Indian markets is that of financial services firms which are chased as growth stocks because of a sustained bull run in the market for the last four years. They command high valuations. A highly brokered market with severe competition is bringing down the brokerage rates and at the same time the compensation packages are hitting the roof due to a heavy demand for managers and analysts. On January 4, 2008, a newly listed full service brokerage firm Motilal Oswal Financial Services Ltd. enjoyed a market capitalization of Rs. 6128 crores, which was close to the combined market capitalization of multinational giants, Gillette and Proctor and Gamble, at Rs. 6795 crores. The former is a growth stock while the beaten down latter companies are the value stocks.

This brings us to the most important question of the sustainability of the competitive advantage. In a free and a competitive market economy, any business activity which earns high returns on capital cannot be expected to continue doing the same in the future. Competitive forces will drive down the higher returns to a level where at best they earn market risk-adjusted returns most of the time.

The concept of growth stock is a product of a bull market. It dies when the bear market sets in. Bear markets create values.

Growth Stock

The term 'growth stock' is meaningless since a 'growth stock' can be identified only in retrospection: it is merely a stock that went way up. For most of us, our greatest richness always has been and will continue to remain in dreams. Stocks go to particularly high levels when a lot of people think they might equal their dreams. 'Growth stocks' are perhaps, better termed as 'dream stocks'.

When a stock becomes a fancy and a fad in the markets, it is chased by one and all. The steep rise in the stock price makes it a growth stock.

Before the rise how many would call it a growth stock? It is only when the price moves very fast it is evident that it has found fancy and is thus termed as a growth stock.

Since it is easy to sell a dream story of a growth stock, it is also possible to create a large band of followers chasing the growth illusion. Moreover, growth stock investing does not require any hard work associated with value investing. It is based on hunches, dreams, illusions or popular opinion.

When the dream of a new industry is translated into reality, the dream ends and stocks start selling more conservatively. At present financial services, real estate, infrastructure and telecommunications stocks fall in this category of 'dream stocks', as it is very difficult, as of now, to understand their business models and the future profitability potential is still a mystery. This brings us to that particular moment when the value of mystery is at its greatest—a special moment when everyone sees something amazing coming out of mystery and are thus willing to pay a lot more to know about these strange things. Later on, when the mystery ceases to be and they do know a lot more, they will pay less. Most internet and technology stocks the world over were booming in 1999–2000. They were riding high on the value of mystery. However, when these companies started fulfilling their vision as is happening today, they are selling for less in relation to their earnings. Gradually they tend to be associated with the rating of knowledge rather than mystery.

Behavioral Traits for Pursuing Growth Strategies

Availability Heuristics

Human beings tend to rely on the most recent or the most readily available information. That is the reason that front-page advertisements command a hefty premium to other pages in a newspaper.

We have more people following growth strategies and chasing growth stocks as compared to value investing strategies. Hence, the information on growth stocks is very readily available. More brokers recommend them, their volatility makes them take headlines, more fund managers and analysts discuss them on TV shows, and more investors chase them, making them press worthy and popular.

Investors are more likely to act on this readily available information. Growth stock is a very hot story and everyone likes a stock that goes up very fast. Individuals as well as Institutional investors fall prey to this availability heuristic, start believing in the growth story and chase growth stocks.

Follow the Herd

This availability heuristics creates such a huge following that we have all sorts of investors joining the bandwagon.

Individuals or institutional investors are known to buy what others are buying. This gives them the confidence that if anything goes wrong they are not the only ones affected. They take solace in the fact that they are not alone when they take such risks of putting their money in growth stocks.

This creates a herd mentality amongst the investors and they all buy what others are buying. Since this buying frenzy does not arise out of some firm conviction, it is subject to fear and doubt. So, if a few investors are noticed to be selling, all will follow and would want to sell faster than the other. This herd behavior is one of the reasons that growth stocks go up very fast and attract investor attraction. They also fall very fast as the herd comes to sell.

Chasing Fads and Fancies

As discussed earlier, growth stocks are dream stocks. It is the value of the mystery that excites investors. It is the lure of the new and the unknown that fascinates investors. Hence when such opportunities come in the market there is a ready set of buyers chasing these fads and fancies. Investors are always looking at something new, as they believe that novelty can fetch them more money. This novelty becomes a fancy when more and more investors chase it. This is also the effect of availability heuristic and herding. Thus, a fad and a fancy start quoting at fancy prices. This is termed as a growth stock as there is no available explanation to justify the steep rise in price.

Growth stocks become fads and fancies of the market and investors are known to run after them.

Novelty Over Familiarity

People in their pursuit to grab a piece of something novel forget the inherent conventional wisdom of time-tested principles of investing.

This fascination with something new is as old as the stock markets. From Tulip mania to the south Sea Bubble to the recent Tech bubble of 2000. Once upon a time they all promised immense growth.

Instant Gratification

We are always looking at short cuts or quick fixes. That is the way the environment works. Take the case of a game like cricket. Initially, we had the five-day test match which was replaced by a one-day 100-over match, and today we have a three hour, forty-over match known as Twenty–Twenty. People like quick results. Why wait for the result for five days when you can have it within three hours.

This allure of instant gratification plays an important part in investor stock preference. Value stocks are like five-day test matches while growth stocks are like the 20- 20 matches. Growth stocks are able to give instant gratification. The number of growth stocks in the market multiplies this instant gratification. That is the reason we have more growth stocks and more growth stock investors than value investors.

Rationalization Trap

The following observation by Benjamin Franklin highlights the rationalization trap brilliantly, "So convenient a thing it is to be a reasonable creature, since it enables one to find or make a reason for everything one has a mind to do."

Rationalization trap manifests in various forms, in the business and investment research space, as well. It is very common to come across businessmen seeking evidence to support the decision they have already made. Tata Nano is just one example, where having decided that they have to come out with a Rs. 1 lakh car, they seem to have placed all the other considerations, including the feasibility of such a project from the viewpoint of shareholders, as secondary.

Inspite of realizing severe losses by chasing a fancy by paying a fancy price, a growth investor continues to chase more emerging fancies and keeps on losing money by buying at ridiculous valuations. What explains this behavior? The answer lies in understanding a behavioral tendency known as 'Rationalization Trap.' It says that when one is faced with an unexpected outcome or failure, one attributes one's failure to external factors and not to oneself, which might not be the case, and continues to keep on repeating the mistakes. This is what happens in growth investing. Instead of realizing the consequences of one's behavior of ignoring the price commanded by a company in a fancy while making a buy decision, one will blame the promoters or market experts or business news channel for having misled him. This sort of behavior might help one deal with the psychological pain associated with holding oneself responsible for one's losses, but it ensures that when the next fancy sector emerges, one will be ready with one's hard-earned money to chase another fancy sector and lose it all over again. One will again start blaming somebody else for one's losses rather than one's emotional indiscipline.

Expectations Investing

Stock prices reflect expectations and the key to generating superior returns is to successfully anticipate expectation revisions. An important thing to understand is that neither a good high return business nor a bad low return business is inherently attractive or unattractive. Investors need to assess the stocks of all companies versus expectations.

The return on stocks depends not on earnings growth but solely on whether this earnings growth is more than what the investors expected. And are these growth expectations already reflected in the PE ratio?

The long-term return on a stock depends not on the actual growth in earnings but on how those earnings compare to what investors expected.

Stock markets reflect the sentiments of the investors. When the sentiments are bullish, the expectations are high and when the sentiments are bearish the expectations run low. Understanding these expectations and assessing their impact on the price is the key to good stock picking.

3.4 RETURNS

Investing is all about earning a return. For that we have seen two styles of investing. One is the difficult one requiring a lot of hard work and patience known as value investing. The other one is more fashionable and thrilling and is known as growth investing. Growth investing is investing in new ideas, new technology, new sectors, new initial public offerings, new additions to the indices, new fads and fancies etc. It is with a hope that a new breakthrough innovation or an idea will result in higher returns. However, when everyone is thinking on the same lines and trying to chase such ideas, these ideas become expensive and the investors start paying a higher price. This act of buying such overvalued growth stocks is falling into the growth trap.

Actually, there is nothing wrong with investing in new ideas and innovations. That is what capitalism is all about. There would be no innovations if investors shied away from investing in such companies. Many have made fortunes investing in such companies.

There is nothing wrong in buying a growth stock in its early stage, but such early phase is reserved for the venture capitalists and the private equity investors. They are the ones who enter early, and when they see the opportune time to exit, they get the stock listed and sell it on the stock markets when the markets are in a bull phase. In such markets, there is frenzy and least importance is given to valuations. The stocks start going up on investor demand. The steep rise in the price of a stock makes it worthy of being called a growth stock. This is when the investors get trapped. They tend to pay a much higher price, and even if they have invested in a good company, their overall returns suffer in the long run. Common sense would demand that they ask one question: If it's a growth stock and expected to do well why are the insiders selling?

Well they are selling because there is a sucker willing to buy and pay a fancy price. They had bought a value and are reaping the rewards because the fancy name of "Growth" is getting them a fancy price.

3.4.1 What Constitutes Stock Returns?

Stock investing is akin to buying a business with a sustainable business model. This business sells goods or services at a profit. This profit is distributed amongst its shareholders as dividends, and the remaining profit is again ploughed back to grow the business. This growth of the business is shared with the existing shareholders by issuing bonus (split) shares to them.

However if these shares of the business are listed on the stock market their price not only captures the fundamentals of the business but also the future growth expectations. This is dependent on the sentiments and the expectations of the investors in general in the market. In bullish times the investors are willing to pay a much higher price than the fundamentals justify, and in bearish times they would be willing to pay a much lower price than the fundamentals. This leads to volatility in the stock price of a company.

For an investor there are two components of stock returns:

1. The dividend one gets from the stock.
2. The capital appreciation of the stocks.

However, both these sources of returns are dependant on the price one pays when one acquires the stock. If one buys a stock in a bull market when prices are high, then one takes a hit on the dividend yield, and capital appreciation would take much longer as the base price is higher.

So, it is very important that the acquisition price is lower for one to have healthy stock returns. Hence, buying stocks without taking into consideration the value of the stock and the price one is paying for that value is a sure way to take a hit on one's long-term returns.

Stock returns multiply over time. Hence, patience and discipline are its best friends.

The Fallacy: Of late, investors have been accustomed to calculating returns on their speculative activity in stocks. Buying and selling stocks has become a fashion especially with the advent of online trading. When one makes a profit in buying and selling a stock one calculates the profits made as a return. It is actually a speculative profit. In the guise of speculating people believe that they are investing and hence the fallacy of confusing stock returns with speculative gains. However, a stock which is appreciating due to speculative activity may find fancy with the investors as the returns on the investment in that stock seem good. However, inherently the company may not be worthy of investment if one were to look at the value.

Reliance Natural Resources Ltd. (RNRL) is a stock that has good investor fancy and has appreciated from a low of Rs.18 in early 2007 to a high of Rs.240 in January 2008. Investors who bought at lower rates have had good returns in the stock. But, should one call these returns or speculative profits?. At a price of Rs. 240 per share, with an EPS of Rs. 0.40 per share, RNRL was quoting at a PE ratio of 600. Is this price justified? But investors who have made money in the stock will swear by it. This is just one example but there are so many stocks that come in to this category.

Moreover, this anomaly has been reinforced with the advent of open-ended mutual funds. These funds talk about long-term investing, but allow the investor to withdraw funds at 24 hours notice. This design itself induces the fund manager to speculative trading. His performance is based on the profits he makes in such trading and speculative activities. This is reported as returns generated on the investment activities of the fund. Some of the most reputed mutual funds that talk about long-term value investing have also bought RNRL. They are also speculating and not investing.

Having experienced a bull market for the last four years till the onset of bearish conditions in the recent past, we have been fed with all sorts of data by the media on investor returns. They all concentrated on the speculative and the trading gains. Availability heuristics made investors understand returns this way. They missed out on the larger and the true picture of stock returns.

3.4.2 Growth is not Returns

Most investors suffer from the false impression that higher the growth, higher the returns. Therefore, investors buying high PE stocks are under the impression that they are paying more for the expected growth. But what really determines a PE ratio? A company's value is a function of market expectations for its growth rate and its economic returns. This fundamental concept explains why looking at growth in isolation can be misleading. Growth can be good when a company earns a return in excess of its capital, and bad when the returns are below the cost of capital. One must have a clear sense whether or not a company is earning appropriate returns before one can judge the impact of growth. Companies can and do grow their way to bankruptcy. The IT boom and the bust brought out many such growth stories going downhill. Visual Soft, Pentafour, DSQ Software, Himachal Futuristics are just a few of them. There were no profits in their business models and the investors justified their high valuations as growth. Studying growth in isolation of economic returns is an invitation to failure.

Here is a case study of the returns and growth mismatch in Bharti Televentures Ltd., a hot stock in the market as it is in the hot sector of telecommunications. The stock has performed exceedingly well in the last three years and has been the favorite of the investors. The company is excellent and well-managed.

The more one pays for the current stream of earnings, the more one has to rely on future growth to reap profits from the investment. There is nothing inherently wrong in this setup except that one has accepted promises of returns for one's money and in the business world, future promises are easily made but take great effort to be met with.

Good Company vs Good Stock

Bharti Tele: A Unique Company:

Conventional Wisdom Belied

Most of the times we look at an industry and try to make sense of how a company in that sector would do. Every decision is governed by the information readily available to everyone. This is more evident when new technologies enter the market. Technology can enhance the productivity of an existing service or a product. But, when it is looked at in that fashion we really miss out on how a new technology would change the rules of the game for a particular industry. Take the case of the telecommunications industry. With the advent of mobile telephony a host of companies were vying for a piece of the action. We had six players with deep pockets vying for a dominant place in the Indian market having a huge population of prospective mobile users. The competition was so severe that the mobile talk charges were going down practically every quarter. Conventional wisdom was that if talktime charges are regularly falling, how could companies in this sector make profits—more so when we had six powerful players competing with each other.

One of the players in this highly competitive market dominated by international players was a first generation company by the name of Bharti Telecom promoted by Sunil Mital. Bharti stock was appreciating and was a favorite of the stock markets. Quarter to quarter it was posting healthy profits. The way its stock was going up it did not match any value parameters and was termed as a growth stock. No doubt when you cannot justify the valuation of a company one would term it as a growth stock. But here was the major difference. Bharti Telecom was in the business of creating a wireless infrastructure.

Technology was changing everything. It was paving the way for the new by destroying the old. The old way of looking at the rates of talk-time and then valuing the company was dead. The way to look at was how this infrastructure of the mobile telephony will change the lives of people. In the industrial world we talked about economies of large-scale production. Enabling mass use of mobile telephones was the goal to change the behavior of people. The demographic change due to the use of technology changed the way people looked at paying for services. Moreover, the ease of use of mobile phones empowered the people to be confident of the new technological revolution. This in a way was also educating the people on the new advantages of technology. As people became more confident of using the technology, the technology revolution itself enabled the companies to bring down the cost of services so low that even the poorest people were able to use it. This penetration enabled the people to realize the value of communication. This created a communication revolution unheard of even in the developed world. Most of the large international players were caught napping as they missed out on the big communication revolution in India. They went by the conventional wisdom that a poor country like India was not a market for mobile phones. However the converse has been true. The mobile revolution was supported by China and India, the most poor and populated countries. Mobile telephony was a big failure in the US and it took years before being accepted by the people.

A poor country like India suffered from poor infrastructure facilities like roads and transport. However the birth of the wireless infrastructure in the form of mobile phones mitigated a lot of problems of the people. The ability to connect and communicate enabled small businesses to offer value-based services, professionals to be effective in their professions, businesses became customer-centered. Even small vegetable and fruit vendors were able to service their clients efficiently and effectively. This also improved the overall customer service and satisfaction. Villages are effectively connected to cities with the wireless infrastructure while the road and the rail infrastructure could not keep pace.

Mobile phones have changed the behavior of people. This mobile phone has become a habit, to be connected at all times. A difficult habit to change. This has changed the fortunes of Bharti Telecom, an Indian company born just after the liberalization process started in 1991.

This is where the investors get trapped when they chase such innovative companies and pay fancy prices for their breakthrough success. Can Bharti go on repeating what it has done? Technology was a wealth creator for Bharti in the initial stages and this same technology when used by the competitors and when new technologies started replacing it, become a wealth destroyer for the company. The company has to go on reducing the talk-time rates and the customer is the beneficiary. Such breakthrough companies do change the rules of the game and make life easier for the consumers. We salute such companies. But it would be foolish to think that the stock of the company is also very good when the built-in expectations of people are very high.

The initial investors reaped huge fortunes for investing in a company like Bharti. They had foresight and they paid the right price for a company expected to grow in a new domain having the first entrant advantage. In fact they were buying a value and that is what got them the profits. But paying any price for even a growth company like Bharti will hit returns. Growth does not translate into returns.

3.5 CONCLUSION

In spite of such strong evidence why do most individual and professional investors not change their behavior to embrace value-investing strategies? It is amply evident that growth investing is risky although majority follows it.

I was with a fund manager of a large mutual fund and discussing the type of services we could offer. In the course of the decision the fund manager categorically stated that though he believed in my value strategies he wanted me to give him ideas on stocks that will go up in the short run. When I expressed my inability to do so as it did not match with my investing beliefs and principles, he curtly informed me that for him keeping his high profile and high-paying job was more important and thus he had to rely on momentum strategies rather than be a contrarian and underperform in the short run. His organization will not tolerate underperformance. Knowing fully well that he was not doing the right thing he lacked the courage to stand up.

One answer offered by Lakonishak, Schleifer and Vishny is that being a contrarian may be too risky for the average individual or a professional.

If you are wrong along with everyone else, the consequences professionally and for one's self-esteem are far less than if you are wrong and alone in your choice of action. It's safer to be with the herd as it allows for the comfort of safety in numbers.

Another reason is that individuals tend not to change courses if they are happy. Individuals can be happy with sub-optimal performance so long as it is not painful. Moreover, individuals who tend to be unhappy and prone to making changes often do so for the wrong reasons and end up being just as unhappy in their new circumstances. Resistance to change and fear of failure may simply be forces too great to overcome.

Greed and envy seems to be the biggest sins for investors getting trapped in the growth trap. The lure to make a fast fortune drains them out of any rationality and common sense. Looking at others' success without knowing the risks taken by them, people try to emulate them thinking that they too shall be as successful as them.

It is evident that no rationality works in the stock markets, as they are inefficient especially in the short run. What works in the stock markets is one's ability to understand one's emotional and psychological weaknesses. This is the first step. Thereafter, understanding the irrational behavior of others and benefiting from their mistakes is the second step. And the third step is to have the courage and conviction to stand away from the crowd. That is why value investing works. It's a contrarian approach and few follow it. The herd very often falls victim to the growth trap.

Value investing is knowledge and growth investing is mystery.

FOUR

4

CONTRARIAN INVESTING: THE PSYCHOLOGY OF GOING AGAINST THE CROWD

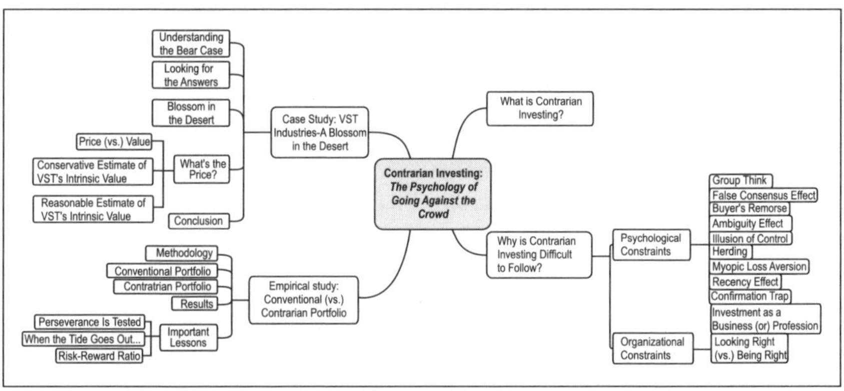

4.1 What is Contrarian Investing?
4.2 Why is Contrarian Investing Difficult to Follow?
4.3 Empirical Study: Conventional vs. Contrarian Portfolio
4.4 Case Study: VST Industries—A Blossom in the Desert

4.1 WHAT IS CONTRARIAN INVESTING?

"If everybody else is doing it one way, there's a good chance you can find your niche by going in exactly the opposite direction. [But] be prepared for a lot of folks to wave you down and tell you you're headed the wrong way"—Sam Walton

> **A contrarian investor can be defined as one who attempts to profit by betting against conventional wisdom, but only when the consensual opinion appears to be wrong.**

What exactly does 'contrarian investing' mean? Does it mean that the investor has to be somebody who believes that conventional wisdom is *always* wrong? Also, among the majority of investors who subscribe to the fundamental school of comparing the price of a security to its intrinsic value, what is it that differentiates the minority of contrarian investors?

A contrarian investor can be defined as one who attempts to profit by betting against conventional wisdom, but only when the consensual opinion appears to be wrong. What really differentiates the contrarian investor is his emphasis on looking for opportunities where consensual opinion has led to mispricing. When I say looking for mispriced bets, I mean that they are looking to exploit areas where consensual opinion is not wrong *per se* in its stand, but has led to an exaggeration of problems at hand. This exaggeration is often the result of mass psychology that is prevalent in the stock market to varying degrees.

At the heart of the argument of betting against the crowd when the consensual opinion appears to be wrong, is the belief that markets—which are more often than not efficient—sometimes err on the side of inefficiency. To understand this anomaly, it helps to think of the stock market as an aggregator, where people of diverse opinions, expectations and incentives, bet against each other, leading to more or less efficient markets. But sometimes this diversity amongst its participants breaks down, due to factors like excessive fear or greed, leading to the majority set of participants acting as an individual. It is at times like this that a contrarian investor starts to see an opportunity to consider betting against the crowd, if he has reason to believe that it is not the fundamentals but fear and greed that are driving the current markets.

Before we discuss the results that can be expected by a contrarian investor betting against the consensus opinion when it appears to be carried to excesses, let us discuss the psychological and organizational aspects which make it difficult for him to go against the crowd to which he himself belongs.

4.2 WHY IS CONTRARIAN INVESTING DIFFICULT TO FOLLOW?

As an investor, or even as a speculator for that matter, the aim is to profit by buying low and selling high. The foundation that is the basis for making those buy and sell decisions can be divided into two types: fundamental analysis and technical analysis. A fundamental analyst will compare current price with historic and prospective earnings. The fundamental approach can be further sub-divided into: top-down approach, a bottom-up approach, growth, value, country-specific, and commodity. On the other hand, the technical analyst will compare current price and volume patterns to the price and volume patterns from the past, along with many other indicators pertaining to supply and demand for shares of a specific company.

An above average PE ratio is generally indicative of optimistic future prospects from the enterprise and a below average PE ratio indicates a pessimistic outlook.

Among the fundamental analysts—who constitute a majority of the investment community—what is it that differentiates contrarian and value investors from the rest? And why is it that people who subscribe to this school of thought only constitute a minority, despite no major distinction in their basic foundation? Possible answers to these questions can be found in the form of two types of constraints, psychological and organizational.

4.2.1 Psychological Constraints

"*You can think of investing as a long-term journey with many starts, stops, changes of scenery and occasional bumps. We believe that you are much more likely to enjoy the journey, or at least endure it, and reach your destination safely, if you know what to expect along the way. Your own psychology and ability to handle the emotional ups and downs of investing are likely to be important determinants of your long run investment success.*" Tweedy Browne

One of the most important aspects of successful investing is to ensure that closer attention is paid to the risk-reward ratio, and not just to the reward alone.

Individuals often use heuristics to help themselves get on with their daily lives, by making things easier to accomplish. But for us as investors, these shortcuts can be detrimental to our investment performance by affecting the way we make decisions. The important heuristics which make contrarian investing a difficult task to accomplish are described in the following sections.

Group Thinking

One of the advantages of being an individual investor is that there is no pressure to sacrifice your own views to be a part of any group or to have people agree with you. It is a different matter that individuals sometimes create their own groups, among friends or colleagues, and succumb to group thinking; but there is no obligation on their part to be a part of a group. However, when they belong to fund houses, the most common behavioral anomaly affecting individuals is 'group think'. They all think alike, and even if they don't agree with something, for fear of being reprimanded in the group, they hide their true perspective about something rather than stick their necks out.

False Consensus Effect

The false consensus effect highlights a tendency common amongst us to overestimate the percentage of people we think would agree with us. As an investor, the decision we reach about an investment opportunity does not necessarily have to be in accordance with most other people. Their motives for investing in the stock market might be different, their philosophy might be totally different, their risk-appetite might be different, and their expectation from business might be different from ours. The bottom line is to remind ourselves of the false consensus effect when we have people disagreeing with us, and to weigh our decision based on the facts we have on hand and our reasoning, and to not let other people's perceptions affect us unless they point to something wrong in our reasoning.

Buyer's Remorse

What makes sticking to a contrarian philosophy so difficult? Buyer's remorse, a tendency that is common amongst everybody to varying extents, partly answers that question. Buyer's remorse is that after we commit our capital to anything, self-doubt triggers a sort of remorse to the extent that we feel we may have done something wrong. In times like this, unless we have a deep conviction in our stand and are ready to face the uncertainty, it becomes very difficult to continue with our stand, as most people we would come across would be hell bent on proving us wrong. Thus, a deep-rooted conviction, leading to being patient with such an approach is a key to following a contrarian approach to investing.

> **For an investor, the financial statements representing the recent performance of the enterprise constitute an indispensable tool. But the value is a function of the ability of the enterprise to generate cash flows in the future.**

Ambiguity Effect

Investing involves facing uncertainty in the form of changes in price movements and unexpected performance from the underlying businesses. In short, it can be said that while investing one is faced with lots of uncertainty coming from all corners. Under such circumstances, most people lack the conviction in their reasoning and seek social proof or authority supporting their stand to get over the ambiguity. This irrational behavior, born out of ambiguity or confusion, can be termed as the 'ambiguity effect'. This effect can range from ignoring cheap stocks from out–of-favor sectors to buying into speculative stocks based on widespread acknowledgement through media and experts to justify one's stand.

Illusion of Control

How many of us can say that we reached our present state by putting in effort towards this particular end? None of us, I suppose. Chance plays a critical role in governing the exact outcome of our endeavors. Our job is to ensure that good work will eventually be rewarded in the long run. The same applies to stockmarket investing. Yet it is common to note that people have a tendency to act as if they have everything under their control, especially when it comes to investing.

For example, sometimes a well-implemented investment strategy takes years to justify one's choice, whereas at other times luck saves one from suffering a loss even where one has made a mistake. In such a scenario, we should not fool ourselves by believing that we have destiny under our control. Taking on leverage which can wipe you out if you get something wrong highlights that 'illusion of control' is not as uncommon as one might want to believe.

Herding

As an investor, it is difficult to think out-of-the-box or to stand outside the pack for consistently longer periods of time. It requires an unflinching conviction in one's belief and the ability to withstand being called a failure until the culmination of the struggle. And contrarian investing requires one to be able to have attributes such as being patient through the periods of uncertainty before the final outcome, which could eventually prove one right.

Considering the above, it is only normal that people tend to converge towards an opinion which forms the foundation of the conventional wisdom, irrespective of its validity. Moreover, the ability to withstand such social pressures and hold contradicting views should be considered an extraordinary behavior on the part of the individual.

Myopic Loss Aversion

'*If you cannot stand 50% paper loss on your stock, stay away from the markets*' Warren Buffet

'Loss aversion' refers to the fact that people are more upset when they experience losses as compared to the satisfaction they derive from a similar gain. This tendency leads to a behavior wherein investors, faced with the prospect of temporary quotation loss, tend to forgo investing in such situations even if, in the long run, such an approach leads to higher returns.

Seen in this light, the difficulty of following a contrarian approach surfaces, as its very foundation is based on the notion of betting on something whose prospects are not good in the short- to medium-term. Moreover, as a contrarian investor, the ability to withstand temporary losses is a necessity rather than an exception.

Recency Effect

People are not blessed with unlimited circuitry in their brains to simultaneously consider many things to reach a decision about something. The best way to go about making a decision under such physiological constraints is to use the data that is readily available. More often than not, memory brings to the fore data that is most recent. Unless one consciously puts in an effort to consider things from the past, it is a normal behavior to fall into the trap of believing the recent past to be an appropriate representation of the ultimate reality. To be a contrarian investor, one needs to have the ability to place the present situation in the context of not only the present or the recent past, but also to go far into the past and put things in perspective. This can be termed as abnormal behavior and helps explain the minority status of such investors.

Confirmation Trap

There is generally a lag between an action and its desired outcome. And there is never a surety that a particular action will lead to a particular outcome. Under such circumstances, it is only natural to validate one's stance by seeking confirmation from the actions of other people. In the absence of such evidence and the inability to confirm our actions, one is left to face great uncertainty until the culmination of the outcome. Inability to withstand such pressures, in the form of psychological turmoil, is a natural behavioral reaction. But as a contrarian investor, one has to learn to stick to and to test one's own views and stance, and this makes contrarian investing difficult to successfully implement.

4.2.2 Organizational Constraints

A vast pool of capital to be invested in capital markets takes the route of institutions—mutual funds, private equities, insurance companies, pension funds, NRIs, FIIs, etc.—where the investment decisions are taken under the purview of agendas set by authorities primarily looking after the interests of the institutions. Secondly, these agendas are followed by individual asset managers, whose interests might not be in alignment with those of the stakeholders of the institutions. The general areas of conflict of interest can be divided into two: (i) between the institution and the segregated stakeholders, and (ii) between the asset managers and the institutions.

Investment as a Business or Profession

The simple distinction between investment as a business and as a profession can be understood from the basic mode of profit-seeking by the institution. Does it earn a profit only when the stakeholders—say, unit-holders in mutual funds—make a profit? Or does it take a simple route of keeping a considerable portion of assets-under-management as a management fee, reaching as high 3-5% of assets every year, irrespective of benchmarking the performance of the fund with the broader indices over the same period? The answer is the amount of money made by asset management companies are directly linked to the amount managed by them and is not linked directly to the performance.

Operating under such misaligned incentives, the authorities might be more interested in attracting more capital under management than working towards increasing the chances of making more money *for* the current stakeholders, particularly when it involves sitting on the sidelines and going against conventional wisdom, which leads to temporary periods of looking foolish.

Looking Right versus Being Right

"*Worldly wisdom teaches that it is better for reputation to fail conventionally than to succeed unconventionally*" – John Maynard Keynes

Let us discuss the second constraint, which exists in the form of conflict of interest between the individuals making decisions on behalf of institutions and the stakeholders. This conflict prevents the decision-makers from following contrarian investing.

These individuals are more interested in making themselves appear right in the eyes of authorities and colleagues in order to increase their chances of moving up in the professional hierarchy, rather than to bet against the crowd—which could involve sitting on the sidelines, appearing foolish, having conviction in their actions, until the tide eventually turns to prove them right.

For example, take the case of the late-1990s, when people who were skeptical of the dawn of a new era with the advent of the Internet, in terms of creating sustained levels of growth and shareholder value-creation, proved to be right in the end. It should not be forgotten that many of these people lost their jobs and faced harsh criticism by being called outdated, when the markets continued to exhibit irrational exuberance for an extended period. What little consolation would it have been in the end, after having lost their jobs and appearing foolish for a year or two, while betting against the crowd? Many of them did not manage to get back their lost jobs or to get the credit which they deserved in the first place.

When faced with the prospect of saving your job versus making an extra few percentage points of profits for your stakeholders, it does not take the knowledge of rocket science to choose the first option. And as long as there exists this conflict of interest, people ready to bet against the crowd would continue to be few and far between.

Having discussed the constraints, let us now discuss the results that can be expected by a contrarian investor with the help of a study conducted by our research team at Parag Parikh Financial Advisory Services Ltd.

4.3 EMPIRICAL STUDY: CONVENTIONAL VERSUS CONTRARIAN PORTFOLIO

"*Those who do not learn from history are condemned to repeat it*" - Santayana

The broader index, the BSE Sensex, is constituted from a group of 30 leading companies representing the important sectors of the economy. The performance of the Sensex and its underlying companies is generally considered to be a reflection of how well the economy is functioning. At any given point in time, there are sectors with optimistic prospects just as there are a few with pessimistic prospects.

For an investor, what should be the rational approach in taking a stake in a business, through the equity medium, when the sole aim is to profit from such an initiative? The answer that seems right at first instance is to buy a stake in the leading players in the sectors, especially where the outlook for the future growth seems imminent, and avoid laggards in terms of recent performance and with a poor outlook, as the surest way to ensure superior performance. However, the study under consideration aims to prove that the seemingly obvious answer does not lead to the expected financial results.

Even though the Sensex PE ratio is taken very seriously by the market participants in forming a view of the attractiveness of the investment scenario, one thing that is not properly utilized is to compare among the constituents of the Sensex. For example, currently the Sensex trades at a PE multiple of around 22 times the recent earnings. But on a closer look, it emerges that the range of PE ratios starts from 9 and ends at 160 times the recent earnings. This range, of course, reflects the difference in quality of the recent trend in earnings but also, more importantly, the differential in the expectations from these businesses.

An above average PE ratio is generally indicative of optimistic future prospects from the enterprise and a below average PE ratio indicates a pessimistic outlook. Extending this line of thought, it can be observed that a high PE ratio is also a result of a good outlook for the industry it represents, from whose growth the enterprise in consideration is expected to reap huge benefits. Is positive outlook an appropriate indicator in deciding which enterprise deserves to be considered a long-term investment opportunity? Or a possibility of reversal of the fortunes and investor interest should make one believe that low PE stocks should turn out to be better bets as a long-term investment opportunity?

The following study was carried out to find answer to these questions. The aim was to observe, using the most recent decade, whether companies with a positive outlook and current high PE ratio have superior long-term results or whether the low PE stocks, with a pessimistic outlook of the future, tend to outperform the other group. Based on the results of this study, we can design a prudent way to invest by taking selective exposure to sound players, from either low PE or high PE stocks.

4.3.1 Methodology

Let us time travel in the past and calculate the returns of two portfolios constructed using PE ratios as a measure. The portfolios constructed for this purpose would try to replicate the performance of each of the following two strategies:

(1) Conventional or High PE Strategy:

Invest Rs 1 lakh in the 10 highest PE stocks, from the Sensex, at the start of the exercise, i.e., financial year 1995, and sell at the end of the year, and repeat this methodology of picking stocks, by investing 10% of the resulting value from then on in each of the 10 stocks chosen this way from 1996–97 to 2005–06.

(2) Contrarian or Low PE Strategy:

Invest Rs.1 lakh in the 10 lowest PE stocks, from the Sensex, at the start of the exercise, i.e., financial year 1995 and sell at the end of the year and repeat this methodology of picking stocks, by investing 10% of the resulting value from then on in each of the 10 stocks chosen this way from 1996–97 to 2005–06.

(3) Results:

Compare the results of the two strategies and draw important lessons.

4.3.2 Conventional Portfolio

The reason for using the word 'conventional' in the context of high PE ratio stocks is as follows: PE ratio is one of the most popular valuation metrics used by the financial community. A high PE ratio is only possible when the majority of the investor community thinks that the prospects of a given industry and its representative stocks offer a good investment opportunity.

In the process, investor interest results in high appraisal of recent earnings, leading to a high PE ratio. Considering the fact that conventional wisdom involves the opinion of the majority, we have named the portfolio resulting from the strategy of investing in high PE stocks of the Sensex in any given year as 'conventional portfolio', deriving its name from the foundation that such a strategy is based on conventional wisdom.

Before we get to the results of the study, let us take a quick look at the nature of the portfolio by reviewing the average PE ratio of such a portfolio constructed, at the start of each financial year, during the last decade. The average PE ratio for a given year is the average of the PEs of the 10 stocks selected in the portfolio.

Table 4.1 Average PE of Conventional Portfolio Stocks

Portfolio Year	Average PE
1995–96	36
1996–97	36
1997–98	30
1998–99	45
1999–00	62
2000–01	79
2001–02	37
2002–03	28
2003–04	20
2004–05	25
2005–06	37

As can be observed from the preceding table, the average PE of the conventional portfolio has ranged from a low of 20 at the start of financial year 2003 to a high of 79 at the start of financial year 2000. The average PE ratio of the 11 such portfolios, constructed between 1995 to 2005 is 40 times the trailing twelve months' earnings.

4.3.3 Contrarian Portfolio

The reason for using the word 'contrarian' in the context of the strategy involving low PE ratio stocks is as follows: PE ratio is one of the most popular valuation metrics used by the financial community; a low PE ratio is only possible when the majority of the investor community thinks that the prospects of a given industry and its representative stocks offer unattractive investment opportunities.

In the process, investor interest fades from these sectors and associated companies, resulting in low appraisal of recent earnings and lower expectations from the future, leading to low PE ratios. Considering the fact that contrarian wisdom is founded on the notion of betting against the opinion of the majority, we have named the portfolio resulting from the strategy of investing in such neglected stocks of the Sensex in any given year as a 'contrarian portfolio'.

Just as we did in the conventional portfolio, let us take a quick look at the nature of the portfolio by reviewing the average PE ratio of such a portfolio constructed, at the start of each financial year, during the last decade. Again, the average PE ratio for a given year is the average of the 10 stocks selected in the portfolio.

Table 4.2 Average PE of Contrarian Portfolio Stocks

Portfolio Year	Average PE
1995–96	16
1996–97	18
1997–98	13
1998–99	14
1999–00	14
2000–01	11
2001–02	15
2002–03	11
2003–04	11
2004–05	13
2005–06	13

As can be observed from the above table, the average PE of the contrarian portfolio has ranged from a low of 11 at the start of financial years 2000, 2002, and 2003 to a high of 18 at the start of financial year 1996. The average PE ratio of the 11 such portfolios constructed is 14 times the recent twelve months' earnings.

4.3.4 Results

Let us now get to the results that a conventional (or high) PE portfolio and a contrarian (or low) PE portfolio would have delivered during the period of the evaluation. The results are depicted using a chart indicating the cumulative value of Rs.1 lakh invested using each of the strategies over the 11-year period.

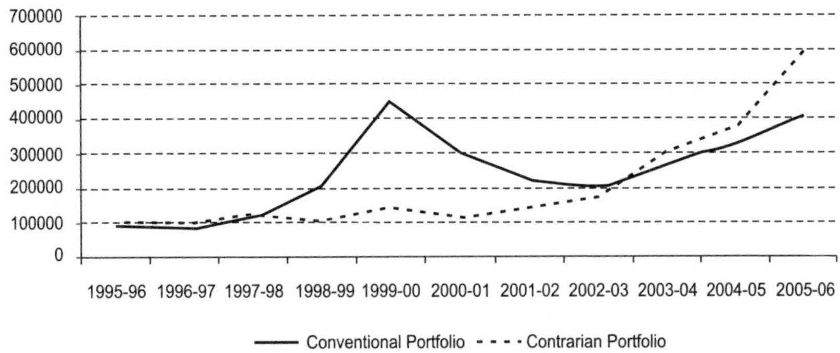

Figure 4.1 Results of Conventional versus Contrarian Portfolios

The chart indicates two key things:

(1) The contrarian (or low) PE portfolio has—in spite of its underperformance vis-à-vis the conventional (or high) PE portfolio during the IT bubble period—managed to easily beat the conventional portfolio over the long run.

(2) The rise in the contrarian portfolio is steadier and indicates less risk, in terms of severe losses in the interim, as compared to the conventional portfolio. This reduces financial and emotional strain as we go about leading our lives. At the end of the day, isn't it true that financial rewards are a means to achieve better lives?

For a more detailed analysis of the quality of results, let us take a look at the year-wise performance. The conventional portfolio has delivered a compounded annual rate of return of around 13.6% during the period under consideration. A 13.6% annualized return ensures that Rs.1 lakh invested at the start of the financial year 1995 would have grown to Rs. 4.06 lakhs by the end of financial year 2005.

Table 4.3 Returns from Conventional Portfolio

Year	Average PE	Returns %	Cumulative Value of Portfolio (Rs.)
1995–96	36	*–7.6*	92,379
1996–97	36	*–9.4*	83,665
1997–98	30	*41.9*	1,18,690

(Contd.)

Year	Average PE	Returns %	Cumulative Value of Portfolio (Rs.)
1998–99	45	*72.0*	2,04,141
1999–00	62	*120.4*	4,50,012
2000–01	79	*–32.3*	3,04,588
2001–02	37	*–25.8*	2,26,111
2002–03	28	*–10.9*	2,01,507
2003–04	20	31.9	2,65,755
2004–05	25	21.3	3,22,448
2005–06	37	25.9	4,05,896
Average PE	**40**		

On the other hand, the contrarian portfolio has delivered a compounded annual rate of return of around 17.7% during the period under consideration. A 17.7% annualized return ensures that Rs.1 lakh invested at the start of the financial year 1995 would have grown to Rs. 5.99 lakhs by the end of financial year 2005.

Table 4.4 Returns from Contrarian Portfolio

Year	Average PE	Returns %	Cumulative Value of Portfolio (Rs.)
1995–96	16	*–3.7*	96,259
1996–97	18	*–1.6*	94,742
1997–98	13	*28.1*	1,21,411
1998–99	14	*–13.9*	1,04,484
1999–00	14	*38.0*	1,44,179
2000–01	11	*–20.9*	1,14,018
2001–02	15	*23.2*	1,40,484

(Contd.)

Year	Average PE	Returns %	Cumulative Value of Portfolio (Rs.)
2002–03	11	*23.2*	1,73,125
2003–04	11	*71.8*	2,97,468
2004–05	13	*26.4*	3,76,068
2005–06	13	*59.3*	5,99,164
Average PE	**14**		

4.3.5 Important Lessons

Having seen the difference in the quality of results emanating from the two strategies, let us review the key takeaways from the whole study.

Perseverance is Tested

It can be observed that out of 11 years evaluated under the study, the conventional (or high) PE portfolio has outperformed the Contrarian (or low) PE portfolio in only three instances; viz., the financial years 1997 to 1999.

During this period, as is a well-established fact, we saw one of the greatest mass manias in recent times, with the evolution of information technology as a so-called 'new era'. The comparative performance of the two portfolios during that period can be seen from the table below.

Table 4.5 Comparative Performance of Portfolios during 1997–2000

	Conventional Portfolio		**Contrarian Portfolio**	
Year	**Average PE**	**Returns %**	**Average PE**	**Returns %**
1997–98	30	41.9	13	28.1
1998–99	45	72.0	14	–13.9
1999–00	62	120.4	14	38.0

During this period, holding onto the laggard stocks would have hurt you in two ways. First, it resulted in significant underperformance and secondly, looking like a fool for standing outside the crowd. But the true rewards of such a stance would have been felt during the ensuing years.

When the Tide Goes Out

As the legendary investor, Warren Buffett appropriately said, "*It is only when the tide goes out that we know who has been swimming naked*", the true reward was realized by the contrarian investor during the next four years as the conventional portfolio continued to lose money because of the correction in IT stocks, while the low PE stocks representing sectors that were neglected during the IT bubble attracted investor interest and considerably out-performed the IT stocks. This can be seen from the table below.

Table 4.6 Comparative Performance of Portfolios During 2000–2004

	Conventional Portfolio		Contrarian Portfolio	
Year	Average PE	Returns %	Average PE	Returns %
2000–01	79	–32.3	11	–20.9
2001–02	37	–25.8	15	23.2
2002–03	28	–10.9	11	23.2
2003–04	20	31.9	11	71.8

Risk-Reward Ratio

One of the most important aspects of successful investing is to ensure that closer attention is paid to the risk-reward ratio, and not just to the reward alone. The failure on the part of an investor to follow this principle has to be the main cause of the under-performance of the conventional portfolio as compared to the contrarian portfolio.

Take a look at the table below, which highlights the performance during the years when broader indices gave a negative or negligible return to investors, indicating overall bearish sentiments towards equity investing. On a closer look, it emerges that in every single year the contrarian portfolio has out-performed the other portfolio by a significant margin.

Table 4.7 Portfolio Performance During Bear Market Years

	Conventional Portfolio		Contrarian Portfolio	
Year	Average PE	Returns%	Average PE	Returns %
1995-96	36	–7.6	16	–3.7
1996-97	36	–9.4	18	–1.6
2000-01	79	–32.3	11	–20.9
2001-02	37	–25.8	15	23.2
2002-03	28	–10.9	11	23.2

The out-performance of the contrarian portfolio when the sentiments are negative is highlighted by the fact that even though the conventional portfolio has shown a stellar return of 120.4% in 1999, negative returns of 32.3% and 25.8% in subsequent years were enough to wipe out very nearly all the gains made during the year 1999. as IT stocks retreated to more reasonable levels.

In essence, the contrarian portfolio's out-performance can be attributed to the fact that while it exposes one to laggard stocks considered less rewarding, the risk is curtailed which seems to have led to its overall superior performance.

Having discussed, with the help of the above example, that time may be well-spent looking for an attractive contrarian pick among the neglected stocks, let us now spend some time on an investment opportunity that qualifies as a contrarian pick. The following discussion highlights various aspects of contrarian investing in practice.

4.4 CASE STUDY: VST INDUSTRIES — A BLOSSOM IN THE DESERT

During the last few years, we have witnessed one of the major bull markets in the history of the Indian equity markets. The impetus behind this bull market seems to be two-fold. First, increased economic activity leading to impressive growth realizations for corporate India and secondly, the possibility of positive re-rating* happening across most of

* Positive re-rating' denotes the expansion of PE ratio. For example, when the Sensex moves up from a PE ratio of 12 to PE ratio of 25, it is denoted as being positively re-rated.

the companies trading on the bourses. This has created huge wealth for the shareholders as a whole.

A natural consequence of an extended bull market is the shift in the risk-reward ratio on opportunities available in the market. Before the onset of the bull market, when in a bear (or consolidation) phase, mass psychology makes people fixated on the risk, all the time, without comparing the huge rewards that are there to compensate for the risk taken. As the bull phase progresses and the inherent risk factor increases, the mass psychology being totally fixated on recent rewards achieved by investors, loses its focus on the inherent risk quotient of the markets. Here we have a classic case of mass psychology leading to mis-appraisal of the risk-reward ratio, inbuilt in the stock valuations, at various stages of the market cycle because of behavioral anomalies leading to excesses and resultant painful contractions leading to great losses to people who forget to think in terms of the inherent risk and reward factors of an opportunity. It is no different in this bull market also.

As a contrarian investor—whom the legendary investor, Warren Buffett, appropriately defined as somebody who gets greedy when others are fearful and one who gets fearful when others are greedy—one should not forget the important principle of comparing the reward against the risk, while making investment decisions.

In effect, as the market and stocks start to fully discount the fundamentals of the business and future prospects, one would do well to shuffle one's portfolio by replacing stocks with deteriorating risk-reward ratios with opportunities that offer attractive risk-reward prospects. This involves constantly looking for businesses where the true value of the business is not fully reflected in the stock price. This approach of striking the right balance between price and value involves betting against the conventional wisdom because if conventional wisdom followed the same principle, investors would end up driving markets to become *fully* efficient; i.e., every business would be valued appropriately based on its underlying fundamentals and expectations to deliver risk-adjusted rate of return.

But as long as mass psychology drives the market, there are going to be areas where the businesses will be mispriced, and the prospects of earning an above-average return will exist. One of the best places to look for such mispricing, led by mis-appraisal of a security, is the '52-week low' list published in all the business newspapers. It must be remembered that most of the stocks on the list deservedly make it there because of deteriorating fundamentals and business prospects; but occasionally a neglected stock, with strong fundamentals and prospects, also makes it to the list.

One such stock, which has been a part of the 52-week low list many a times during the last year is VST Industries. The extent of pessimism, or lack of interest, towards this stock is evident by taking a look at the chart below, comparing the performance of the Sensex and VST Industries during the last two years. As the Sensex has gone up around 80% during the two years, VST Industries has lost 30% of its market value during the same time.

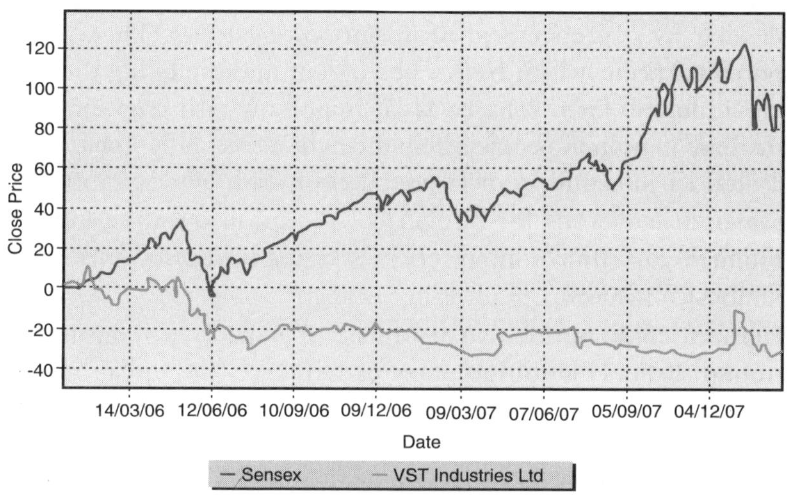

Figure 4.2 Price of VST Industries versus the Sensex, 2006-2007

4.4.1 Understanding the Bear Case

Just as it pays in sports to learn as much as possible about the opponents, it also pays in investing to understand the rationale behind the stance taken by the opponents. In the context of investing, opponent is somebody who holds an opposing view to the one held by you. Now, in the case of VST Industries, it would involve understanding the reason behind the lack of investor interest towards this enterprise.

Understanding the bear case would involve seeking answers to the following questions: Does it operate in a business with bad economics? Is it a company whose financial stability is in a questionable state? Is it a business facing intense competition, which makes the competitive advantage susceptible to invasion by new entrants and causes deterioration in its earnings power? Is it a business with questionable management practices being practiced leading to misappropriation of assets? Does the current price fully discount the recent performance and future prospects of the enterprise?

4.4.2 Looking for the Answers

VST Industries belongs to the tobacco industry, being one of the four main cigarette manufacturers with a 10% market share. Let us start with a discussion of the tobacco industry to which VST belongs, before discussing its respective area of operation, cigarettes. There are two important aspects, which have a bearing on understanding the nature of the industry. First, tobacco is an important cash crop employing more than 60 million people across the nation. Secondly, tobacco as an end product in the form of cigarette, cigar, bidi, gutka, snuff etc., is considered dangerous for human consumption over the long run, resulting in government intervention in trying to control consumption by indirect measures.

Cigarette consumption, as a percentage of total tobacco consumption, is around 20%. This consumption pattern gives the Indian market a unique structure, as in other countries the percentage of cigarette consumption as a percentage of total tobacco consumption is more than 80%. Part of the reason for this anomaly is that chewing tobacco has been a tradition in India and a large number of consumers still prefer this to cigarettes. Also, government has taken a strong stance against cigarette manufacturers, in the form of levying a high excise duty and VAT on cigarettes as compared to other tobacco products, leading to a shift in consumer preference from cigarettes to bidi and chewing tobacco. This explains the fact that cigarette companies generate around 80% of the total tax generated from the tobacco industry, inspite of their relatively negligible share of the overall tobacco market. But with increasing per capita income, the consumption pattern is expected to change in favor of cigarettes, leading to reasonable growth prospects for cigarette manufacturers.

But what about the competition and pricing power in the face of consistent increase in excise duty levied on cigarette manufacturers. Would they be able to withstand such measures and continue to maintain their profitability?

High Barriers to Entry

In 2004, Government of India banned all forms of advertisements by cigarette manufacturers, to curb cigarette consumption. Inspite of its seemingly negative implication for the cigarette manufacturers, this holds a significant positive for the incumbent players as it resulted in two things:

(1) It became improbable for a new player, without consumer awareness and loyalty, to establish a new brand in the market, leading to a stronger competitive position for the incumbent players.

(2) It resulted in lower advertisement expenditure, and thereby improved profitability.

Brand Value - Share of Mind

The consumption of cigarettes is more an act of habit, rather than one of choice which can be put on hold or changed. Under such circumstances, the addicted person develops a certain utility from a given brand, which is not calculable nor alterable by external means, unless he himself shifts from one brand to another, based on changes in his economic well-being. This allows the major brands to effect price increases in the face of increasing costs, resulting in the maintenance of their profitability. Moreover, as the new breed of youngsters start getting addicted, the basic nature of consumption behavior and brand loyalty makes it unlikely that brand deterioration and the resultant pricing pressure will be a major concern.

4.4.3 Blossom in the Desert

Conclusively, it can be said that, even though the cigarette industry is operating in a challenging regulatory environment with government not in favor of its progress and reasonable growth prospects, the incumbent players enjoy a considerable moat around themselves, in the form of their ability to pass on the excise duties to some extent resulting in favorable overall economics to work with. An appropriate analogy that comes to mind when trying to put things in perspective regarding the cigarette industry is that of a blossom in the desert, where the industry *per se* might have the attributes of a desert but the players have the attributes of a blossom in the form of good cash flows, high return on capital employed, dividend payouts, and future prospects.

4.4.4 What's the Price?

The story is still mid-way as it involves answering an important question: Would VST Industries make a good investment at current market price? Before we start with the process of comparing the price with the value behind the enterprise, let us review the basic parameters of the security at the closing market price as at the time of this writing—31st March, 2008. In the following table,

- Treasury indicates the excess cash, which is not deployed in the business towards the operation, held in the form of liquid funds.
- Cash from Operations = (Operational Cash after Working Capital Changes) – (Capital Expenditure)
- Growth is measured as annualized growth rate in earnings per share and book value over four years, from 2003–07.

Table 4.8 Financial Data on VST Industries

VST Industries Ltd	
Market Price (31st March, 2 008)	Rs. 309
Book value	Rs. 133
Market Capitalization	Rs. 475 cr
Debt	-
Treasury	Rs. 175 cr
Enterprise Value	Rs. 300 cr
Ratios	
EV* /Cash from Operations	3.7 x
Debt/Equity	-

(Contd.)

VST Industries Ltd	
Return on Equity	28%
Price/Book value	2.3 x
Price/earnings	8.8 x
Price/sales	0.65 x
Dividend Yield	6.5 %
Growth (4yrs; annualized)	
EPS	10%
BV	15%

* EV stands for 'Enterprise Value.

The enterprise value of Rs. 300 crores is used, as against the current market capitalization of Rs. 475 crores, in the intrinsic value calculations done later in the discussion. This is because the cash figure is the operational cash flow and the current market capitalization of Rs. 475 crores includes excess cash of Rs. 175 crores, which does not add anything to the operational cash flow. In effect, it means that if somebody is buying 100% of VST Industries, even though he would pay Rs. 475 crores, he can encash Rs. 175 crores worth of liquid funds and still continue to earn the Rs.80 crores cash that the enterprise is earning at present.

Price versus Value

For an investor, the financial statements representing the recent performance of the enterprise constitute an indispensable tool. But it must be remembered that the value is a function of the ability of the enterprise to generate cash flows in the future. So one has to ensure that the enterprise has the ability to withstand operational or regulatory hiccups of massive impact, which are outside one's ability to predict—at times even so for the management of the company—and continue its good run when times turn favorable. This judgment on the company's financial stability can be made by looking at its balance sheet.

In the case of VST, the fact that it is a zero debt company with plenty of excess cash, which—inspite of its negative aspect in terms of contracting the return on equity by generating suboptimal returns—

can be considered a factor in attracting the highest rating of creditworthiness. Also, given the fact that the current capacity utilization is below 50%, with no major expenditure in the form of advertising expenditure, it can be inferred that VST Industries will not require major capital outlays in the foreseeable future for any expansion or upgradation. As a result, the majority of cash generated from operations will be translated into free cash flow.

Having established that VST is a sound enterprise in terms of its financial stability, let us move on to an equally important question involving the calculation of its intrinsic value. Before we proceed further, it is important to note that the intrinsic value is an illusive concept. Two people working with even the same mind-set but with slightly different expectations from the future and discount rate, can get a huge divergence in the intrinsic value for an enterprise. But this lack of precision can be overcome by calculating a range for intrinsic value, to provide us with a basis to decide the favorability of the opportunity.

Conservative Estimate of VST's Intrinsic Value

In the case of VST, even though it has managed to grow its earnings at an average of 10% per annum during the last few years, let us make a conservative assumption that it would not grow its cash flow at all over the next 10 years. The discount rate that we shall use for discounting the cash flow is 10%, which we can say is our required rate of return from an investment. Using these estimates, the cash inflow and the net present value (NPV) is shown in the following table. Let us further assume that the enterprise would be sold at the end of the 10-year period; i.e., in 2018, at Rs. 360 crores, or 4.5 times Rs. 80 crores (cash flow in 2018), which in itself is a very conservative estimate. This Rs. 360 crores to be got in 2018 translates into Rs. 142 crores at a 10% discount rate.

Table 4.9 Projected Cash Flows of VST Industries with No Growth

(in Rs. Cr.)

Year	Amount	NPV
2009	80	73
2010	80	66
2011	80	60
2012	80	55

(Contd.)

Year	Amount	NPV
2013	80	50
2014	80	45
2015	80	41
2016	80	37
2017	80	34
2018	80	31
Sale in 2018	360	142
	Total	**633**

Thus, the intrinsic value of VST Industries based on the conservative estimates comes to Rs.633 crores; i.e., paying this should result in a 10% return from the business during the next 10 years. But the current enterprise value is Rs.300 crores, which ensures that the rate of return expected could turn out to be much higher. In conclusion, it can be said that VST Industries is available at around 50 % its conservative estimate of intrinsic value.

Reasonable Estimate of VST's Intrinsic Value

As already indicated, intrinsic value is an illusory concept, and it is advisable to calculate intrinsic values using various expectation measures representing the ground reality, to derive a range of intrinsic values and give us a better idea of the opportunity at hand. Thus, let us calculate the intrinsic value using a growth rate of 5%, which is very reasonable considering that it hardly covers the inflation rate and VST has the ability to pass on this increase to its customers. In this case also, let us assume that the enterprise would be sold at the end of the 10-year period; i.e., in 2018, at Rs.558 crores, which is 4.5 times Rs.124 crores (cash flow in 2018), which in itself is a conservative estimate. And Rs.558 crores to be got in 2018 translates into Rs.215 crores at a 10% discount rate.

Table 4.10 Projected Cash Flows of VST Industries with 5% Annual Growth

(in Rs. Cr.)

Year	Amount	NPV
2009	80	73
2010	84	69
2011	88	66
2012	93	63

(Contd.)

Year	Amount	NPV
2013	97	60
2014	102	58
2015	107	55
2016	113	53
2017	118	50
2018	124	48
Sale in 2018	558	215
	Total	**811**

Under these reasonable assumptions, the current market capitalization values VST Industries at 37% of its intrinsic value. Considering the above calculations it can be estimated that the intrinsic value for VST Industries lies in the range Rs.633 to Rs.811 crores, based on the conservative and reasonable expectations from the future offering an extensive margin of safety.

4.4.5 Conclusion

Having discussed VST Industries Ltd as a contrarian investment opportunity, let us end the discussion with an added advantage in VST Industries that acts as an icing on the cake. It pays out a considerable part of its earnings every year as dividends. During the financial year 2008, it paid out 50% of its earnings as dividends to shareholders translating into a dividend yield of 6.5% at current market price of Rs. 309.

This measure has two implications for equity shareholders. First, we are paid to wait for the closure of the price-value gap. Secondly, it indicates the quality of earnings behind the enterprise and the lack of capital required by the business. What more can a contrarian investor ask for: getting paid to wait until the market participants realize the true value of the enterprise!

FIVE

5

GROWTH TRAP

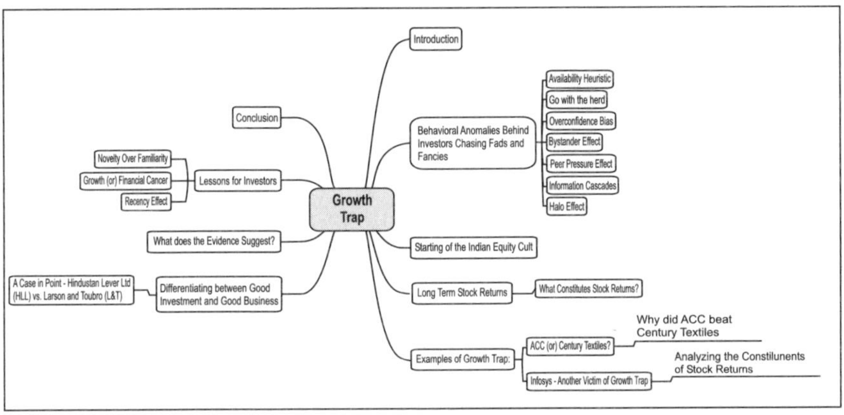

5.1 INTRODUCTION

It is in our pursuit of making quick gains that we tend to take short-cuts that lead us into difficult situations. There is the law of the farm: you cannot reap today and sow tomorrow. A seed when sown has to go through various seasons before it turns into a fully-grown tree. This takes time.

So is the case in investments. You cannot have short cuts to making money by buying stocks that will go up fast. However, in the world of investments "growth stocks" offer such opportunities. It is the promise of a dream to make big and fast money. Who does not like an opportunity like this? There are many takers for it. This leads to a scramble for such growth stocks and investors fall into the "growth trap".

> When everyone is chasing growth stocks, these stocks become favorite and expensive, and investors tend to ignore the basic parameters of investing, like valuations, earnings and dividends.

When everyone is chasing growth stocks, these stocks become a favorite and they become expensive. However, investors believe that since they are growth stocks the expensive price is justified, as the stocks have the potential to go still higher. When chasing growth stocks, investors tend to ignore the basic parameters of investing, like valuations, earnings and dividends. Their focus is only on buying a stock, which they will be able to subsequently sell at a huge profit to some other investor.

When a high price is paid for an asset compared to its intrinsic value, the returns on that asset are bound to suffer. This is what happens when investors chase growth stocks. They get into the growth trap and their returns take a hit over the long run.

One would argue that if the entry level in a growth stock has been right, one might not get into the growth trap. But such entry levels are reserved for the promoters, angel investors, private equity investors and the venture capitalists. You have initial public offerings because these investors need to exit. These offerings are usually timed in bull markets, when people are willing to pay high valuations and get into the growth trap.

Stock markets offer all sorts of opportunities where investors are either able to invest at throwaway prices or at ridiculous valuations. Stock markets are known for their frenzies from time to time. Sometimes the frenzy comes from a new idea or a technology (as happened during the technology boom), sometimes it comes from an idea heavily marketed by an operator (Harshad Mehta's theory of replacement cost took cement company ACC to Rs.10,000), sometimes it comes from changes in government policies (the financial services company boom in 1994–1995 due to the liberalization process and the opening of the financial services sector), sometimes it comes from the contagious effect of the global scenario (the telecommunications boom in the late 1990s and early 2000), and sometimes it is just a change of investor perception and sentiment like what happened during 2004–2007 when we had a commodity boom, a real estate boom and a stock market boom the world over. There was a mad rush for investing in these sectors. All these fads attracted investors who rushed in to buy stocks of companies which were "fancied", only to lose fortunes when the fancy waned. Even if they bought with an idea of the longer term, their returns would suffer.

When a high price is paid for an asset compared to its intrinsic value, the returns on that asset are bound to suffer.

5.2 BEHAVIORAL ANOMALIES BEHIND INVESTORS CHASING FADS AND FANCIES

Why do investors get trapped in spite of having the knowledge that investment returns are dependent on the acquisition price? When greed starts to dominate, intellectual reasoning paves the way for emotional behavior. The heart starts ruling over the mind and investors start making mistakes which, in the long run, harm their financial interest. The following heuristics and biases explain why investors get swayed in chasing fads and fancies.

5.2.1 Availability Heuristic

Growth stocks are supposed to make investors very rich and hence they become fancies of the market. What is a growth stock? It is a stock that went way up. It is always in hindsight that we know that it was a growth stock. A stock which goes way up could be because it is in a new industry or has a new technology and becomes the investors' fancy. Normally investors in stock markets tend to go for new ideas and thus are built new fads and fancies. Investors start chasing these new ideas, the stock price starts going up and people start believing that it is a growth stock. Investors believe that money is to be made in such new ideas and start investing. How does a concept of a new idea or a new technology catch the attention of investors? The media play a very important role in creating hype. When one is bombarded with the same type of news everyday on a continuous basis, one falls prey to the availability heuristic. That is, one starts believing and relying on readily available information. This availability heuristic gets so strong that it becomes the talk of the town and everyone starts advocating it.

> **The key lesson in investing is to look for businesses which have the fundamentals to beat the expectations built into the prices.**

Remember the "India Shining" story. It had become so strong that every one started believing in it and talking about it. When the NDA government lost the election it was clear that India was not shining. It was only shining in the cities. In the early-1990s we had this fancy for plantation stocks and these were so hyped up that people were willing to invest in any plantation company. The fancy lasted for a couple of years resulting in huge losses for the investor. How can we forget the IT fancy in the late-1990s? The internet was supposed to change the economy and the way people do business. Every one talked of the emerging 'new economy'. It was such a hyped-up affair that everyone not only started believing it but also started advocating and investing in the new economy companies. When reality dawned that there was nothing like a new economy, investors as well as businesses lost heavily. This is what happens when one gets swayed by the popular judgment and joins the herd. In such times when one makes investments, one is bound to take a hit on one's returns.

5.2.2 Go with The Herd

The other day I was waiting at a traffic signal, as the light showed red. Since no other car was coming from the other direction, which was green, the car next to me broke the signal and raced ahead. The signal was still red. Other cars also followed the car breaking the signal. Then from behind me all other cars were honking, signaling others to go and break the signal. And many other cars broke the signal in spite of it still being red. Not only that, I was cursed by the ones behind me for not going ahead. Now how does one explain this behavior? Just one driver broke the law and the others followed him blindly not realizing that it is not the right thing to do. This is what we call is going with the herd or in behavioral terms it is known as 'herd mentality'.

> **For a rational investor who thinks in terms of business behind the stocks, the best time to buy a business is when it is available at a deep discount to its value.**

The availability heuristic makes people think in the same direction and, thus, they do what others are doing. Chasing technology stocks was more acceptable because everyone was chasing them. When you become a part of the herd, you lose your own common sense, and you do not want to be seen doing something different lest you look foolish. Moreover, misery loves company. In case of a negative outcome, the pain of regret is mitigated by the fact that many others also behaved similarly.

In the driving case above I was the one who looked foolish. The others who were breaking the signal did not mind being got caught as they had company.

5.2.3 Overconfidence Bias

People are normally highly overconfident of their knowledge and abilities. Ask a group of your friends how confident they are about their driving skills and you will find that most of them would put themselves as above average. You ask the same group of their chances of dying before the age of 80 and you will also find that the majority was confident to live beyond 80. This overconfidence is dangerous, especially when it comes to money and investing to make money. When one is overconfident, one under-reacts to any new information that comes because one believes that one is smarter than one actually is. Sift through the track records of a few outstanding intelligent fund managers and you will find that their losses have been more because of behavioral biases stemming out of over-confidence, rather than lack of knowledge or intellect.

> Investment opportunities don't come daily. However, the noise of the markets offer mispriced securities from time to time.

5.2.4 Bystander Effect

Human beings seem to take great comfort being in groups. For example, it is very common to have a large group of people surround a tragic accident spot and not do anything to help the victim. The reason cited is "nobody is coming forward to help so it must be dangerous to act like that", or "why should I go forward when no one else is doing so". In effect, we let other people's behavior influence our decision.

When it comes to investing, such behavior might not be the apt thing to do because a crowd never seems to be doing the right thing. It only leads stocks to ridiculous valuations, either over or under. Listening to other people's talk, interviews on the media, information on the internet, newspaper reports, brokers' tip sheets—should all warn one to remind oneself not to fall prey to Bystander Effect.

5.2.5 Peer Pressure Effect

Two common occurrences that trigger envious behavior are (1) Somebody looking over our shoulders to see how we are doing in our professional lives, and (2) we wasting our time and energy tracking how the other person is progressing in his professional life.

Using peer pressure to move in the right direction is always welcome, but being outcome-oriented and trying to better the peer in everything you do might not be a good thing for your emotional and financial well-being. Being envious and jealous of others invariably triggers the urge to seek rewards and not care for the effort required, leading to irrational behavior. Each one of us would get what we deserve and what we deserve is what we work towards. So it might not be a good idea to track the performance of peers without focusing on what they seem to be doing to get those results.

5.2.6 Information Cascades

During speculative excesses, a common behavior observed amongst investors provides an interesting example of information cascade. What happens is that participants seem to cease to reason on their own and simply imitate the actions of other people, believing that to be the most appropriate way. It is like simply copying somebody else's actions, using those as a substitute for reliable information, while simply ignoring the true motives behind their actions. When a large majority of the public gets into this sort of behavior, information cascade results in reality diverging from fundamentals.

During the Harshad Mehta boom we had a whole lot of investors blindly following him and buying stocks recommended by him. They believed that he was a great stock-picker to have amassed so much wealth in stocks. This information was not correct. Money was siphoned off from banks and channeled into the stock markets. We never knew what was actually his and what belonged to the banks. It was assumed that all his wealth was made in picking winning stocks. So was the case with the Ketan Parekh K10 stocks. He was known as the pied piper of technology stocks. His cover was blown when the technology boom ended and it soon became evident that his funds were illegitimately diverted from different banks. They both had a huge investor following and some even worshipped them. These are just two examples, but such things happen very regularly in stock markets.

> **Being in control of one's impulses and keeping the urges in control will help one to spot mis-priced opportunities and avoid the growth trap.**

5.2.7 Halo Effect

'Halo effect' denotes the tendency where the perception about something is based on a single variable rather than considering the overall picture. As an investor, every time you hear somebody say that "XYZ Ltd is a good buy because it is a growth stock" or "ABC Ltd is a good buy because it is an infrastructure company", you can say that it is an example of the halo effect. Because after all, a good investment has to have many more factors to make it investment-worthy, in terms of management quality, valuation, payout policy of the company, business model, etc. So beware of judging a stock on a singular piece of information.

5.3 STARTING OF THE INDIAN EQUITY CULT

The late-1970s witnessed the start of the equity cult in the Indian stock markets.

During those times, textiles was a hot sector and the industry had a weightage of over 20% in the BSE Sensex. Reliance Industries entered the capital markets in the late 1970s and with its state–of-the-art ultra-modern facilities was about to change the rules of the game. It did so. The public issue came with much fanfare. There were various rumors regarding the sustainability of Mr. Dhirubhai Ambani (the founder of Reliance Industries), but he proved his critics wrong. The company saw a spectacular rise with a huge following from the retail investors. He was the darling of the investors. Mr. Dhirubhai Ambani set the equity cult in the Indian markets by being very investor-friendly and handsomely rewarding his shareholders.

Ironically the other proponent of the equity cult was a socialist leader, Mr. George Fernandes. The year 1977 saw the fall of the Congress government and the Janata Dal government came to power. Mr. George Fernandes, one of the constituents of the Janta Dal government, became the Industries Minister. The Foreign Exchange Regulation was enacted and all foreign companies were asked to either list their shares on the Indian bourses or quit India. Some companies like Hindustan Lever (HLL), Nestle, Colgate obliged, but others like Coca Cola quit. This was the beginning of a new era in equity investing in India and all these companies, which got listed, were known as 'FERA'(Foreign Exchange Regulation Act) companies. They soon became the stock market favorites and almost all of them commanded high PEs. Indian shareholders had, for the first time, an opportunity to invest in foreign-ownership companies. Since the Controller of Capital Issues controlled the pricing of new public issues, the Indian shareholder got these shares at ridiculous valuations. For instance, HLL was forced to offer its shares to the Indian public at Rs.16 (face value of Rs.10 at a premium of Rs.6.). These companies made a lot of wealth for the Indian shareholders. With the success of these initial listings, we saw a flood of international companies entering the Indian capital markets. Their listing gave Indian investors an opportunity to share the wealth created by such international companies. What was once the domain of a few individuals or business houses now spread to the equity investing class. Companies like Digital, Xerox, Tektronix, Wartsila, Diesel, ZF Steering, to name a few, entered India and made issues of shares to the Indian public.

Mr. George Fernandes, a hard-core socialist, was thus responsible for enacting a law that helped capitalism, and laid the foundation of the equity cult in India. These international companies were the ones who understood early the power of the Indian consumer and the potential for growth that India offered. This was the starting point when Indian companies first tasted international competition.

Foreign companies like the engineering giant, Siemens, and the pharmaceutical innovator, Glaxo, were listed in the Indian stock markets. These companies were most sought after by the Indian investors, as they were able to get the right ideas and technology from their parents and had a very good global reach. They were considered future growth stories. Glaxo commanded 3.21% weightage in the index and Siemens had a weightage of 0.06%. Another FERA company was HLL an FMCG giant, a part of the Unilever group, which had a weightage of 7.92% in the Sensex.

The name of the industrial icons of India, the Tata group and the Birla group, also commanded considerable respect with the investing class. Hence, their stocks were also the fancy of the investors and they also commanded a premium in the markets. The Tata group had the following companies with their respective market weightage: Indian Hotels 2.66%, Tata Power 1.63%, Tata Steel 4.71% and TELCO (now Tata Motors) 7.98%, making a combined weightage of 16.98% in the Sensex. The Birla group had Century Textiles 6.53%, Gwalior Rayon(Grasim) 7.00%, Hindustan Motors 1.33%, Hindalco 2.39% and Indian Rayon 12.48%, making a combined weightage of 29.73% in the Sensex. Thus, the Tatas and the Birlas had over 45% of the market capitalization of the Sensex.

It will be interesting to study the returns generated by the investors. The following is the list of the different companies and their weightage in the BSE Sensex.

Table 5.1 Composition of Sensex in 1979

Sr. No.	Name	Sector	% of Index
1	ACC1	Industrial	4.75
2	Asian Cbls	Electricals	0.35
3	Bharat Forge	Automobile	0.41
4	Ballarpur Industries	Materials	3.94
5	Bombay Burma	Diversified	0.79
6	Bombay Dyeing	Textiles	4.70
7	Ceat	Automobile	0.83
8	Century Textiles	Textiles	6.53
9	Crompton Greaves	Electricals	2.61
10	Glaxo	Health Care	3.21
11	GSFC	Materials	5.60
12	Gwalior Rayon (Grasim)	Diversified	7.00
13	Hindustan Motors	Automobile	1.33
14	Hindalco	Metals	2.39
15	HLL	Consumer Goods	7.92
16	Indian Hotels	Consumer Services	2.66
17	Indian Organics	Materials	1.48
18	Indian Rayon	Textiles	12.48
19	ITC	Consumer Goods	4.44
20	Kirloskar Cummins	Industrial	0.87
21	L&T	Industrial	3.61
22	M&M	Automobile	1.43
23	Mukand	Metals	1.56
24	Nestle	Consumer Goods	0.80
25	RIL	Materials	2.80
26	Scindia	Consumer Services	1.15
27	Siemens	Electricals	0.06
28	Tata Power	Energy	1.63
29	Tata Steel	Metals	4.71
30	Telco	Automobile	7.98

The hot sectors of that era were led by Textiles with 23.71 % weightage in the Sensex, followed by Materials at 13.82%, Consumer Goods at 13.16%, Automobiles at 11.98%, Industrials at 9.23% and others at 28.10%.

Common sense would say that most of the stocks belonging to the hot sectors and owned by the famous houses of Tatas and Birlas and the upcoming Reliance group of Dhirubhai Ambani would have rewarded the shareholders immensely.

Will you pick Indian Rayon (Textiles and Birla Group) over Bharat Forge (Forgings and Kalyani Group) or Reliance Industries (Textiles and Ambani Group) over Glaxo (Pharmaceutical and multinational)?

5.4 LONG-TERM STOCK RETURNS

Table 5.2 shows the returns of the 1979 Sensex over a 27-year period from 1979 to 2006. The results are startling. Bharat Forge was an ordinary forging company and Mahindra and Mahindra (M&M) was just a tractor and jeep manufacturing company. Both these companies were in mediocre businesses and did not command any fancy in the stock markets. Their sectors also did not command any fancy. Although both of them were classified into the Auto and Auto Ancillary sector which was a hot sector, both had very mediocre businesses; forging for Bharat Forge and Tractors and jeeps for M&M. This was evident from the fact that Bharat Forge had a weightage of just 0.41% in the Sensex while M&M had 1.43%. In fact, Bharat Forge saw its exit from the Index in 1982, just three years later. Their managements were not any great icons in the capital markets but understood their businesses and ran them efficiently. No great technology was required and entry barriers for potential newcomers were also low. They were just old economy companies run very efficiently.

Table 5.2 1979 Index Ranked by Returns to 2006

Sr. No.	Name	Sector	Returns (%)
1	ITC	Consumer Goods	31.69
2	Bharat Forge	Automobiles	31.50
3	Nestle	Consumer Goods	28.70
4	Kirloskar Cummins	Industrials	28.15
5	HLL	Consumer Goods	26.98
6	Siemens	Electricals	26.73
7	M&M	Automobiles	26.68
8	Hindalco	Metals	26.10
9	ACC	Industrials	25.67
10	Indian Hotels	Consumer Services	24.60
11	Glaxo	Health Care	24.17

(Contd.)

Sr. No.	Name	Sector	Returns (%)
12	Tata Power	Energy	23.00
13	Crompton Greaves	Electricals	21.94
14	L&T	Industrials	20.79
15	GSFC	Materials	20.10
16	Gwalior Rayon (Grasim)	Diversified	19.52
17	Century	Textiles	19.33
18	Indian Rayon	Textiles	19.24
19	Bombay Burma	Diversified	18.65
20	Telco (Tata Motors)	Automobiles	18.59
21	RIL	Materials	18.57
22	Bombay Dyeing	Textiles	18.48
23	Tata Steel	Metals	14.32
24	Ceat	Automobiles	13.24
25	Mukand	Metals	13.16
26	Hindustan Motors	Automobiles	10.00
27	Ballarpur Industries	Materials	8.44
28	Indian Organics	Materials	2.61
29	Asian Cables	Electricals	2.21
30	Scindia	Consumer Services	–1.61

It is interesting to note the returns to the shareholders who invested in the above companies. If one were to go by the popular thinking and fast recall value of big names, one would assume that Reliance Industries, Bombay Dyeing, Larsen and Toubro (L&T), Tata and Birla group companies and the FERA companies like HLL and Siemens would have earned maximum returns for the investors. However, the picture is totally different when one looks at the above table. Not so well-known companies in mediocre industries, run by uncharismatic and simple management, have performed better than the fancies of the market. The returns from investments in Bharat Forge, Kirloskar Cummins and M&M far exceeded the returns of their peers.

Bharat Forge has returned 31.50% and Mahindra and Mahindra (M&M) 26.68%. As against that, Reliance has returned only 18.57%, L&T (Larsen and Toubro) 20.79% and Glaxo 24.17%. During the same period, the BSE Sensex has returned 20.02 per cent. Both these once insignificant companies have beaten the most sought-after companies. Bharat Forge has stolen the show by beating its rivals by a huge margin. M&M has also beaten its rivals by a considerable margin. However this difference over a period of 27 years is very significant with the power of compounding. The table below shows what Rs.10,000 invested in a company would have become at the end of 27 years.

Table 5.3 Returns from Different Companies for the Period 1979–2006

Return Rank	Company	Annual Return (%)	Final Accumulation of Rs. 10,000
1	ITC	31.69	Rs. 1,69,01,511
2	Bharat Forge	31.50	Rs. 1,62,55,313
3	Nestle	28.70	Rs. 90,91,191
4	Kirloskar Cummins	28.15	Rs. 80,98,461
5	HLL	26.98	Rs. 63,21,989
6	Siemens	26.73	Rs. 59,94,386
7	M&M	26.68	Rs. 59,30,857
8	Hindalco	26.10	Rs. 52,39,711
9	ACC	25.67	Rs. 47,78,082
10	Indian Hotels	24.60	Rs. 37,93,038
11	Glaxo	24.17	Rs. 34,55,019
12	Tata Power	23.00	Rs. 26,75,704
13	Crompton Greaves	21.94	Rs. 21,18,103
14	L&T	20.79	Rs. 16,39,972
15	GSFC	20.10	Rs. 14,04,951

Kirloskar Cummins returned 28.15% and HLL returned 26.98%, a difference of only 1.17%. Nevertheless, Rs10,000 invested in Kirloskar Cummins would have fetched Rs 80.98 lakhs and the same investment in HLL would have given Rs 63.21 lakhs— a difference of Rs 17.77 lakhs.

It also needs to be mentioned that the FERA companies like ITC, HLL, Siemens, Nestle and Glaxo have also given spectacular performance even though they were a part of the hot sectors. Their returns would have been much higher if they were not the most sought-after stocks. Three of them have been in the FMCG sector, with strong brands and distribution networks. I have always been a strong proponent of that sector and we will discuss the same in the chapter on sector analysis. Siemens in the engineering sector and Glaxo in the pharmaceutical sector have also given good returns to the shareholders, but not as much as would be expected from big multinationals as compared to their peers.

5.4.1 What Constitutes Stock Returns?

What are the main factors that comprise stock returns? Fundamentally, a stock return is a function of two variables: price appreciation and dividend. Increase in the price of a stock will lead to returns by way of price appreciation, and dividends are yearly cash flows from the stock that you hold. Re-investing these dividends to buy more of the scrip will lead to a rise in the number of units of stocks held. Reinvested dividends form a major part of stock returns.

Let us take a case study of ITC Ltd., originally known as the Imperial Tobacco Company Ltd. ITC Ltd. has given a healthy return of 31.69% from 1979 to 2006.

Let us assume that 100 shares were purchased at the then prevailing price of Rs.25 per share on 1 April 1979 (Table 5.4). Subsequently, the company declared a dividend of 15% on the face value of Rs.10 on 24 August 1979, resulting in a total cash inflow of Rs.150. This money was then used to buy additional shares of the company. Six more shares were bought at the then prevailing ex-dividend price of Rs.23.50. Thus, the total holding of ITC shares increased to 106. In the year 1980, the company issued bonus shares in the ratio of 1 for every 5 shares held. Thus the shareholding increased from 106 shares to 127 shares.

Table 5.4 Returns from ITC Stock, 1979–1980

Date	Face Value (Rs.)	Price/ Share (Rs.)	Dividend (%)	Total Dividend Received (Rs.)	Additional Shares (no.)	Total no. of Shares	Remarks
01-Apr-79	10	25.00	-	-	-	100	Initial investment
24-Aug-79	10	23.50	15	150.00	6	106	6 shares bought using Rs.150 dividend
01-Aug-80	10	22.00	-	-	21	127	Bonus issue: 1 share for 5 shares held
29-Aug-80	10	22.50	15	190.50	9	136	9 shares bought using Rs.190.50 dividend

Subsequently, a dividend of 15% was declared on 29 August 1980, resulting in a cash inflow of Rs.190.50. When the said money was again reinvested, 9 more shares were bought at ex-dividend price of Rs.22.50, taking the total holding to 136 shares.

In a matter of less than two years, the number of shares increased by 36 per cent (from 100 to 136). On further scrutiny, we can see that the stock price fell to Rs.22.50 on 29 August 1980. After considering the 21 shares received as bonus shares and presuming that dividends were not re-invested, the value of the initial investment of Rs.2,500 would have increased to Rs.2,722. However, with the dividends reinvested, the value of the investment was Rs.3,060 (136 shares times Rs.22.50) with the reinvested dividends. Thus, reinvested dividends have appreciated the value of our investments. From this perspective, we can say that reinvested dividends act as a hedge against depreciation of stock price when used correctly, that is, at right valuations.

Dividends play a very important role in the determination of stock returns. In olden times, when technology was not available, the best way to understand the profitability of a company was not the cash flow statements or balance sheet analysis. What the company distributed as dividends was the real test of the company's earnings. Only earnings and positive cash flow will enable the company to distribute dividends. This conventional wisdom still holds true. A chicken for its eggs, bees for their honey, cow for her milk and a stock for its dividend. Why does one invest in stocks? To earn a return which is by way of a dividend. The stock being listed on the stock market will also enable the investor to get more return by way of capital appreciation only when he sells the shares.

5.5 EXAMPLES OF GROWTH TRAP

5.5.1 ACC or Century Textiles?

To understand the growth trap better, let us look at another example. In the 1970s and 1980s, the textile industry witnessed a spectacular boom in India. Textile companies were mushrooming all over the country. If you were in the stock market in 1979, you would have at least some of your money invested in textile stocks and you would have been a firm believer that the future of India lies in textiles.

There were three textile companies in the Sensex; viz., Century Textiles, Indian Rayon and Bombay Dyeing. Century Textiles had over 6.50% per cent of the weightage in the Sensex.

It is 1979. You are given a choice to buy one of the two stocks from the index to plan for your retirement. One is Century Textiles. It is the stock market favorite and happens to be in a promising sector, Textiles. The other one is Associated Cement Company (ACC) an ordinary cement company classified as commodities. The stock would be governed by the prices of cement in this cyclical industry.

Assume that you would be reinvesting all the dividends and subscribe to all the right issues if any. The returns of this investment will be calculated a quarter of a century later and will be used for your retirement. Which company will make you comfortable and rich?

To help one decide better, let us have a look at the textiles and the cement industries. The textile industry is a steady sector and is devoid of any industrial cycles. There is demand for textiles throughout the year and consumers spend on clothes more frequently than on cement. Cement being a pure commodity industry is highly cyclical in nature. The cement industry is directly dependent on the infrastructure sector, and any fall in the construction and infrastructure spending will hit the cement industry. At the same time, it is extremely difficult to predict the boom and bust of a cyclical industry. If one were to ask a professional, one would be advised to go for Century rather than ACC. All the arguments are in favor of Century and it is the most talked about and hot stock in the market. It had all the characteristics of a growth stock. A high PE signifying high investor expectations and a lower dividend yield. A growth stock where one could benefit from a higher capital appreciation and which was the market favorite would be the natural choice.

However, in reality, 27 years later one would have been better off had one bought ACC. Buying Century would have got one into the Growth Trap. ACC beat Century by a wide margin in returns to the investor. Chasing a fancy and following the herd is a sure way to pay an excessive price and thus get into the growth trap.

Why did ACC Beat Century Textiles?

The answer in short is "valuation". Valuation is nothing but the price that one pays for the future stream of expected earnings and the dividends. Since Century was a growth stock and a market favorite there was too much of investor expectation built into the stock price. Hence, an investor ended up paying a higher price for its future stream of earnings. This resulted in a low yield. On the other hand, ACC being a neglected stock, there were no inbuilt investor expectations in the stock price. This made ACC a high dividend yield stock. This benefited the investor from the time he bought the stock. The average dividend yield of ACC was more than double the dividend yield of Century. ACC's average PE ratio, an important parameter of valuation, was 14 points lower than that of Century Textiles. This made ACC far cheaper than Century. The following table shows the wide difference in the valuation measures of both the companies.

Table 5.5 Valuation of Century Textiles versus ACC

Valuation Measures	Century Textiles	ACC
Average Dividend Yield (1979- 2006)	2.41	5.51
Average PE (1979-2006)	38.94	24.31

A critical component of stock return is the dividend from the stock. In earlier times, when information technology was not available to enable widespread and easy access to data, the best way to understand the profitability of a company was not the cash flow statements or the balance sheet. What the company distributed as dividends was the real test of the company's earnings. Only earnings and positive cash flow will enable the company to distribute dividends. And it is these dividends that matter in the long run.

These yearly dividends can be used to buy more of the same stock. This not only increases the holding in a particular stock but also has a compounding effect of increased dividends. This power of compounding is what has made all the difference.

ACC had a lower price and a higher dividend yield. Thus, more shares could be bought out of its yearly dividends. This has resulted in a return of 25.67 %. As against that Century has returned 19.33% only, a difference of 6.34%.

Table 5.6 Sources of Return (1979-2006)

Return Measures	Century Textiles	ACC
Capital Appreciation	16.92%	20.16%
Dividend Yield	2.41%	5.51%
Total Return	**19.33%**	**25.67%**

To help us put the premium of 6.34%, earned over an extended period of 27 years, let us compare the final value of Rs 1 lakh invested in 1979, at the end of 2006.

Table 5.7 Growth of Investment from 1979 to 2006

Name	CAGR%	Initial Investment	Final Accumulation
Century Textiles	19.33	Rs. 1 lakh	Rs. 1.2 crores
ACC	25.67	Rs. 1 lakh	Rs. 5.1 crores

In the case of Century Textiles, Rs. 1 lakh grew 120-fold to Rs.1.2 crores. However for ACC the Rs.1 lakh grew 510 fold to a whopping Rs. 5.1 crores. At the end of 27 years taking into consideration inflation, this difference is phenomenal for a retired person.

5.5.2 Infosys: Another Victim of Growth Trap

Let us look at another example from the recent past. I think most readers would agree that the very mention of 'Infosys' brings to mind a company that is synonymous with the face of Indian companies that have proven to the world the competence of India in the corporate space, and whose corporate governance principles have set a benchmark for corporations not only in India, but worldwide.

Equally impressive has been the growth of the enterprise, all the while maintaining one of the highest returns on capital employed. Infosys has compounded its bottom-line by as much as 37% over the last 8 years. The phenomenal trend of corporate earnings growth of Infosys can be seen from the chart below.

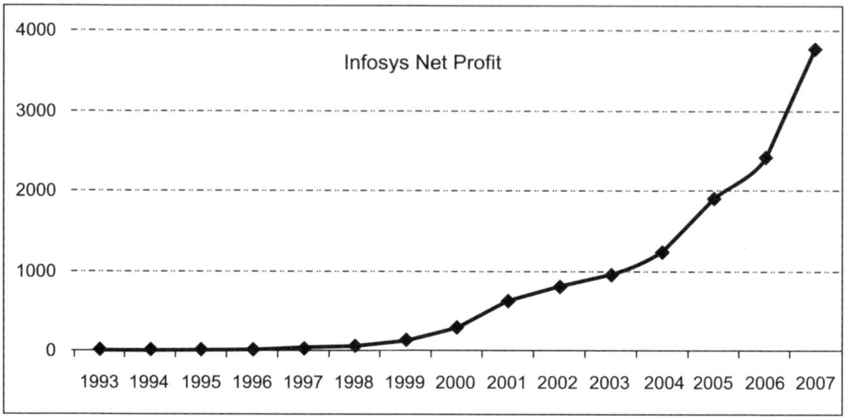

Figure 5.1 Infosys Net Profit, 1993–2007

However, how good have the results been for the shareholders in this excellent company? If a shareholder had bought shares in March 2000 at the height of the IT boom, he would not have seen a stock price higher than his purchase price until June 2006. Moreover, except for a spurt in the stock prices from mid-2006 to the end of 2007, the stock price is still trading below the March 2000 levels.

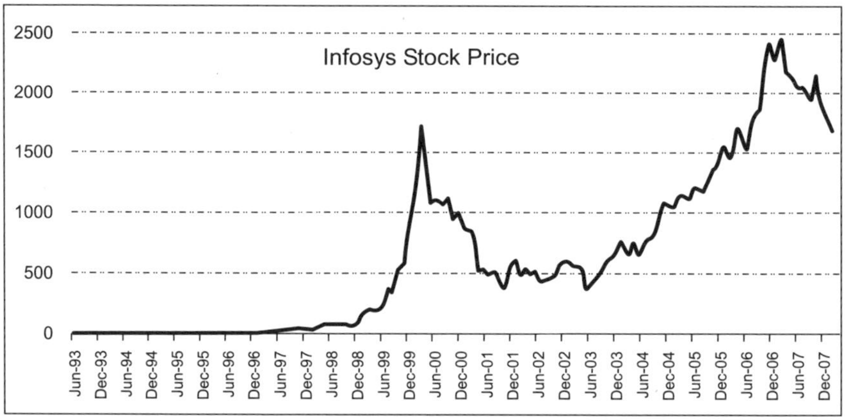

Figure 5.2 Infosys Stock Price, 1993–2007

This underperformance is not due to any depressed market conditions. In fact, during this period, Indian stock markets witnessed the biggest boom period in history. The BSE Sensex went up from around 3,000 in 2003 to 21,000 in January 2008. The fact that Infosys has not generated any capital appreciation over the last eight years is not because of depressed market conditions, but as a result of the growth trap. Investors expecting growth were willing to pay any price for the stock. This greed and irrationality got them into the growth trap.

Analyzing the Constituents of Stock Returns

The two components that constitute total shareholder returns are capital appreciation and dividends. These two components have an interesting difference. The dividend is a function of corporate performance during the year and the general dividend policy followed by the company, and is not dependent on the changes in market participants' perceptions about the business. For example, let us assume that a company has historically paid out 50% of its earnings as dividends to shareholders, and at current market price it results in a dividend yield of 5%. Moreover, if we have reason to believe that dividends will be maintained at 50% of earnings and can also reasonably expect that, with earnings growth, the dividend on our purchase price is set to grow, then the dividend component not only provides an important source of shareholder returns but also acts as a potential downside risk protection agent.

Let us understand the dividend yield component of Infosys. It was a miniscule 0.05% in March 2000. The payout was 10% of the net profit, which is understandable considering that any growing company would have had to infuse as much capital into the business as possible. So the favorability of the dividend yield component was not at all applicable in the case of Infosys, which leaves us with the capital appreciation component to compensate.

On the other hand, the capital appreciation component is not a function of corporate performance *alone* but of the general trend in profitability as well as the market's perception of future trend. This is subject to change as the perception shifts between excessive optimism and pessimism.

In fact, the dividend component is much easier to estimate and more reliable than the capital appreciation component.

Let us take a step forward to understand the importance of these components in the quality of returns one can expect to generate in Infosys in March 2000. As can be seen from the chart below the PE ratio of Infosys ranged between 150 and 300 times during the year 1999–2000.

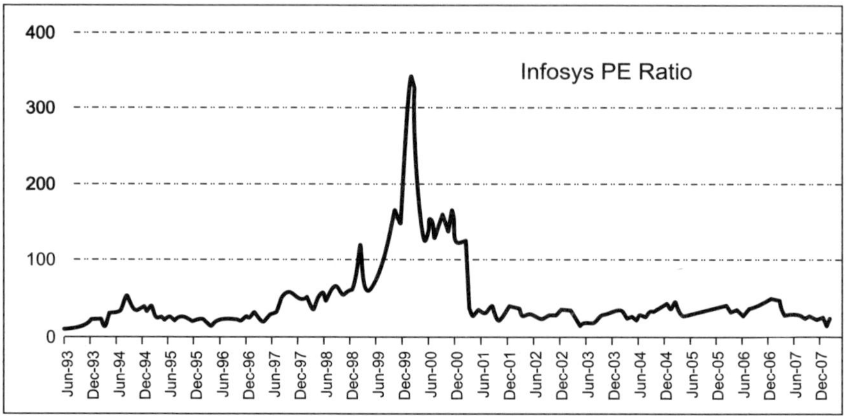

Figure 5.3 Infosys Price-Earnings Ratio, 1993–2007

What does this stellar PE ratio tell us? Investors' expectations were running very high. They were expecting very high growth and were willing to pay high prices for the stock, thinking that this high growth would reward them with higher returns. Investors had become irrational.

The net profit earned by Infosys in March 2000 was Rs 293 crores. Assuming that it would continue its growth sprint of 37%, over the next 8 years, the net profit in March 2007 would have been Rs 3,783 crores.

In March 2000, Infosys was trading at a PE ratio of 201, resulting in a market capitalization of Rs 58,985 crores. For this stellar growth of 37% to be translated into returns for shareholders, the PE ratio would have to be maintained at 201 for the next seven years. Not only that this was not possible but it was not sustainable also. In such a scenario the market capitalization of Infosys would have been a whopping Rs.7,60,383 crores; i.e., $190 billion. This would have been around 15-20% of India's present GDP.

Investors who expected such growth rates from Infosys suffered from the double whammy effect resulting in suboptimal shareholder returns, despite an excellent performance by Infosys. This was because of below-expectation growth rates (in spite of 37% growth rate achieved) and re-rating of the PE ratio based on below expectation results. It is amply evident as to how irrational behavior gets investors into problems, rather than the company in which they invest. Understanding the difference between a good company and a good stock is critical.

5.6 DIFFERENTIATING BETWEEN GOOD INVESTMENT AND GOOD BUSINESS

Equity as an asset class has outperformed other asset classes over the last few decades. Yet a majority of equity investors have not been able to replicate such superior results for their portfolios. Why? Part of the reason lies in the way they approach equity investments—they are often speculating, believing that they are investing, by acting on news, using demand-supply mismatch as a basis to predict future price changes.

Investing is about buying a piece of business at a price where the business offers enough safety in the form of assets owned by it and earnings potential in the form of profits available for distribution to shareholders.

Another reason which acts as a deterrent in achieving superior returns, is holding on to certain misconceptions about successful investing. One such widespread misconception is that successful investing is all about buying good businesses and holding onto them for the long-term. I use the term 'misconception' because the above principle ignores a vital step involved in appraisal of securities—comparing what is being offered for the amount paid.

Buying an exceptional business at an exorbitant price makes it a mediocre or even bad investment and buying a mediocre business at a bargain price makes it a good investment.

5.6.1 A Case in Point—Hindustan Lever Ltd. versus Larsen and Toubro

Let us go back to the year 2001. The technology boom had just busted. People were afraid to enter the stock markets. Loss-aversion was so high that either they chose fixed income securities or if it was equity investments the choice fell on well-known companies with a good long-term sustainable business.

One such stock was HLL. It was a leader in its industry; earning exceptional returns on capital employed, and was expected to continue doing well in the future. It being in the FMCG space had a strong brand and an extensive distribution network.

Another such stock was L&T. It was a leader in its industry, earning mediocre returns on capital employed and was expected to tag along in the difficult space of capital goods and infrastructure. It was a neglected stock, being in a mediocre business, earning average return on capital employed, whose prospect for growth and improvement in operational efficiency were overlooked.

However, four years down the line there emerged a very different picture (Table 5.8).

Table 5.8 Comparative Performance of HLL and L&T, 2001 to 2005

Name	ROCE (Dec 2001)	ROCE (Dec 2005)	PE (Dec 2001)	PE (Dec 2005)	Performance %
HLL	66.0	55.0	32.5	32.7	-11.8
L & T	11.5	29.5	17.8	36.0	422

ROCE: Return on capital employed

PE: Price to earnings ratio

Hindustan Lever— A Star that could not Rise beyond the Horizon

As the above table shows, an investor actually lost money by investing in HLL. First, it was due to the exceptionally high price paid for HLL. Investors paid 32.5 times its earnings. They were expecting that these earnings would be sustainable, as they had been in the past. Investor expectations from HLL were very high and when those did not materialize investors lost interest. Investors expected it to do exceptionally well, without considering the fact that high returns attract competition and if the customers are sensitive to price changes, no matter how strong the brand value, profitability gets impacted. And it did, as the ROCE declined from 66% to 55%.

Larsen & Toubro – An Unexpected Winner

In the case of L&T, the investor paid only 17.8 times its earnings. Investor expectations built in to the price were not high. It had a low ROCE of just 11.5%. This positioned the company as a mediocre business and it did not command any investor fancy. On the contrary this low ROCE acted as an entry barrier to the industry and newcomers were not attracted to enter. Little competition, together with a firm foothold in the market, enabled the company to take advantage of the change in the environment. This gave a sudden boost to the ROCE, which has gone up from 11.5% to 29.5% in just four years. This is what the market likes and it has become an investor fancy. Investors have started extrapolating this performance too long into the future and are willing to give it a PE of 36.

Investor returns in L&T are due to increase in the profitability of the company and also in the rating of the company. This re-rating is due to investor behavior and the change of sentiment.

Here again there is evidence of a growth trap when investors pay a higher price for the foreseeable growth and ignore inexpensive companies with potential growth.

5.7 WHAT DOES THE EVIDENCE SUGGEST?

There is actually nothing like a growth stock. It is an invention of analysts and investment bankers to sell expensive stocks to investors. Ultimately, when one buys a stock for investment one has to look at the following:

- Quality of the management
- Sustainability of the business
- Good cash flow to enable dividend payments
- Reasonable return on investment
- Right valuations

The first two are qualitative and would depend upon individual judgment. However, the other three are quantitative and quite easy to calculate and understand. But investors are so carried away by the trends in the market that they do not make decisions out of their minds but out of their hearts. When this happens, it is emotional investing. Investors tend to be with the herd and do what others are doing. Thus they start chasing fancies or the next hot thing in the market. This gives the stocks they are chasing a momentum, and these stocks start moving up. More people start buying as they see that others have made money and thus the stock becomes a growth stock. Why? Because it is appreciating. Moreover how does one justify such foolish buying of stocks at ridiculous valuations? Simple: you call it a growth stock, as you are unable to justify the valuations.

That is why even if you have bought a good company, if you bought when it was a fancy or so-called growth stock, you tend to lose out on the long-term returns as you invariably paid a higher price than justified by its valuations. The return on stocks depends on growth in earnings. But in reality, we need to check whether the growth in earnings exceeds investor's expectations and those growth expectations are embodied in the PE ratio. Thus we tend to pay a much higher price for growth or fancy stocks because of unreasonable growth expectations of the investing class. This is not only true of companies but also of sectors.

5.8 LESSONS FOR INVESTORS

The key lesson to take away from the above examples is to look for businesses which have the fundamentals to beat the expectations built into the prices. The larger the gap between the intrinsic value based on quantitative analysis and the expected value built into the price, the better the results would be for an investor.

At any given point in time, very few of the businesses traded on the stock exchange would qualify the above test of expectations game. But if one can train oneself to spot the behavioral anomalies that lead to mispricing, one could expect to spot some bargains. Some of the behavioral anomalies common among all the fads and fancies that lead investors into the "growth trap" are discussed below.

5.8.1 Novelty Over Familiarity

The stock markets' fascination with something new is as old as the establishment of stock exchanges. Right from the Tulip mania, when a flower became so important to investors for no utilitarian reason, to the South Sea bubble, when the company promised to amass gold that exceeded the estimated quantity of gold on earth, to the more recent Tech bubble of 2000 when people paid exorbitant prices for technology stocks and earnings seemed to matter little—people believed that there is more to a business than the assets it owns or the profits it can potentially earn from those assets. We are about to see such excesses in the infrastructure and the real estate sectors.

Time has proven again and again that an enterprise is worth the amount it can earn for its owners in the form of distributable earnings over its estimated lifetime. It deviates to excessive levels during boom and bust alike, but this basic law does not change.

During such times, people in their pursuit to grab a piece of something novel forget the inherent strength of time-tested familiar businesses which, in all probability, would continue to do business as they have done in the past. At such times, investing in something that has stood the test of time and has earnings to show for the price payable offers an opportunity for a contrarian investor to prosper.

5.8.2 Growth or Financial Cancer

Expected growth in itself is no indication of value-creation potential of a business. To be able to understand the true impact of growth on the ability of a business to create shareholder wealth, one needs to try and estimate how much cash would be required to produce a unit of growth in earnings.

Only if it is higher than the cost of capital can growth be considered as value-accretive. Otherwise, it can be considered as value-destructive and growth would be a negative factor in the value equation. So, every time you come across growth projections don't forget to ask yourself, how much capital does the business require to grow?

Occasionally, the stock market is involved in a fancy parade where all that matters to participants is that a certain industry will achieve a high growth rate going forward. They forget to ask questions about capital requirement, competition and potential for downward shift in the average ROCE earned by the industry, current expectations built into the stock price as compared to the growth expectations implied in the business, and so on. Neglecting to ask these questions inevitably leads to losses. Avoid mental short-cuts in processing information. Process all information and do not be carried away by hearsay.

5.8.3 Recency Effect

Psychologists define the recency effect as a heuristic where people tend to overweigh events that are recent because they are easy to recall. Investors exhibit extreme forms of this bias at the height and the bottom of stock market cycles. Just before the market crashes, the liquidity and optimism is highest amongst the investor community as a whole.

Conversely, during bear markets, the amount of capital invested in equities as a percentage of total household savings is at its lowest, indicating people's tendency to overweigh the short-term underperformance of the market to defer their investments in equity markets.

For a rational investor who thinks in terms of business behind the stocks the best time to buy a business is when it is available at a deep discount to its value. That is not to say that one could spot the bottom of a bear market. The long-term investing principle is put to the test and one needs to have the conviction to wait patiently from one's buying point until interest is renewed.

5.9 CONCLUSION

Investment opportunities don't come daily. However the noise of the markets offer mispriced securities from time to time. All information on companies is always readily available. This can never be an edge in investing. However, many believe it to be so. But there are a lot of investors who are swayed by the noise of the markets and their crowd behavior gives opportunities to a rational investor. Being in control of one's impulses and keeping the urges in control will help one to spot mispriced opportunities and avoid the growth trap. A growth stock is a stock which went way up. It is always in hindsight.

SIX

6

COMMODITY INVESTING

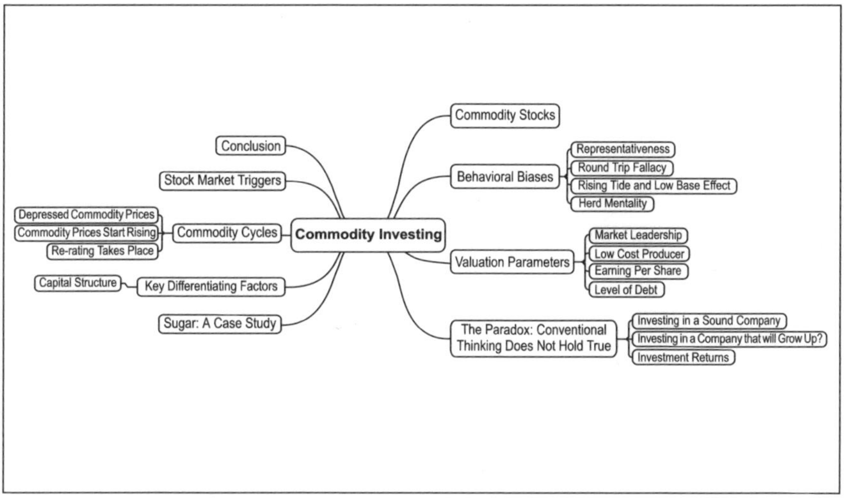

6.1 COMMODITY STOCKS

Why do people buy commodity stocks?

What research does one do about a commodity stock?

If the price of a commodity goes up the stock price of a company producing that commodity starts rising as well.

> **The basic idea behind investing in a business is to calculate how much we are getting for our money's worth as compared to other opportunities.**

Investors keep a tab on the prices of commodities and then make their buy and sell decisions on a commodity stock. If one is doing so much study to track the price movement of a commodity, is it not better for one to buy the commodity itself? Why should one go for a commodity stock? We have commodity exchanges dealing in each and every commodity and the investor or the trader would be better off operating in the commodity directly.

However, commodity stocks are listed on the stock markets. These provide investors an opportunity to earn returns. It becomes important to understand how to value a commodity stock. The valuation parameters have to be very different because the commodity prices are subject to commodity cycles. Moreover, companies in the commodities have varying capital structures.

If you are thinking of applying the conventional parameters like good management, efficiently run, healthy balance sheet, less debt and manageable interest burden to value a commodity stock, you are in for a big surprise.

Things do not work that way for a commodity stock. In fact, the opposite might hold true.

Market valuations are dependant on a host of psychological factors of the investors. Their short-term view to make short-term profits completely changes the conventional parameters. The stock markets are also based on the earnings parameters and the current earnings take precedence over other factors like sustainability of those earnings, the long term health of the company, and the management.

The short-term behavior of investors to only look at immediate gains, has made the concept of Earnings-Per-Share (EPS) as the most effective measurable tool to judge a company, where as in the long run, it is the net cash generated by the business that determines the returns for the shareholders.

This makes a strong case for evaluating commodity companies differently as their prices are subject to volatility in the short run, which is very difficult to predict. Moreover it is this volatility that attracts and excites the speculative tendency of the investors. Understanding investor behavioral biases is the first step to understanding why commodity companies need to be evaluated differently.

6.2 BEHAVIORAL BIASES

If one is looking at higher returns accruing by investing in commodity stocks, the conventional wisdom of buying a good company may not hold true, especially in the short run. Commodities have cycles and most investors make money by getting early in to cycle when the commodity prices start hardening. However, returns from commodity stocks are governed by the perceptions of a large number of investors. Their behavior and their perceptions of the commodity stock are dependent on the bottom line of the company in question. It will be important to understand the various behavioral biases before we go on to analyze the commodity stock valuation parameters.

> **In the sock markets, a small percentage of people end up being successful in the long run, whereas the majority of people, in spite of being successful in the short run, end up losers in the long run.**

Heuristics or mental short-cuts play an important role in framing investor decisions.

"Heuristics are simple, efficient rules of thumb which have been proposed to explain how people make decisions, come to judgments and solve problems, typically when facing complex problems or incomplete information. These rules work well under most circumstances, but in certain cases lead to systematic cognitive biases."
—Daniel Kahneman

6.2.1 Representativeness

When commodity prices start moving up, the trend is reflected in the working results of the leaders in the commodity stocks. The leaders are well-run companies having a healthy balance sheet and a reasonable market share. Due to their market position, they command a good respect and following in the markets and are tracked by a majority of the analysts. They could also be a part of the index. When the leaders start doing well in a particular commodity, the laggards also attract attention from investors, as they are also perceived to be able to deliver good results in view of the hardening commodity prices. Due to the effect of the representativeness heuristic, we have all the stocks of that commodity moving upwards and attracting investor attention. At this point of time, investors do not see if the company is good or bad. They buy it because it is representative of a commodity whose price is rising.

6.2.2 Round Trip Fallacy

Markets are always chasing such growth stories. An exponential rise in the bottom line is mistaken for sustainable growth momentum.

Consider the following statement, "All successful people are hard workers." Can we thus conclude that all hard workers are successful people? Definitely not. Hard work is one of the most important attributes behind successful people, but it is not the singular attribute.

Most of the cheap stocks generally have low or moderate PE ratios and only in exceptional cases have a high PE ratio. By believing that all low PE stocks would necessarily be cheap stocks one is succumbing to the "round trip fallacy".

Coming to the commodity stocks, one would believe that a well-managed commodity company producing at a low cost would generate higher returns for the company. In view of its higher earnings per share it would be able to command a higher PE and thus a higher price. Being a low-cost producer is an integral attribute for the company. However, investors look at other attributes, which may not be integral, but can have a good effect on the bottom line. We will see in the course of this chapter that a well-managed low-cost commodity company may not necessarily generate higher returns for the investor.

6.2.3 Rising Tide and Low-base Effect

A rising tide lifts everybody. When the tide rises every one standing in the water goes up with the tide. A six-foot father with his three-foot son in the water would both go up with the tide; however, the son's rise will be far more significant as his starting point is half that of his father. This is known as the low-base effect.

A commodity cycle turnaround lifts all the players in the industry. This is where the low-base effect becomes very important when we look at returns generated by investors. It is relatively easier to improve PBDT* margins from 5% to 10% than from 20% to 40%. This is where the laggards score over the leaders. Investors are thus more excited with the laggards as they seem to be performing better than the leaders. This makes the stock go up much faster resulting in good returns for the investors.

Value investors would always shun commodity stocks, as they never fit into their valuation parameters.

6.2.4 Herd Mentality

Investors are always chasing fads and fancies in the markets. A turnaround story is good news for the investors. Once a commodity turnaround is identified and the trend shows an upward movement we have the 'herd' of investors chasing it. This leads to a spurt in stock prices, which in turn leads to more investors joining the herd. When such crowd behavior is at work, there is no rationality. The only goal is to buy faster than the neighbor. As certain stocks go up and become expensive, the attention turns to other laggards in the same industry, as they seem cheaper. This again leads to massive demand for such stocks.

6.3 VALUATION PARAMETERS

"Investing is most intelligent when it is most business-like."—Benjamin Graham

*PBDT stands for 'Profit before Depreciation and Tax.

The basic idea behind investing in a business is to calculate how much we are getting for our money's worth as compared to other opportunities. An understanding of the concept of valuation plays an important role in successful implementation of the above principle.

"Price is what you pay, value is what you get."—Benjamin Graham

Investing, thus, is all about identifying strong sustainable businesses capable of giving the investor sustainable earnings over a longer period of time.

The stock market is probably the only place where people develop the habit of paying real money for future promises.

If one goes by the above parameters of valuing a commodity company one gets a bit confused. How does one really understand the business of commodities? Can one really do it? The performance of all commodity stocks is dependent on the price movements of the underlying commodities. The stock price fluctuates with the fluctuations in the price of commodities. Since this is not a very exciting business and cyclical in nature, one can expect to get normal average returns except in abnormal times when there is a run up in the price of commodities due to reasons like excess demand, acts of God, government controls, etc. We have been witnessing such a commodities boom that started in 2004.

If one were to follow Benjamin Graham's business-like approach in stock-picking then commodity stocks would definitely be out.

They may not be investment-worthy, but they could be very attractive for traders and speculators.

We are in a market where all sorts of businesses are listed. If a commodity happens to be one of them, let us identify the salient features of a good commodity company that will give a reasonable margin of safety to the trader or the speculator.

The following parameters would be very important for a commodity company.

6.3.1 Market Leadership

It will be important to invest in the best—the market leader. This has many advantages in the form of scale and size, strong balance sheet, internally-generated resources with less debt, pricing power and the ability to withstand the downturns. In bad times, such companies are able to survive for longer periods and are thus able to ride the commodity cycles. Market leadership ensures staying power and the ability to be efficient and shareholder-friendly. Investors looking at safe, sustainable investment returns will invest in commodity stock leaders.

6.3.2 Low-Cost Producer

How does one make profit in commodity companies? The commodity prices are given and the profits are dependent on internal efficiencies. The lower the cost of production, the higher would be the profits. The ability of companies to utilize their cash, manufacturing facilities, labor and resources ultimately affects its efficiencies. For a company to have such efficiencies, it needs to generate internal funds to undertake its operations. A minimum amount of debt on the books would herald sustainable profits in the future. A low-cost producer has pricing power over its competitors and is able to gain market share. Tata Steel is one such company in the steel industry in India.

6.3.3 Earnings Per Share

What does one look for in a commodity company? The health of the company is judged by its earning capacity, which is calculated by how much a company earns per share. Normally, for judging a company's financial health, a host of ratios are evaluated and dependence cannot be on just one. Nowhere in a commodity business do the earnings per share really become the most important attribute. This is due to the dependence on commodity cycles.

6.3.4 Level of Debt

In a commodity company, what differentiates a high-cost from a low-cost producer is the level of debt and the interest payments outflow. The real test of efficiency and profitability comes when the business does not have a high burden of debt. When one looks at a commodity company, debt becomes an important attribute as it can drastically affect the earnings. Moreover, the cyclical nature of the business does not justify huge debts. It could lead to a debt trap in tougher times.

6.4 THE PARADOX: CONVENTIONAL THINKING DOES NOT HOLD TRUE

When one is looking at returns to be made from investing in a commodity stock, the conventional wisdom of investing on sound financial parameters does not hold true. This is a paradox, and it is due to the fickle-mindedness and the short-term approach of investors who base their decisions solely on short-term profitability as against sustainability of earnings.

6.4.1 Psychological Denial: Speculating in the Name of Investing

A conservative person often happily puts his money in a bank earning him 9% annual interest, but speculates in the market expecting to earn 100% return in two months. How does one explain such an anomaly in expectations? Is it lack of understanding of the effort that goes into successful investing or is it his belief in his ability as a good stock-picker? A majority of people today fall in to this category.

In the stock markets, a small percentage of people end up being successful in the long run, whereas the majority of people, in spite of being successful in the short run, end up losers in the long run. People tend to focus more on the outcome than on the process. This is so evident in commodity stocks.

6.4.2 Investing in a Sound Company?

When one is investing, one looks at the soundness of the business model of the company. The management is important. Financial position plays an important part. The debt component needs to be low if one is looking at sustainability of the earnings. If it is a commodity stock, then the company needs to be a low-cost producer to survive in the long run. A long-term approach is essential.

6.4.3 Investing in a Stock that will Go Up?

There is a big difference in perception when one is investing in a good company and when one is buying a stock that will go up. The former is the investor while the latter is the trader or speculator.

When one is speculating and not investing, what does one look for? One looks for short-term quick fixes. One sees the current trend by looking at the leaders and then sniffs for opportunities in the laggards. If the leaders are doing well it is expected that the laggards will also do well. Moreover, the laggards are cheap, and when the investor fancy grips these laggards, they will go up.

What is the current EPS and what is it expected to be in the next quarter? Is the stock available cheap? If it is a laggard, it is cheap, so buy it. If the fortune turns it could be a multi-bagger in a short time. If a stock is a laggard and is bought at Rs.2, it has chances of becoming a 'three-bagger' if it goes to Rs.6. This will not be the case with a good stock quoting at Rs.30, which is an industry leader. The behavioral factor of low-base effect is at work, especially when one is buying a stock solely with the aim of its price going up.

6.4.4 Investment Returns

The basic goal of an investor, a trader or a speculator is to earn returns from the activity of investing, trading or speculating. The underlying asset may vary.

To earn good investment returns one would naturally invest in a company that is well-positioned to make good profits for its shareholders. To achieve this, it needs to be efficient in its facilities and needs to be the most competitive low-cost producer. It should not have much debt in its books for it could hamper its profitability due to high interest charges.

Conversely, investors would shun investing in inefficient high-cost producers who have a high debt. The higher interest charges are bound to eat into their profits.

However, in commodity companies, this logic does not work. In fact, investors would reap low returns when an upside takes place if they have invested in to efficient low-cost producers. And high-cost producers will be able to give higher returns to investors.

Generally, the PBDT to Sales ratio is used in comparing investment opportunities within an industry. But it is not accorded its proper weight when one does not take into account the fact that two businesses generating different returns on capital employed are expected to perform differently in future, and warrant earning profits at different multiples to sales. The capital structure also influences the multiples assigned to the ratios.

High- and Low-Cost Producers in Commodity Stocks

Contrary to popular belief that low-cost production in a commodity industry leads to higher investment returns, evidence suggest that sometimes investing in high-cost producers leads to higher investment returns. The recent 'Bull Run' in the steel industry is a case in point.

The current steel cycle started in 2003. Assuming that an investment was made during the initial stages of the uptrend and sold out after a period of two years, the performance would have been as summarized in the following table, where market capitalization on March 31, 2003 and on March 31, 2005 is used to calculate performance, after adjusting for split and bonus shares.

Table 6.1 Performance of Steel Companies, 2003–2005

Company	PBDT / Sales (Mar 2003)	PBDT / Sales (Mar 2005)	Performance (Mar 2003–Mar 2005)
TISCO	17.2 %	18.7 %	344 %
SAIL	0.2 %	29 %	600 %
Shree Precoated Steel	6.7 %	7.8 %	920 %
Uttam Galva	3.9 %	5.4 %	1,250 %
Bhushan Steel	7.5 %	9.8 %	740 %

What could possibly lead to such an anomaly? How could the market leader, a well-run efficient company under good management, fall so short of returns to investors as compared to its inefficient peers?

The following factors play a crucial role in leading to such a difference in investment returns.

Low-Base Effect

A commodity cycle lifts all the players in the industry. It is relatively easier to improve PBDT margins from 5% to 10% than it is to improve from 20% to 40%. This improvement in margins gets translates into

EPS growth, provided depreciation and tax outgo remain similar, resulting in better performance for high-cost producers.

High Debt Companies

The main differentiating factor between a low-cost producer and a high-cost producer is the level of debt. Interest payment is a fixed cost, and when things improve, the relative size of the interest component gets reduced, leading to higher bottom-line translation of revenues.

Debt Reduction

In good times, high-debt companies use the positive cash flows to pay back the debt or use the favorable business conditions to rotate the debt at favorable terms, resulting in lower interest cost and higher translation of revenues into profits.

Losses Carried Forward Resulting in Lower Taxes

Generally, the high-cost producers have a tough time surviving the consolidation phase as the impact of high-cost and lower realization leads to losses. But when the tide turns, the same losses have a positive impact on the bottom line, as those losses are adjusted against profits in good years, resulting in higher EPS.

Re-rating

Last but not least, market participants who worry about the ability of a company to survive the bad times value a high debt, operationally incompetent business at a lower multiple, indicating lower expectations, and rightly so.

It is when things become good that market participants re-rate the entire industry, and this gets translated into price appreciation even for not so good businesses.

6.5 SUGAR: A CASE STUDY OF LOW-COST VERSUS HIGH-COST PRODUCERS

The table below tries to depict the leverage employed in each of the five sugar companies at the start and end, (i.e., 2003 and 2006) of the last major sugar industry cycle and the impact it subsequently had on the post-interest profitability of the company.

One thing that becomes clear from the table is that Dhampur Sugar and Oudh Sugar, which had debt-to-equity ratio of 5 and 7, respectively, on their balance sheets, were performing very badly in 2003, i.e., just before the start of the cycle.

Table 6.2 Comparative Performance of Sugar Companies, 2003–2006

Company	Debt / Equity (2003)	*PBDT / Sales (2003)*	Debt Equity (2006)	*PBDT / Sales (2006)*
Balrampur Chini	1.4	*12.9%*	0.6	*24.3%*
EID Parry	0.6	*10.7%*	0.6	*15.5%*
Dhampur Sugar	5.3	*1.8%*	0.8	*9.8%*
Sakthi Sugar	1.4	*-14.0%*	2.4	*13%*
Oudh Sugar	7.2	*-3.0%*	1.7	*16.7%*

Debt / Equity: Debt to Equity

However, when the cycle turned, they ended up not only regaining their profitability but also managed to show a higher *percentage* gain in profitability as compared to low-cost producers like Balrampur Chini and EID Parry.

Low-Base Effect

This marked improvement led to higher appreciation in their share prices as compared to low-cost producers, who did well by themselves but not as well as the high-cost producers. This is depicted in the table below.

Table 6.3 Stock Performance versus Growth of Sugar Companies, 2003–2006

Company	Market Capitalization Mar 2003–Mar 2006 (Rs. Crores)	CAGR (%)
Balrampur Chini	232–4,658	185
EID Parry	134–2,550	166
Dhampur Sugar	24– 900	235
Sakthi Sugar	22–693	265
Oudh Sugar	9–400	240

The Effect of Compounding:

The difference in the compound rate of return may not appear to be large. However, that money would have compounded at these rates for three years, which is enough for small differences in rates to produce remarkably large differences in the end pool of money. Let us assume that Rs.1 lakh was invested in each of the companies at the start of the cycle, and compare the results to better understand the difference in the quality of results obtained in this study.

Table 6.4 Results of Investment of Rs. One Lakh in Sugar Companies

Company	CAGR%	Result (Rs. lakh)
Balrampur Chini	185	23.14
EID Parry	166	18.82
Dhampur Sugar	235	37.50
Sakthi Sugar	265	48.62
Oudh Sugar	240	39.30

Another example, of the cement industry, further reinforces the argument.

Table 6.5 Low-Cost versus High-Cost Cement Producers, 2003–2006

Company	Debt/ Equity (2003)	PBDT / Sales (2003) %	Debt/ Equity (2006)	*PBDT / Sales* (2006) %
Ambuja Cement	1.1	20.0	0.5	27.0
Madras Cement	2.6	14.2	1.5	17.5
JK Lakshmi	1.8	11.0	2.1	20.0
ACC	1.3	7.0%	0.8	11.5
Birla Corp	1.6	2.0	0.6	31.0
India Cement	4.5	– 23.0	1.8	7.4

Table 6.6 Stock Performance versus Growth of Cement Companies, 2003–2006

Company	Market Capitalization Mar 2003–Mar 2006 (Rs. crore)	CAGR (%)
Ambuja Cement	2,479–13,991	78
Madras Cement	416–2,616	85
JK Lakshmi	58–643	120
ACC	2,372–14,578	82
Birla Corp.	91–2,457	200
India Cement	180–3,146	160

Table 6.7 Results of Investment of Rs. One Lakh in Cement Companies

Company	CAGR %	Result (Rs. lakh)
Ambuja Cement	78	5.6
Madras Cement	85	6.3
JK Lakshmi	120	10.6
ACC	82	6.0
Birla Corp.	200	27.0
India Cement	160	17.5

As can be observed from the results in the preceding table, the theme also holds in the case of the recent cement sector cycle from 2003 to 2006, as the highest-cost producers in 2003, Birla Corp and India Cement, have outperformed the low-cost producers, Ambuja Cement and Madras Cement, by a significant percentage (with absolute capital appreciation being more than three times). Moreover, the reason for the high cost structure of Birla Cement and India Cement—apart from their high debt—is their lower productivity leading to higher manufacturing expenses.

6.6 KEY DIFFERENTIATING FACTORS

"When a rise in the price of a commodity occurs, there will ordinarily be a larger advance, percentage-wise, in the shares of high-cost producers than in the share of low-cost producers. Contrary to the general impression on Wall Street, the stocks of high-cost producers are more logical commitments than those of low-cost producers when the buyer is convinced that a rise in the price of a commodity is imminent and he wishes to exploit this conviction to the utmost." Ben Graham in Security Analysis.

Ben Graham first proposed this counterintuitive idea way back in 1934. Things have not changed since then, and possibly they will not change, as long as companies with varying capital structure and efficiencies operate in the commodity space.

As long as investors approach commodity companies believing that investments in low-cost operators would *invariably* lead to the highest investment returns, thus factoring the future expectations in the prices, and neglect other relatively small and inefficient companies to a level where they don't expect them to improve at all, they are bound to go wrong.

6.6.1 Capital Structure

Varying capital structures and efficiencies form the basis for differentiating companies.

Cyclical commodity companies often commit themselves to projects with huge capital expenditure just when prices are high and hitting a peak. They then proceed to retrench when prices are low.

The cyclical nature of the business affects cash flows in bad times, when inefficient companies become hungry for capital and take on excessive debt. This debt again leads to higher interest costs, which in turn affects the bottom line. The length of the bear cycle leads to carry-forward losses. Investors lose interest in such stocks and such a company's stock price is always depressed.

In contrast, efficient companies are well run and have manageable debt on the books. The interest outflow is reasonable so as not to affect the bottom line. These companies have market leadership due to their financial health and pricing power. They quote at reasonable PE multiples and attract investor interest. When the commodity cycle is upwards these companies' stocks move up as investors start chasing them.

An investor would normally look at investing in efficient and well-capitalized companies to earn handsome returns on his investment. However, the rules in commodity stocks are very different from the conventional, common-sensical approach. Returns to investors from such companies lag way behind the returns from inefficient and debt-ridden companies, especially during an upward inflection point. Why this anomaly? To understand this let us look at how the commodity cycle works.

6.7 COMMODITY CYCLES

Commodity stocks follow the commodity cycles, and investors track the trends in commodity prices to invest in commodity stocks. Companies in the commodity space are prone to significant swings in profitability and present challenges for investors trying to value such companies.

Companies in these cyclical industries—like steel, paper, chemicals, sugar, cement—challenge the fundamental principles of valuation. The use of the discounted cash flow technique creates hurdles due to the cyclical fluctuations and the uncertainty in the price of the commodities.

6.7.1 Depressed Commodity Prices

In depressed conditions, commodity prices are low. The overall business environment is pessimistic. Profits are hard to come by. Low-cost producers benefit, as they are able to undercut the competition. This makes them strong and they have less debt on the balance sheets. They are well-capitalized and their interest outflows are under control. These are the efficient companies, with efficient means of production and a healthy capital structure. They survive the hard times and reasonably reward their shareholders. The investors are happy with the margin of safety they enjoy with such companies.

On the other hand, inefficient companies suffer due to their huge debts and high cost of production. The bad times take their toll and decreased profitability makes these companies take more debts that result in more interest outflow. They go into the red and their losses mount. They are a neglected lot and command very low PE multiples.

6.7.2 Commodity Prices Start Rising

The inflection point comes and commodity prices start hardening. The fortunes of the industry seem to be changing and, in such a situation, the leaders would start doing much better and the laggards and the high-cost producers would start coming out of the red. Of course, a rational investor would invest in the leader, who is a low-cost producer, and with the changing fortunes the said company would yield handsome investment returns.

6.7.3 Re-rating Takes Place

If you are a conventional thinker, you are in for a rude shock. With the change in the commodity cycle from depressed prices to rising prices, re-rating of commodity companies starts.

The high cost and low cost differentiation vanishes as the commodities prices start rising. Investors no longer use this yardstick. It was a good tool in depressed conditions.

With the change in fortunes, companies are differentiated on the basis of their capacity to earn. Thus the concept of EPS becomes the tool for judging commodity stocks.

This change in investor behavior leads to a reversal of perception, and a re-rating of commodity stocks take place.

This re-rating makes the stocks of high-debt and inefficient companies most sought after, as they will be able to show healthier bottom lines than the efficient and low-debt producers. Expectations run high from these laggards and they become the investors' fancy. The low-base effect reinforces their fancy as their bottom line increases exponentially.

High-cost manufacturers with a high-debt component report higher EPS. The high interest payments are a tax shield and so are the carry-forward losses. Since expectations run high, investors are optimistic about the laggards, as good times will enable them to pay off their debts and add to the bottom line. Interest payments would also go down. The analysts start presenting a very optimistic picture of the future. Since such companies start from a very low base, a slight improvement has an exponential effect on their bottom line. Markets are always chasing such growth stories. An exponential rise in the bottom line is mistaken for sustainable growth momentum.

6.8 STOCK MARKET TRIGGERS

Stock price movements are subject to various kinds of news and information flowing about a company. Since most investors fall into the category of financial addicts, their time horizon is short. The data they look at is also short-term. Hence EPS becomes the dominant valuation metric. All high-cost producers with heavy debt are able to show strong earnings due to higher interest charges and carried forward losses. The following triggers are associated with higher EPS, and they are positively extrapolated by the investors.

Debt Reduction

Good times would also make the investors optimistic about a company's ability to reduce its debt. During good times, high-debt companies use positive cash flows to pay back the debt, or use favorable business conditions to rotate the debt at more favorable terms.

Interest Burden Declines

With the reduction in debt comes the reduction in interest obligations, which again increases the profitability and this is reflected in the EPS.

Lower Taxes

Generally, high-cost producers have a tough time surviving the consolidation phase, as the impact of high cost and lower realization leads to losses. But when the tide turns, the same losses have a positive impact on the bottom line as the losses are adjusted against profits, resulting in higher EPS.

6.9 CONCLUSION

Shareholders always look at returns when they are investing. If an investor had used the conventional parameters of valuations to make investment decisions, he would have bought shares of low-cost producers with a lower debt component. However, his returns would have suffered because these valuation parameters do not work in the case of commodity companies, where production efficiencies and capital structures vary. Value investors would always shun commodity stocks, as they never fit into their valuation parameters.

Traders and speculators would love commodity stocks. These stocks give them the thrill of momentum investing. The short-term nature of the markets and excessive reliance on quarter-to-quarter bottom line earnings thrills the majority of investors who can be classified as financial addicts. This majority forms the crowd, and the standard set by the crowd becomes the popular following. That is precisely the reason why commodity stocks cannot be valued using the conventional valuation models.

SEVEN 7

PUBLIC SECTOR UNITS

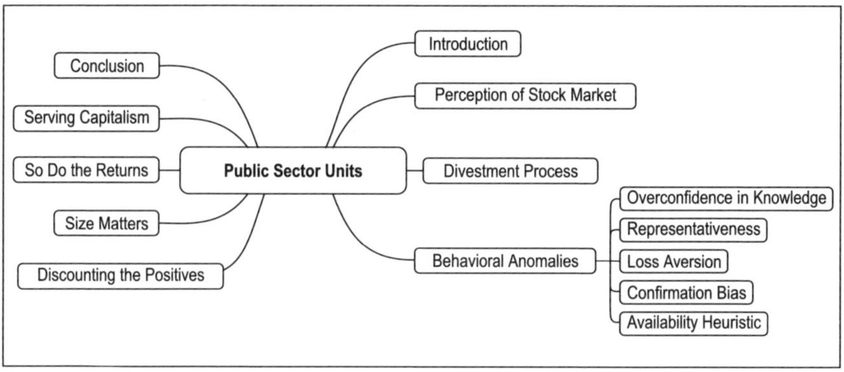

7.1 INTRODUCTION

PSUs are an inseparable part of India Inc., and deserve a bigger space in the investor's mind, as these are the companies to watch for long-term returns.

Public sector units (PSUs) are an inseparable part of India Incorporated. Although at present they are not getting their fair share of attention, they deserve a bigger space in the investor's mind, as these are the companies to watch for long-term returns. They have already rewarded the shareholders who were the early ones to enter during the divestment process or those who understood the business landscape and were willing to hold on for the long run.

These companies are unlikely to come up in discussions on corporate India nor are the media or the analysts covering them. They are not the current 'flavor' and that is what makes them very interesting for an investor. If one is a long-term investor it will be foolhardy to ignore such opportunities.

The popular belief is that corporate India is all about private enterprise. The fact is that PSUs account for as much as 43% of the combined net sales of the ET 500 companies, although the total number of PSUs in this list is only 59. This is a clear indication that most of these PSUs are not only a major chunk of India Inc. but are also corporate giants. In terms of net sales, a typical PSU is almost three times bigger than its private counterpart. Seven of the top ten Indian companies and 33 among the top 100 companies are PSUs.

Table 7.1 Top Ten PSUs by Turnover and Net Profit

Top 10 PSUs	Turnover FY 07 (Rs. crores)	Net Profit FY 07 (Rs. crores)
Indian Oil Corporation (IOC)	217,534	7,499
Bharat Petroleum Corporation Ltd. (BPCL)	98,872	2,140
Hindustan Petroleum Corporation Ltd. (HPCL)	94,681	1,674
Oil and Natural Gas Corporation (ONGC)	87,491	17,462

(Contd.)

* Economic Times.

Top 10 PSUs	Turnover FY 07 (Rs. crores)	Net Profit FY 07 (Rs. crores)
State Bank of India (SBI)	68,377	6,364
National Thermal Power Corporation (NTPC)	36,652	6,898
Steel. Authority of India Ltd (SAIL)	36,194	6,261
Mangalore Refineryand Petrochemicals Ltd. (MRPL)	28,637	526
Chennai Petroleum Corporation Ltd.	24,717	565
MMTC	23,225	127

Source: ET Intelligence Group, "Top Ten PSUs by Turnover and Net Profit", www.etintelligence.com

In terms of net sales, a typical PSU is almost three times bigger than its private counterpart.

PSUs account for 37% of the combined net profit of all ET500 companies, which is less than their share of turnover. But this is due to the lower profits of oil marketing companies like IOC, BPCL and HPCL. From the above table, it is evident that their profitability is low. The government's cap on retail fuel prices adversely affects their margins.

However, on a like-to-like basis, government companies such as National Aluminum (NALCO), National Thermal Power Corporation (NTPC), Steel Authority (SAIL), Gas Authority of India (GAIL), Bharat Heavy Electricals (BHEL), State Bank of India (SBI), Shipping Corporation of India (SCI) have the same level of profitability as their private sector counterparts.

Even the oil companies are well managed and efficient, comparable to the best in the industry.

However, the stock markets are not giving them the true credit they deserve. Markets like growth, and critics argue that growth is more important than profitability. They do not find these companies capable of grabbing the growth opportunities and growing fast. If one asks what

* Economic Times Intelligence Group.

is growth, I doubt they can offer an explanation. It is the common jargon used in the markets.

Last year, the turnover of PSUs was up by 25%, compared to 32% combined growth shown by ET500 companies. Profit growth for PSUs was lower at 31% compared to 43% of the ET500 companies. This could signify that the PSUs are slow and sluggish in spotting opportunities. However, this could also be due to the nature of the business, and slower decision-making with regard to major investment decisions, which require clearance from ministries concerned, and often face bureaucratic delays.

Moreover, PSUs have a negligible presence in the so-called high-growth businesses like IT, construction, real estate and telecom services.

If one is a long-term investor interested in good returns, then this is definitely an opportunity.

No doubt, government interference with the pricing policy of the oil companies has dented the profitability of these efficient, well-run giants. This has led to the PSUs losing credibility with the investors. There is always a fear of government interference.

While size may be attractive when it comes to the private sector, the stock markets do not show a similar faith in PSUs.

The ET500 companies are valued at around 19 times their trailing net profits, while PSUs are valued at only 12.4 times their earnings. This is a 40% discount to the private sector players. Is this an opportunity or is the market seeing it differently?

If one is a long-term investor interested in good returns, then this is definitely an opportunity. We will explore this in detail in this chapter.

7.2 PERCEPTION OF STOCK MARKET

There is always a gap in the valuation of a company between its actual worth and the worth with the built-in expectations of investors who make up the market. These built-in expectations can be too positive or too negative.

The market-perceived negatives are the following:

1. Political interference as is happening with the cap on retail prices of fuel with the oil companies.

2. Political risks and uncertainties related to government ownership. Can populism overrule business considerations? Are coalition governments capable of pushing through the divestment?
3. Cyclical nature of businesses. Most of the PSUs are in commodity businesses—like oil and gas, steel, metals—and banking, which are generally accorded poor valuations as compared to the hot growth sectors like consumer goods, IT, IT services, capital goods and infrastructure.
4. Will they able to survive the onslaught of foreign and domestic competition? Most of them are a product of a socialist *raj*, and became monopolies in their industries. Their vulnerability is most visible in the services sector like telecom and banking, where speed of decision-making and execution and operational flexibility matter the most.

7.3 DIVESTMENT PROCESS

Investors are not risk-averse, but they are loss-averse.

Opportunities take birth in distress situations and PSU divestment was one such opportunity for long-term investors. The year 1991 saw the country going into financial bankruptcy and, thus, was born the process of economic liberalization. The economy needed to be freed from its shackles and the only way to save the country was to go ahead with the reform process.

Money had to be raised to make up the fiscal deficit, and what better way could there be than to sell the government stakes in the huge PSUs. These companies were a product of our socialist society and, with the liberalization process and embracing of market economy, they had to be restructured to function in a market economy.

The divestment process soon started and the government finalized a list of PSUs for divestment to the Indian public. However, the mood of the market was bearish and there were no takers for such offerings. The government-run financial institutions came to the rescue and picked up sizeable stakes in various government-run companies. The idea was to let the government tide over the existing crises, and when the market conditions improved they would off load the shares in the market.

The opportunity for an astute long-term investor was immense.

7.4 BEHAVIORAL ANOMALIES

We have seen the positives and the negatives of the PSUs. No doubt size matters, but the markets are giving a very heavy discount of 50% in valuing the PSUs as compared to the valuations given to comparable private sector companies.

One reason for the market giving such valuations to the PSUs is that it does not see them in a growth phase. This is just a condition of the mind. If one were to ask the growth strategists to define lack of growth, most of them will come up with a typical answer of the sales, profits and stock price not moving fast enough. We all know that the stock price is a function of how 'Mr. Stock Market' perceives the stock. This 'Mr. Market' comprises of the sentiments and the cognitive illusions of market participants.

If one is making a decision to invest, does one not look at the returns one would make if one invests in the companies? As we have seen in the chapter on growth trap, investors chasing growth are bound to get into the growth trap and suffer on their returns.

The Indian growth story is on and the markets are in a correction mode. The government also understands the need to divest its shareholding from PSUs.

There is a PSU commodity company, Minerals and Metals Trading Company Ltd. (MMTC). Its EPS for March 2007 was Rs.32 and at a price of Rs.33,000 on 26th November 2007, it was at a PE of 1,027. At its 52-week high of Rs.56,931 on 12th November 2007 its PE was 1,779. If it is a PSU and in a commodity sector, why this spurt of valuation? There are no definite answers with anyone, but this rise can be attributed to speculative investor behavior.

As far as PSU investment is concerned, there is a mind set amongst investors to refrain from such stocks. However, here lies the opportunity if one is a long-term investor. Investors are so averse to PSU-stock investment that when, in 1994-95, the government came out with divestment of its holdings in select, good PSU companies, it met with such a lukewarm response from the investors that the shares had to be placed with government-owned financial institutions (FIs).

What cognitive defects or anomalies make investors behave in such a way? Understanding them would help one to understand one's own defects and at the same time to use this knowledge for formulating one's investment strategies.

7.4.1 Overconfidence in Knowledge

One of the most significant and irrefutable findings of behavioral psychologists is that people are overconfident in their judgments and over-estimate the reliability of their judgments. What else can explain the valuations of telecommunications, media and technology companies during the 1999–2000 technology boom? Or the rise of MMTC to Rs. 56,000 in November 2007? People are confident of their abilities and also of their knowledge. When it comes to doing things like driving, it is their ability. When it comes to investing or business it is their knowledge. People make changes in their portfolio or day-trade because they are confident of their knowledge on a particular stock or the markets in general. This tendency of being overconfident manifests itself in high portfolio turnover rates, and is reflected in the tendency to time the markets. This overconfidence is evident even amongst the institutional professional investors.

> **Investors are so lured by the quick short-term gains of the stock markets that they are willing to bet on corporations built like a pack of cards.**

This overconfidence bias is obvious in investors shunning the PSU companies. Investors are overconfident of their knowledge that all PSUs are inefficient because they work in a protected environment. They are overconfident that these companies will not survive domestic and foreign competition. They are overconfident of their knowledge that these are mediocre investments as they are not in the growth sector. They are overconfident that only a growth stock is a good investment. They are overconfident that government interference will harm the interests of the shareholders.

7.4.2 Representativeness

Resemblance to a certain attribute or quality is termed as representative of that particular group. This is known as "representative bias". This is a heuristic, a mental shortcut that the brain takes when processing information. It does not process the full information. Thus, decision-making is biased.

All PSU stocks are representative of a government-controlled environment. All PSU companies are representative of inefficiencies due to their monopolistic status. All PSU companies are representative of low-growth businesses. All PSU companies are representative of ministerial and bureaucratic interference leading to delayed decision-making in a competitive world. All PSU companies are representative of government interference.

Thus the market's perception of PSU stocks is very negative. These stocks represent all that is not good. This is also extrapolated too far into the future. It is just assumed that things will never improve.

7.4.3 Loss Aversion

The pain of a loss is three times greater than the joy from an equal amount of gain. Investors are not risk-averse or else they would not enter the markets. But they are loss-averse. They will shy away from any opportunity where there is a loss. For any investment, one must weigh the risk-reward ratio and then come to a decision. However, investors become loss-averse when even the slightest hint of a loss lurks in their minds.

Investors believe that inefficiency and government controls are a sure sign of a mismanaged company and investment in such companies will lead to losses. Moreover, in the past, divestment in PSUs had met with failure, and the bear markets from 1996 to 2003 had severely punished these stocks. This was due more to the market conditions than the individual stocks. The loss-aversion bias in 2003 was so strong that people were getting out of stocks and investing in fixed income securities. PSU stocks were never a fancy in the stock markets and were perceived to be risky investments. This made the investors loss-averse. Government's price control on oil companies has impacted their profitability to a great extent. This has also made investors loss-averse to PSUs.

7.4.4 Confirmation Bias

People tend to only think in the way that suits their original thinking. They only look at information that conforms with theirs. Any information challenging the original hypothesis is discarded. This bias stems from the overconfidence bias.

There are many attributes of PSUs that have merit, but investors are blind to them. Moreover, with a strong negation of the mind, all the positives are discounted.

It is not that PSUs have not rewarded the shareholders, or that these PSUs are unable to withstand competition. PSUs like SBI, Indian Oil

Corporation, Bharat Electronics and BHEL have done exceedingly well in a free market and, at the same time, investors have been handsomely rewarded.

However, investors are more focused on the PSU laggards like MTNL and Indian Airlines, which have been unable to compete with the private sector.

We do have a mixed bag in the PSUs, but that is so with the private sector also.

7.4.5 Availability Heuristic

When all the information around you is either positive or negative, you tend to be swayed by the information you receive. The mind recollects all that is recent and all that is recently frequent. The mind's ability to recollect vivid and recent information is strong, and this makes us prone to availability bias.

PSUs are not the fancy of the media so they get very scarce coverage in the media. Nor are their CEOs the favorites of media shows. Not many analysts follow PSU stocks, as they are not glamour stocks. Brokers do not recommend many PSU stocks, as they do not find favor with the clients. Lastly, and most importantly, they are not growth stocks.

The recall value in the minds of the investors for PSU stocks is very low and, thus, they do not capture the attention of the investors. Moreover, the available information is neutral to negative, rather than positive.

7.5 DISCOUNTING THE POSITIVES

PSUs like NTPC, Engineers India, BHEL, Bharat Electronics and Dredging Corporation of India Ltd. continue to flourish despite the competition. The stock market is giving respect and healthy valuations to most of the listed PSUs

In sectors like commodities and oil and gas, PSUs continue to dominate.

Investment returns are all about buying a stock at the 'right' price, and this price does not reflect any built-in expectations of the investors. Since most of these PSU stocks carry past baggage of certain behavioral anomalies discussed above, they are not the fads and fancies of the market. This is the positive, which is ignored by the investors.

Another important positive omission is that these PSUs represent very crucial and challenging sectors, where creating critical mass is of utmost importance. Banking, oil and power sectors are cases in point. Mining, engineering and defense sectors, which were virtual monopolies and had stiff entry barriers, were another big positive ignored by the investors.

It was always assumed that the PSU culture would be impossible to change and the unions would play spoilsport. But this also had a big positive. Once the reality dawned that it was a question of survival, these PSUs and their unions bounced back to action by gearing up for the competition with the private sector companies. This is amply evident in the performance of the PSUs. Most of them have performed exceedingly well. It shows that they have changed with the changing times. Their inability to change fast was more due to 'red-tapism' at the ministerial and bureaucratic levels than within themselves.

Another big positive ignored was the valuation metric of the replacement cost theory. Huge investments had gone into creating huge capacities, and the sheer size of these PSUs gave a big advantage over the private sector enterprises. Moreover, these facilities were in the commodity sector, where technological obsolesce played a minor role. In the banking sector the large size of the branch network was not reflected in the profits of the banks. However, this extensive branch network was the key to success in a liberalized environment. Creation of such huge capacities and branch networks were the entry barriers ignored by investors in valuing the PSUs.

Moreover, it was assumed that the PSUs would not be able to withstand competition from private sector players. However, no worthwhile private sector competition existed for them. By the time such players would be established, the PSUs had enough lead to change the rules of the game. This they did, and this is reflected in their performance, which we will see in the later part of the chapter.

Cognitive anomalies of "all or nothing", "discounting the positives" and the "fly mentality" played a major role in investors' decision-making on PSU investments. No doubt, some companies did suffer from the onslaught of liberalization; but some bounced back to become stock market favorites. Investors and the media only focused on the negatives of the PSUs and thus investors' expectations were always very low. This led to such stocks being ignored.

The evidence shows that out of the 61 PSUs that were listed, only 18 companies gave negative returns. These negative returns were due to the fact that most of these companies happened to be in government-controlled and subsidized sectors like oil, refineries and fertilizers. The rest were in sectors like commodities and paper, which were going through tough times and required resources and technological upgradation.

Nineteen companies have given excellent, positive returns and have beaten the Sensex returns. Of these, 10 have been from the banking sector alone.

The rest of the 24 companies have given mediocre to average returns.

7.6 SIZE MATTERS

One basic fact, which the investors missed, was the way they looked at the PSUs. The old yardstick, of valuing the company on the basis of profitability alone, has waylaid many investors. Here, the test was to look into the future and imagine what such huge-sized companies could do when the liberalized era would unfold.

Socialism enabled the creation of an important asset in terms of size and scale. These PSUs were huge undertakings. The darker side was the inefficiencies due to strong unions, inefficient work force, lack of discipline, outdated modes of production, etc. These factors were responsible for the low productivity, which in turn resulted in lower profits. Subsidies and government controls also played a major role in making the PSUs less profitable.

However, most of these PSUs were in the commodity sectors including oil exploration, oil refining, oil distribution, steel, mining, banking, defense, and infrastructure. These companies had built up sizable scale and distribution networks. The oil companies had their pipelines and the distribution network in place, which would be the most valuable hidden asset. Similarly, the PSU banks had branch networks in place, which would be very expensive for a new entrant to copy. In addition, these PSUs were sitting on acres of real estate, which is now fast appreciating. Added to these were other, intangible assets in the form of mining leases, telephone lines, defense contracts, etc.

The replacement cost concept was totally ignored by the investors. It was all about size and scale. In times of rising inflation how could one ignore the fact that the replacement of the assets becomes costlier? One would argue that a plant would have a life and new technological developments would render the old machines useless. However, that would hold true only in industries where technological innovations and improvements would be crucial. In the case of commodities—where most of the PSUs dominated—these were not very important. Moreover, the assumption that these companies would not embrace new technologies and change was also baseless. Ultimately, it has been proven that the bricks and mortar cannot be ignored in times of rising inflation and restructuring of the economy.

What made investors shun this wisdom was the emergence of technology and the internet. The stock market boom driven by the IT sector in 1999–2000 gave an illusion that the old economic model was dead and the new economic model based on services was replacing it. The valuations of the old economy companies had reached ridiculously low levels as investors were chasing the new economy companies. The availability heuristic for the new economy was so strong that everyone assumed that the old economy order was over. This led to a total rejection of the bricks and mortar model. The important cognitive defect evident was the 'all or nothing'. It was assumed that the new economy would replace the old and, hence, the focus shifted to the intangibles. In hindsight, we find that it was a totally flawed thinking. But in stock markets this is how certain fad and fancies rule investor behavior.

SBI the country's premier banking company was shunned by the investors and was available at as low a PE as 8. Investors only saw profitability. If one would have had the vision to see the hidden values of its work force, banking culture, the branch network spread over every nook and corner of India, its real estate portfolio—one would have been a very wealthy investor now. An insight into how reforms in the financial sector would change the rules of the game was also missing. Opportunities opened up and the PSUs were also quick to reform themselves and take on the competition. Even today, SBI is a good buy at the current PE of 21, if one is optimistic about the India growth story.

7.7 SO DO THE RETURNS

None of the PSUs was considered a growth stock and, therefore, was never a fancy with the investors looking for great upsides. Nor were they value stocks, as investors always believed them to be government monopolies that would not survive in a competitive market. The investors least expected them to do well and, hence, the prices of these stocks did not reflect any investor expectations. On the contrary, these stocks were so negatively weighed that they were available at ridiculously low valuations. The prices of these stocks did not even reflect their fair potential. If one had a vision of the potential of these companies in a liberalized era and if one had looked at the valuations at which they were available then, today they would have been giving excellent returns. Investment returns are all about buying investments at the right valuations, which are not reflecting any in-built investor expectations.

Performance of PSUs after 1991

Out of the sample size of 61 PSUs, 10 were listed before 1991 and the remaining got listed after 1991. We have measured the performance of the 51 PSUs, which got listed after 1991, from their date of listing on the Bombay Stock Exchange to 21 December 2006. The performance of the 10 PSUs, which were listed prior to 1991, has been measured from 1991 to 21 December 2006. Out of the total 61 PSUs, 19 are banks and FIs and 11 are from the oil and gas sector. The banks have performed better than other PSUs, while the oil and gas companies have given, on average, negative returns. Only 19 out of the 61 PSUs have given more returns than the Sensex during the same period (Table 7.2).

Table 7.2 Sectoral Perfomance of PSUs from 1991 to 2006

	All (61)	Banks & FIs (19)	Oil & Gas (11)	Others (31)
Mean Returns (%)	13.64	20.32	-0.72	13.91
Maximum (%)	79.77	53.26	18.61	79.77
Minimum (%)	-17.11	-14.91	-14.50	-17.11

The banks have given the best returns of all the other PSUs. Ten out of 19 banks have outperformed the Sensex. UTI Bank (renamed Axis Bank), Indian Overseas Bank, and Jammu & Kashmir Bank have given 20% higher returns than the Sensex for the same period. From the oil and gas sector, only NTPC has given 14% higher returns than the Sensex for the same period. Dredging Corporation of India Ltd. and National Mineral Development Corporation Ltd. (NMDC) have recorded the best performance, with annual average returns of 79.77% and 77.15%, respectively, and have outperformed the Sensex by 61.87% and 52.88%, respectively (Table 7.3).

Table 7.3 Performance of PSUs that Outperformed the Sensex from 1991 to 2006

S. No.	Name of Company	Average Annual Returns (%)	Sensex Returns for the same period (%)	Excess Returns (%)
1	Dredging Corporation of India Ltd.	79.77	17.90	61.87
2	NMDC	77.15	24.26	52.88
3	Maharashtra Electrosmelt Ltd.	61.09	34.27	26.82
4	Allahabad Bank	53.26	34.92	18.34
5	Union Bank of India	47.79	35.05	12.73
6	NTPC Ltd.	42.89	28.59	14.30
7	UTI Bank	42.05	19.48	22.57
8	Canara Bank	41.81	34.68	7.13
9	Indian Overseas Bank	38.91	19.23	19.68
10	Container Corporation of India Ltd.	38.51	17.60	20.91
11	Jammu & Kashmir Bank	37.48	17.91	19.57
12	Andhra Bank	37.45	23.00	14.44

(Contd.)

S. No.	Name of Company	Average Annual Returns (%)	Sensex Returns for the same period (%)	Excess Returns %
13	National Aluminum Co. Ltd.	32.19	17.24	14.95
14	State Trading Corp. of India Ltd.	31.39	19.90	11.50
15	Bharat Electronics Ltd.	27.44	16.76	10.68
16	Vijaya Bank	27.41	19.84	7.57
17	Syndicate Bank	24.54	14.66	9.88
18	BHEL	19.08	11.05	8.02
19	Swaraj Mazda Ltd.	18.61	17.83	0.78

Table 7.4 Performance of All PSUs from 1991 to 2006

S. No.	Name of Company	Average Annual Returns (%)	Sensex Returns for the same period (%)
1	Hindustan Organic Chemicals Ltd.	-17.11	11.72
2	Andrew Yule & Company Ltd.	-15.63	22.17
3	IFCI Ltd.	-14.91	9.61
4	Mysore Paper Mills Ltd.	-14.50	20.62
5	Hindustan Copper Ltd.	-12.17	22.76
6	Tourism Finance Corp. of India	-11.77	10.66
7	Kochi Refineries Ltd.	-10.06	17.59
8	Madras Fertilizers Ltd.	-9.90	12.61

(Contd.)

S. No.	Name of Company	Average Annual Returns (%)	Sensex Returns for the same period (%)
9	BPCL	-8.82	10.57
10	Bongaigaon Refinery & Petrochemicals	-6.26	13.49
11	ITI Ltd.	-5.23	13.40
12	Tamil Nadu Newsprint & Papers Ltd.	-4.86	17.45
13	IDBI Ltd.	-4.26	12.16
14	Engineers India Ltd.	-4.20	15.27
15	Rashtriya Chemicals & Fertilizers Ltd.	-2.20	11.56
16	Punjab Alkalis & Chemicals Ltd.	-1.16	18.34
17	Gujarat State Fertilizers & Chemicals Ltd.	-0.80	17.60
18	Neyveli Lignite Corp. Ltd.	-0.56	17.96
19	HMT Ltd.	0.95	13.43
20	Indian Oil Corp. Ltd.	0.98	14.51
21	Bank of Maharashtra	0.98	30.96
22	Gujarat Alkalis & Chemicals Ltd.	1.21	17.65
23	SAIL	1.70	10.26
24	MTNL	2.16	13.76
25	Dena Bank	3.09	14.04
26	ONGC	3.61	12.36
27	Chennai Petroleum Corp. Ltd.	3.97	12.49
28	LIC Housing Finance Ltd.	4.37	9.99

(Contd.)

S. No.	Name of Company	Average Annual Returns (%)	Sensex Returns for the same period (%)
29	GAIL (India) Ltd.	5.53	13.38
30	Gujarat Narmada Valley Fertilizers Co. Ltd.	6.83	17.51
31	Oriental Bank of Commerce	8.02	10.48
32	Shipping Corp. of India Ltd.	9.24	16.07
33	Gujarat Mineral Development Corp. Ltd.	10.32	14.41
34	IBP Co. Ltd.	10.58	19.32
35	Bank of Baroda	11.07	14.23
36	Bank of India	11.93	13.30
37	Bharat Earth Movers Ltd.	12.95	15.69
38	Corporation Bank	14.24	15.04
39	Balmer Lawrie & Co. Ltd.	15.73	20.31
40	UCO Bank	17.02	32.95
41	Swaraj Mazda Ltd.	18.61	17.83
42	National Fertilizers	18.87	25.89
43	BHEL	19.08	11.05
44	Scooters India Ltd.	22.25	33.88
45	Syndicate Bank	24.54	14.66
46	Vijaya Bank	27.41	19.84
47	Bharat Electronics Ltd.	27.44	16.76
48	State Trading Corp. of India Ltd.	31.39	19.90
49	National Aluminum Co. Ltd.	32.19	17.24
50	Andhra Bank	37.45	23.00
51	Jammu & Kashmir Bank	37.48	17.91

(Contd.)

S. No.	Name of Company	Average Annual Returns (%)	Sensex Returns for the same period (%)
52	Container Corporation of India Ltd.	38.51	17.60
53	Indian Overseas Bank	38.91	19.23
54	Canara Bank	41.81	34.68
55	UTI Bank	42.05	19.48
56	NTPC Ltd.	42.89	28.59
57	Union Bank of India	47.79	35.05
58	Allahabad Bank	53.26	34.92
59	Maharashtra Electrosmelt Ltd.	61.09	34.27
60	NMDC	77.15	24.26
61	Dredging Corporation of India Ltd.	79.77	17.90

The liberalization process started in the year 1991. It started with reforms in the financial sector. This paved the way for reforming the banking sector and several measures were announced to deregulate this sector. Private banks were also allowed to enter the Indian markets. As their survival was in question, the public sector banks started gearing themselves up for the competition by perceiving it as an opportunity. They also started accessing the capital market to raise resources. The PSU banks, with their vast branch network and a pool of skilled staff, ventured aggressively. Initially, since the enthusiasm for the PSU banks was low, they did not have much investor following. But once they started posting healthy profits, the investors' belief started growing, and so did the valuations of these banks, as is evident from the above figures. Out of the listed 19 banks, 10 have out-performed the Sensex. Only Dena Bank and Bank of Maharashtra have been underperformers. Maybe these banks were not able to capitalize on the opportunities, or they were victims of red-tapism and labor unions.

The oil and gas sector PSUs have done badly and underperformed the Sensex. This is not because they were not able to survive in a competitive environment, but because they were not allowed to do so. They have world-class production and refining capabilities and capacities, a pool of skilled engineers and a dedicated work force. Moreover, they have scale and size. Oil and gas being a very sensitive political tool, these companies have always suffered due to government interference in the pricing of petroleum products. This has bled these companies and, with oil prices continuing to rise, investors see no hope of these companies being able to post economic profits. Investors who were early enough to see the potential of these companies have suffered. However, considering the environment today and the way the India growth story is emerging, these stocks are good investment opportunities as there are no built-in expectations. Oil companies like Bharat Petroleum and Hindustan Petroleum have been given oil bonds by the government to offset their losses due to price controls. This is a big plus for these companies.

Nine companies have given returns in excess of 10%. Another 18 companies have posted negative returns as compared to the Sensex. However, it must be noted that most of them were in industries that saw a declining trend. Two such industries were fertilizers and paper. Fertilizer pricing was always controlled and this killed those industries. Even the private sector companies suffered in this sector. Paper and newsprint was also a fading sector.

Telecommunications companies, like ITI and MTNL, suffered heavily due to the deregulation in the sector and their inability to adapt and compete. This was one sector where technology played an important part, and these companies were not able to quickly embrace change due to labor unions and lack of political vision. Where technological change, technology adoption and speed to the market were crucial factors, the PSUs lost out.

FIs, like IFCI and IDBI, carried heavy baggage of non-performing assets. In spite of the liberalization of the financial sector, they could not shed their past legacy.

But, overall, these PSUs provided great opportunities to long-term investors by posting higher returns. It again proves the point that ultimately a return is growth.

The Indian growth story is on and the markets are in a correction mode. The government also understands the need to divest its shareholding from PSUs. A host of offerings came to the market in 2007, including:

1. Power Grid Corporation of India Ltd. (Rs. 51,869 crores)
2. Central Bank of India (Rs. 4,372 crores)
3. Indian Bank (Rs. 7,723 crores)
4. Power Finance Corporation (Rs. 28,849 crores)

However, investing in them might not have given expected returns, as investor expectations were running high in these offerings due to the bull market conditions and the past returns given by the PSUs. Moreover, the IPO markets had been very hot, and steeply-priced issues have also attracted investor interest—especially when all these companies happened to be in the fancied sectors like power, banking and finance.

7.8 SERVING CAPITALISM

What is real capital formation in a capitalist society? It is not stock market capitalization for sure.

This term is highly misunderstood in the current times. During the past five years, the world has been experiencing an economic boom and the stock markets of all countries have been doing exceedingly well. Stock prices have been soaring, commodities prices are spiraling, oil is at a triple-digit dollar price, real estate prices are appreciating, and food shortages are surfacing. The divide between the rich and the poor is widening.

In spite of all these factors the stock markets are still showing strength. Most of the wealth creation was due to paper profits reflected in stock prices. Stock market manipulations; increasing use of derivative products and the futures and options market; and the speculative tendencies amongst qualified institutional investors, the retail investors, corporations, banks and FIs, created a society where insanity works. Greed is so dominant that investors have lost their rationality and are willing to pay ridiculous valuations for stocks. This surge in stock prices has led to a race for market capitalization. Unknown companies with hardly any track record on the markets are able to be listed on stock exchanges and find a place in the indices. In fact a more dangerous trend amongst the big corporations is rewarding the CEOs, COOs and key personnel based on the market capitalization. Stock options are another cause for worry. CEOs reward themselves by manipulating earnings. The future costs are ignored in their anxiety for short-term earnings. Faceless corporations are the worst hit. In the absence of any 'owner', managers are only interested in enriching themselves.

This is the worrisome state of the private sector where thousands of crores of rupees are invested by retail and institutional investors either directly or through mutual funds. Is this capital formation?

On the other hand, let us take a look at the PSUs. Yes, they are government owned, inefficient, have strong labor unions, lack productivity and are subject to red-tapism and bureaucratic interference. However, these corporations have made investments in land, machinery and infrastructure, and their capital is channelized into productive use. Productivity may suffer, but there are visible, tangible investments. Yet, investors are reluctant to give any value to them. On the contrary, investors are so lured by the quick short-term gains of the stock markets that they are willing to bet on corporations built like a pack of cards. Investors are willing to pay any price for someone who is selling them dreams. This situation is something like the technology boom, but on a much larger scale.

Companies like Reliance Power, Reliance Natural Resources Ltd., India Bulls Realty, Reliance Infrastructure, and ICICI Bank command a market capitalization not at all worthy of their true business or future potential. These companies are not in any way aiding capital formation. Sectors like real estate, financial services and entertainment do not help capital formation. They help speculation.

On the other hand, the various PSUs have been responsible for capital formation in the country. Unfortunately, investors shun such companies. In the long run, it will be amply clear that market capitalization achieved due to capital formation creates shareholder wealth, and not stock prices based on market manipulations.

This state of the market depicts unusual investor behavior, where good values are ignored. This presents a wise investor with immense opportunities for good investment.

7.9 CONCLUSION

The markets are efficient in the long run but they are inefficient in the short run. The nature of the markets has changed due to the advent of technology and the Internet, and financial borders disappearing.

Returns are a function of buying a value at the right price. However, in reality it is not as simple as it sounds. When such an opportunity comes we dislike the opportunity, as our decisions are controlled by our emotions, which, in turn, are controlled by the environment. It is not that the PSU investment opportunity was not understood by most of the long-term investors. It was the courage to look at the long-term that was lacking. And returns are always a function of the long-term.

Coming to the environment part, investors were worried about the government's lack of political will to get on with reforms. The fertilizer industry was under price control and was killed. This anchor was too strong in the minds of the investors and it did prove such cautious investors right if one looks at the woes of the oil marketing companies.

What has generated the returns in certain sectors like banking, mining, container, defense? One was that these sectors were opened to reforms faster. Secondly, they were in monopoly sectors. Thirdly, and most importantly, they were able to attract investor attention over time. This was achieved by steady growth in profitability and size.

Size and scale have played an important role for most of these successful PSUs. It is the market capitalization game that works in the market today. Since there are investors from the world over who are looking at investments in various countries, they look at a certain size to invest. Even a great 'blue chip', if it does not have a sizeable market capitalization, will not be in the investing list of such investors. This is where the PSUs have an edge in their visibility in the markets. They also have assets, infrastructure, knowledge, client-base and network to back their claims.

This also makes it easier for them to access the capital markets. Such large issues will feed the appetite of large foreign institutional investors. Foreign institutional investors, as a group, are allowed to hold shares up to a certain limit and that limit has already been exhausted in SBI. Again, this scale and size helps a company to get into the index. Index traders, and those looking at country exposure, normally invest in index stocks only. This again helps the PSUs to get a good investor-following, as the analysts start covering such highly capitalized index stocks.

Stock markets are all about the herd. When you have a herd following a stock because it is a large-cap stock and has a place in the index, it is considered a fancy stock. And fancy stocks have high built-in expectations and hence their stocks gain in value. You have good returns on your investments when you buy them early.

The BSE Sensex has a representation of four giant PSUs, with SBI leading with a weightage of 4.21%, followed by ONGC with 3.90%, BHEL with 2.74% and NTPC with 2.12%, as on 23rd April 2008. All of them combined have a weightage of over 12%, which is quite low considering the scale and the size of PSUs in India. The NSE Nifty has a representation of nine PSUs, with a weightage over 22%. More PSUs will get listed in the future, offering investors good investment opportunities.

Definitely, a wise long-term investor cannot ignore PSU stocks.

EIGHT 8

SECTOR INVESTING

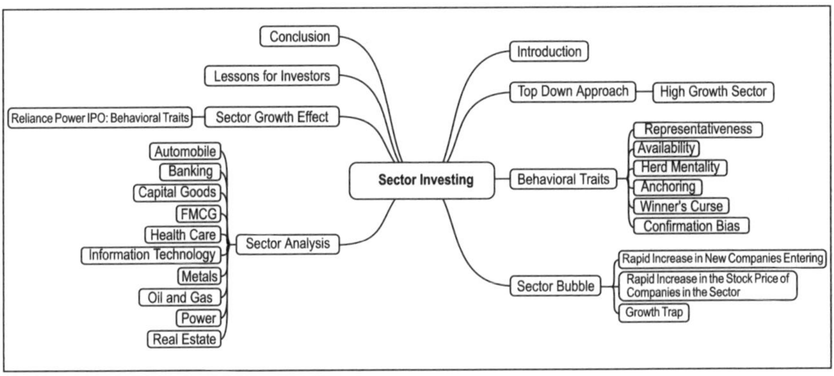

8.1 INTRODUCTION

A host of companies is listed on the stock markets, and if one were to look for a good investment opportunity, one would definitely try to narrow the search by first identifying the industry or the sector that looks promising, and then identifying various companies in that particular industry or sector. Growth in a particular sector would signify that companies in that sector would also enjoy high growth and would attract investments from investors.

> **Stock markets are all about discontinuity and creative destruction. From time to time, different sectors dominate investor interest.**

Stock markets are all about discontinuity and creative destruction. From time to time, different sectors dominate investor interest. No sector has a permanent appeal amongst investors. It is the inherent nature of investors to get enamored by the new, as it signifies growth opportunities, which in turn would lead to abnormal returns.

How do new sectors happen and catch the fancy of investors? It could happen with the change in fortunes of a particular sector, due to factors such as change in business environment, change in price of raw materials as we saw in the recent commodities boom, change in government policies, economic growth in an economy and shortages due to natural disasters.

Alternatively, it could be due to the advent of new technology, as we saw with the internet, the birth of the technology sector, the telecommunications sector and the hardware industry. This technological revolution could also spell the death knell for certain industries like the ones we saw in the telecommunications industry. For example, optic cables replaced the wire cables industry, mobile or wireless telephones are replacing the old fixed-line telephones. The digital revolution has changed the music industry and the way we live our lives.

Over time, such changes do happen, and the stock market is a place where such new ideas get funded. Investors are always looking at getting into a new sector, as they firmly believe that these future growth sectors would make them immensely rich. Investors have a penchant for chasing the new, and thus new sectors soon become the stock market favorites.

8.2 TOP-DOWN APPROACH

This leads us to the style of investing known as the top-down approach. It seems very simple. Identify a growth sector. How does one identify a growth sector? A sector whose fortunes have changed. A sector which has become a fancy of the stock market. A new sector showing tremendous opportunities in the future. A new sector which can change the lives of people. A new sector built on a new technological breakthrough. A sector which finds mention in leading newspapers, television shows, etc.

> **Right investment principles do not promise short-term and abnormal returns. They are representative of slow and steady, long-term returns.**

Once this identification process is complete, the next task is to invest in companies in the sector. It is assumed that since these companies are in the new growth sector they will also be able to reap the benefits. This mode of investing is very popular, and retail as well as qualified institutional investors follow the top-down approach.

However, when everyone is making investment decisions based on these criteria, there is a demand-supply mismatch, leading to investors paying a much higher price for the stock of companies in the new high-growth sector.

8.2.1 High-Growth Sector

New sectors or transformed sectors always attract investors, as growth is expected. This leads to a mad rush to invest in companies in such sectors. The new excitement and the opportunities of the sector attract more companies to enter. When this happens, the sector weight increases and it signals the growth of the sector. The growth is not in profits, but it is more so because of new entrants. However, when the sector becomes sizeable in terms of market capitalization, its leading companies find a place in the index. Getting into the index gives credibility not only to the company, but also to the sector it represents. This gets the passive institutional investors to give due weight to the sector when they invest in the index. Thus we have a concentrated following of the sector by all types of investors. This leads to the sector growing and this growth reinforces the wisdom of investing in the sector. The sector thus becomes a fancy in the stock markets and grows with the values of the stock prices of the companies in that sector growing, as well as the entry of new companies in the sector.

Stock market capitalization is not the right way to judge the sector, if one is looking at investing for returns in a particular sector.

Investors' expectations run high and the prices of stocks do not reflect true value. Stock prices do not offer investment value. Prices are high as they have in-built investor expectations.

Although we find that the sector is growing rapidly, this growth is marred by the following developments:

1. Larger number of companies entering the sector.
2. Investor frenzy leading to stock prices spiraling.

However, a rational investor will be concerned about decline in profits from a sector due increasing competition from other firms entering, as well as the wisdom of investing in companies at ridiculously high valuations.

In the long run, rising or falling market weights are no indication of rising or falling returns. On the contrary, the inverse could be true. However, stock markets are always interesting because when it comes to money, investors become emotional and their decisions are swayed by the behavioral anomalies we will discuss below.

8.3 BEHAVIORAL TRAITS

The goal of any investment style is to get superior returns over other styles. It depends upon the skill of the user and his or her ability to predict the future. We wish it was that simple. In real life situations, one is swayed by emotions and decisions are made not by the logic of an investment style, but by the current fancy of an investment style. Let us try to understand the different types of heuristics and biases which work in sector investing. This will enable us to understand the reason for mispriced securities. A deeper understanding of the behavioral aspects will further enable us to avoid the pitfalls. Once our minds are able to exhibit the right mental model of the different behavioral and cognitive defects that besiege us, the understanding of the marketplace becomes clear.

8.3.1 Representativeness

A company within a sector is representative of the sector. So if the sector is a fancy of the market and expected to grow, the company being a representative of the sector is also assumed to be in a similar growth phase. Hence, the company also becomes a fancy. Investors believe that it is a good investment, start chasing the stock and pay a fancy price, believing that it is a growth stock. However, in reality, the fortunes of the company may not be in synch with the economics of the sector. The working of a company and its stock price are dependent on a host of factors, like quality of management, capitalization, market standing, employee skills, productivity and customer loyalty. Blindly buying any company just because it is cheap in price and belongs to a growth sector can be very dangerous for an investor. The recent technology boom is a fine example. The IT sector was growing and Infosys was the leader of the pack. However, it was expensively priced as compared with companies like Pentafour, DSQ Software, Visual Soft—to name a few. However, investors bought these companies thinking that they were representative of the IT growth sector and they would be the future Infosys. Representative thinking trapped these investors because when the fancy with the sector receded, these stocks had no buyers and investors' losses were manifold. Even if one had bought a company like Infosys during the sector euphoria in 1999–2000, thinking that it was representative of the IT sector, one would have still suffered on the returns. Because one would have paid a fancy price for it. Surprisingly, there was nothing wrong with the IT sector; in fact, it has grown well even after the stock market bust in the year 2000. The losses to investors were due to their representativeness thinking.

> **Rapid growth in a sector does not mean good investment returns for the investors. Investor returns are dependent on the right acquisition price.**

8.3.2 Availability

Whenever there is a turnaround in the fortunes of a sector, or a new sector is born out of an innovation or a technological breakthrough, we are bombarded with a lot of positive news on the same. It is the talk of the town. It is a favorite subject of discussion at various gatherings, parties and business forums. Everyone seems to have all the information on this hot topic thanks to the media, who are regularly feeding you with information on the same. Moreover, the stock market is the first to react to this news and you suddenly find that all the stocks in the sector become active, analysts start tracking them, and brokers start recommending them. Ask anyone in the markets and you will hear the same tune: the hot sector and the companies in the sector. Initially, the euphoria starts with the representative thinking and it gathers steam as the availability heuristic comes into play. All the available information on the sector is positive, and one not only starts believing in the sector but also starts recommending the sector. This reinforces the information loop and the information gains credibility as stock prices in the sector start going up, leading to a growth in the sector weight. This available information gets more companies to enter the sector, which in turn again increases the sector weight. In the current situation, the availability heuristic on the India growth story is so strong that investors are chasing sectors like infrastructure, capital goods, real estate and power, which would be direct beneficiaries of the growth.

8.3.3 Herd Mentality

There is too much of chaos in the stock markets due to the overload of information. In such times, people prefer to follow the popular thinking. If things go wrong, there is always solace in the fact that you were not alone. You did what everyone was doing. This is how the reinforcement loop in sector investing works. Because it has become popular due to the availability heuristic, it makes sense for people to follow the same. They choose to be a part of the herd rather than be left alone. Most of the time, people are aware that companies in the sector have stretched valuations, but the herd mentality does not allow them to see reason. Lack of self-belief makes them wonder how all others can be wrong. Thus they blindly follow the crowd. We saw similar situations during the IT sector boom. People did understand the excessive valuations of technology companies but chose to stay with the herd, believing in the new economy where the rules of the game were different. In the recent past, was the herd mentality evident in the real estate sector, the infrastructure sector and the power sector—all hot sectors with crazy valuations.

8.3.4 Anchoring

The fortunes of a sector cannot change overnight. However the fortunes of an individual company can change very fast due to various reasons like natural calamity, mismanagement, entry of strong competitors, government or regulatory controls. When investors adopt the top-down investing style, they are so much anchored to the fortunes of the sector that they mindlessly hold on to companies that belong to the sector. Anchoring distorts their thinking. If the sector holds promise, they think that the companies in the sector will also do well.

Again, during the IT boom the people were so anchored to the new economy story that they were unable let go of their IT stocks when the tide was turning. Investors also got trapped by fraudulent companies, which happened to be in the IT sector.

In the recent past with the increase in real estate prices, investors have been so anchored to these high prices that they blindly bought shares in real estate companies. This opened the floodgates for even shady companies to tap the capital markets. Getting anchored to the 9% economic growth, investors blindly bought shares of any infrastructure company. Such was the fickle-minded behavior of investors.

Getting anchored to the right investment principles could save the investors a lot of heartburn. The problem is that right investment principles do not promise short-term and abnormal returns. Nor does the herd follow them. They are representative of slow and steady, long-term returns.

8.3.5 Winner's Curse

The companies in a sector that is doing well are prone to becoming overconfident. The good times make them feel that they are smarter than they really are. In such good times, companies tend to go in for mindless acquisitions. In such a scramble for acquisitions, the company forgets the economics of an acquisition. In so doing, the company falls into the trap of "winners curse". In a competitive bidding the winner ends up paying a very high price for the acquisition because, more than economic sense, the ego and the vanity of winning dominate. When that happens, the winner overpays and destroys the value of the firm. This was aptly illustrated when Satyam bought Sify during the technology boom. It was an acquisition which has heavily burdened Satyam and the company is yet to recover from the same. Similar was Tata Tea's acquisition of Tetley, the strongest brand in the world.

In the present scenario, with the Indian economy booming and steel prices firming, the steel industry outlook seems very bright. Of course to help there is a commodity boom also. Inspired by the fortunes of the sector, Tata Steel went on to acquire Corus Steel, one of the world's biggest steel giants. It outbid the competitors. Winner's curse? Time will show.

8.3.6 Confirmation Bias

Investors are always looking for evidence that will confirm their views. They tend to avoid all information that is against their views. During a sector boom, all available information on a company within that sector is positive. Investors ignore negatives of a company and only seek positive evidence. Here, the positive evidence is the positive information available on the sector growth. Investors tend to base their investment decisions on the sector growth, as it confirms their line of thinking. That is the reason that, during a sector bubble, even the laggards start attracting attention and their stocks start moving up.

One such example was evident in the price movement of the stock of BPL Ltd. during January 2008. The stock was languishing at around Rs.50 as there was no investor interest and the company was not doing any business. However, as the rumor goes, the company had applied for a power license a couple of years back and the same was approved. At this time, the power sector was a very hot sector. This confirmed the views of the investors that BPL was a good company as it was in the power sector. The stock zoomed to Rs.170 within a month. It was back to Rs.40 in the first week of April 2008.

8.4 SECTOR BUBBLE

Fundamentals in a sector do not change as fast as they would change in a company. Therefore, a rapid increase in the weight of a sector is a sure sign of a bubble.

Let us take the recent case of the infrastructure industry. With India's GDP growing at 9%, no doubt it is an important industry with good growth prospects. There will be a lot of infrastructure development taking place in the country in the form of building roads, bridges, dams, ports, buildings, townships, airports, etc. This sector will remain an important sector and the dynamics cannot change very fast. If the GDP growth slackens, there could be a slow-down in the sector; but the economics will remain intact.

However, it will take time for all companies in the infrastructure sector to complete projects and thus reap the benefits. Yes, there could be certain companies in the sector which could suffer huge losses due to reasons beyond their control and go down under in a matter of months. Fortunes of individual companies can change rapidly.

When the weight of a sector increases very rapidly it is a sign of a bubble. This weight increase is more as a result of increased expectations of entrepreneurs and investors alike.

On the other hand, a gradual increase in the weight of sector over time, due to a steady rise in profits of firms is not a sign of a bubble. Such a rise does not exhibit increased investor expectations.

8.4.1 Rapid Increase in New Companies Entering

Whenever a sector becomes hot and attracts investor attention, it signals huge growth potential and excessive profits. Stock markets start giving crazy valuations to companies in the sector. All of a sudden, you find that stock prices of such companies start soaring, creating paper wealth. The profits of the new sector, along with the potential to capitalize on the greed of the investors, attract new companies to enter the field.

There could be companies which really find the sector activities exciting, and which may enter the market as viable business models. Or there could be companies which enter the market just to capitalize on the greed of the investors. During the technology boom we saw many genuine companies entering the markets, but there were many which entered by just affixing "dot com" behind their names and collected crores of rupees from the markets. Investors were willing to pay any price for a technology or an internet company.

With so many companies entering the market, we saw the sector weight of technology and internet companies going up rapidly. This was a sure sign of a sector bubble in the making. We all know the consequences that followed.

This also leads to heating up of the IPO market. Companies seeking to cash in on the sector euphoria come out with initial public offerings as investors are willing to pay hefty valuations. The year 2006–2007 witnessed an unprecedented IPO boom in infrastructure, real estate and power sectors.

8.4.2 Rapid Increase in the Stock Price of Companies in the Sector

Irrational investor behavior plays an important role in the rapid increase in the stock prices of companies in a particular sector. The promise of high growth in a sector attracts investors willing to pay any price for the stocks. Even if the fundamentals don't justify the stock price, investors are willing to pay a higher price as they believe that they are buying a growth stock and such stocks are valued higher. Since these stocks are a fancy, investors are willing to pay a fancy price, and thus the stock prices show a rapid increase.

The entry of mutual funds also adds fuel to the fire. Sector-specific funds collect huge amounts of money and that gets invested in sector companies. This huge demand leads to an increase in stock prices. These high prices again attract new companies to enter the markets and we have a rapid growth of the sector weightage.

Such sector bubbles have been evident in the infrastructure, power and the real estate sectors. Every known mutual fund asset management company has come out with an infrastructure fund and a real estate fund. Power funds will soon follow.

Stock market capitalization is not the right way to judge the sector, if one is looking at investing for returns in a particular sector. Being a contrarian investor could make one wealthier.

8.4.3 Growth Trap

A sector bubble is formed because investors start paying crazy valuations for the companies in the sector. What excites the investors is the thrill of an active sector with prices going up fast every day. There is action. The lure of quick profits attracts investors willing to pay any price to be a part of the sector. Different behavioral tendencies, discussed above, make investors irrational. This leads them to fall into the growth trap.

Believing that the sector is growing and hence companies in the sector are good investments, investors chase the shares of sector companies, and they become the fancy. Too many investors chasing them take their prices higher and higher.

Investors fall into the growth trap as they believe that they are buying growth companies, and are, thus, willing to pay a higher price for this growth. If one is a short-term trader and if one gets in and out of a hot sector, it is fine. If one gets the timing right, one can make good money. However. the question is how sustainable could this strategy be? For a long-term investor, this growth trap would lead to inferior returns. Not only the returns could suffer, but if the sector loses investors; fancy, one could end up with huge losses.

8.5 SECTOR ANALYSIS

The Indian stock markets, though quite old, had their appreciable beginning in 1991 after the liberalization process. This created an environment where new sectors and companies started entering the markets. The giant PSUs also found their way to the stock markets. Financial liberalization got the banking sector an appreciable weightage, as the public sector banks got listed on the stock exchanges. The initial years started with the liberalization of the financial sector and the effects of the same started being felt from the year 2000 onwards. The depth of the stock markets increased from the year 2000 onwards. Hence, reliable data on sectors is available from 1999–2000 onwards. Although the data is not for a very long period, it is still useful for us to understand the effects of investor behavior on the growth in different sectors.

It is important to note that the rise in the growth of all sectors from the year 2004 is partly due to the positive change in sentiments, an increase in GDP growth rate, effects of the earlier liberalization policies, increased funds flow from foreign institutional investors, growth of the mutual fund industry, and favorable government policies for investments in stock markets. This led to the BSE Sensex growing from around 2,800 in 2003 to around 21,000 in January 2008. India was witnessing the biggest bull run in its history.

We have attempted to study the various sectors of the economy and how they have moved. Some have moved up in weightage due to entry of new companies, some have moved due to the sector becoming a fancy and investors chasing, it and others have also stagnated showing lack of investor interest. None of the sectors is showing any decline, as the overall health of the economy is good and expected to grow at a healthy 9% per annum. This optimism is reflected in the bullish conditions in the stock market.

For the long-term investor looking at returns, it is important to understand the trends in the sector. If it is a hot and a fancy sector it can show you dreams and affect your returns in the long run.

8.5.1 Automobile Sector

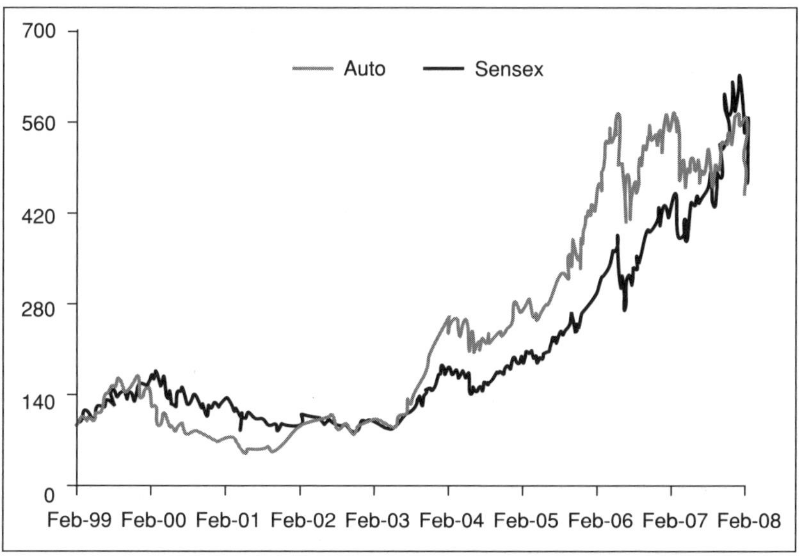

Figure 8.1 Performance of Automobile Sector versus the Sensex

With a base period of February 1999 and a value of 1,000, the BSE Auto Index was launched on 23rd August 2004. As of February 2008, the index was up to 4,147, giving a return of 314%.

It has grown steadily with the Sensex, but from February 2007 it has been losing favor with investors. It has been lagging behind the Sensex and showing a downward trend. The sector has been flat, starting off with a sector PE of 13.72 that has just inched upwards to 15.12 as of February 2008. There is no investor fancy.

However, the opportunities in such neglected sectors come in the form of good, well-run companies that also get beaten down when the sector loses favor.

Mahindra and Mahindra is available at a PE of 10.17, Maruti at 14.60, Tata Motors at 12.98, all much below the current average PE. All these are large cap index stocks. This is how opportunities start coming in neglected sectors.

A company like Bosch is available at a PE of 23 from its high of 54 at the start of the index. I am in no way recommending the stocks. But the idea is to show how value bargains arise when investor expectations are low but a particular company in the sector is doing well.

8.5.2 Banking Sector

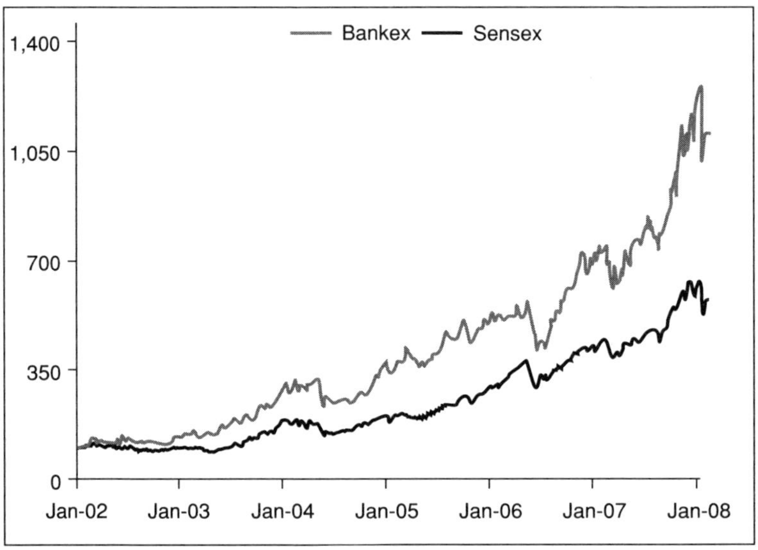

Figure 8.2 Performance of Banking Sector versus the Sensex

The banking sector index, or Bankex, was launched by the BSE on 23rd June 2003, with a base period of January 2002. It has delievered a healthy return of around 900% to investors. However, it must be noted that the returns from this sector are due to the following factors:

1. The liberalization in the financial sector led to the entry of a host of new firms in the market, leading to significant increase in market capitalization.
2. The change in the fortunes of the banking sector attracted investors to this sector in the hope that liberalized policies will help the banking sector.
3. Most companies that entered the market belonged to the public sector and they already had the infrastructure, like branch network, in place. This helped them to compete favorably in the newly liberalized era.
4. The launch of the Bankex coincided with the upward movement of the market, which also started in 2003.

Looking at the chart (Figure 8.2), it is evident that the growth in this sector is in line with the stock market movement, the entry of new firms and meeting investor expectations on performance. There is a steady increase from 2003 to 2006, signifying no evidence of a bubble in this sector growth.

The period from mid-2006 to January 2008 in the chart shows a steep rise in the form of high investor expectations. However, this was more due to the entry of new firms and further issue of capital. Around Rs.3,229 crores were raised in 2006 and a whopping Rs.11,642 crores in 2007. This included the mega issue of ICICI Bank, which raised around Rs.10,000 crores. However, if one looks at the valuations of different companies in the sector, they seem to be reasonable around 17% to 25%.

If one looks at the PE ratio performance, this sector had a PE of around 8.33 at the start. The PE in February 2008 is around 25. However, as mentioned earlier, the expansion in this sector has been due to the entry of new firms. The PEs of most of the stocks in the sector are well below the average of 25. Only the private sector banks attract a higher PE of more than 25. These include HDFC Bank, ICICI Bank, Kotak Mahindra Bank, Axis Bank, Centurion Bank and Yes Bank. All of them command a PE of over 50—that is, double the average. Investors' expectations from the private sector banks, due to the expected high growth in the financial sector, are very high. The rest of the banks happen to be PSU banks and their PEs are well below the average. These banks are not investor fancies. Investor fancy comes when certain events take place. Again this is the case of PSU-aversion discussed in the chapter on PSUs. After the Union Budget of 2008, most of the PSU banks have been further losing favor with investors due to some populist measures like waiving of the farmer loans amounting to about Rs. 60,000 crores.

8.5.3 Capital Goods Sector

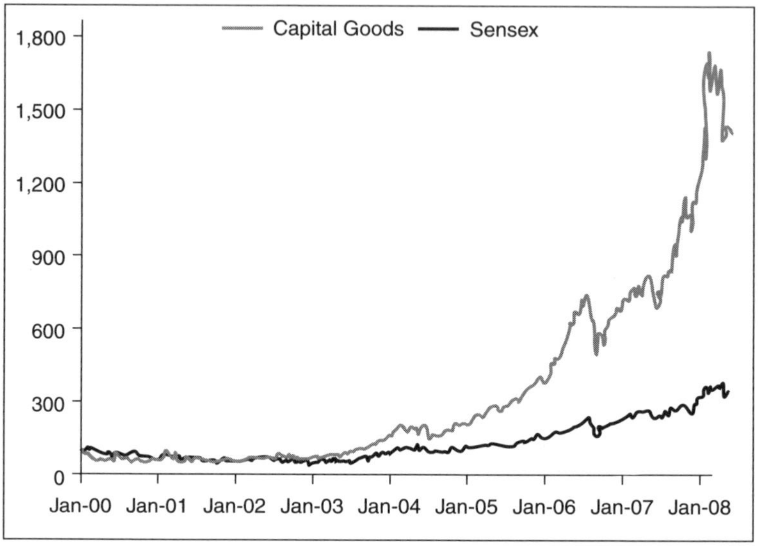

Figure 8.3 Performance of Capital Goods Sector versus the Sensex

The BSE Capital Goods Index was launched in August 1999, with a base period of February 1999. The returns have been a whopping 1,485%. One of the main reasons for the high returns is the bearish conditions prevailing during 1999–2000, when the index was launched. Most of the components of the index are old companies, having a good track record of performance. The depressed stock market did not value these companies favorably. If one looks at the chart (Figure 8.3), it is evident that the sector growth was healthy, with the performance of the companies improving due to increased economic activity. One would notice a steady and smooth increase, from 1,000 to 8,000, until mid-2006. This was in line with the stock markets moving upwards.

However, signs of a steep spurt in the sector are evident when the index moves from around 9,000 in mid-2006 to 21,000 in end-2007. There are no appreciable additions of new companies. This growth is only because of high valuations of these companies due to increased investor expectations. On expectations of higher GDP growth at over 9%, investors were willing to give multiples as high as 50% to companies in the sector. A sure sign of a growth trap for investors.

Moreover, the entry of infrastructure mutual funds added to making the capital goods sector an investor fancy.

The average PE of the sector at the launch was 12.49, which has moved up to 39.74 in 2008. About a third of the companies in this sector are commanding a PE over 40.

One cannot call this a bubble, but definitely evidence of a growth trap.

8.5.4 Fast-Moving Consumer Goods Sector

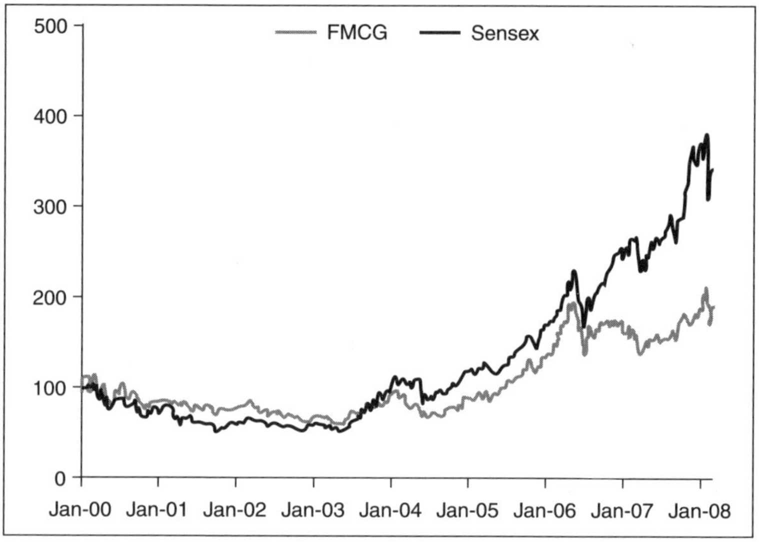

Figure 8.4 Performance of FMCG Sector versus Sensex

The BSE FMCG index was launched on August 1999, with a base period of February 1999. The 1,000 value has appreciated to 2,175 on 8th February 2008, giving a meager return of 117.5%. It has been the most neglected sector, despite the change in stock market sentiment from 2003 onwards. From the above chart, it is evident that the sector has not moved in line with the markets. Especially from 2006, it is showing lack of investor interest. The Sensex returns have been much more than the sector returns. The performance of the companies in the sector has been good, but they are much below investor expectations. Investor returns are least likely to suffer if they invest in this sector.

At the start, the sector PE was 19.97 and in February 2008 it has moved to just 26.58, even though the market has moved seven-fold. This sector has not moved with the markets. Most of the individual blue-chip stocks are available around a PE of 25 to 35. The slow down in GDP growth due to the overall sluggishness in the world economy could hit this sector hard, psychologically. That is how opportunities emerge. This sector does offer value to long-term investors. Index volatility could throw up good opportunities in this sector.

Long-term investors need to invest in sustainable businesses and the FMCG sector offers great investment opportunities. There are excellent companies, including a few multinationals, with a strong brand and a wide distribution network. Fast moving consumer products thrive on branding and distribution. Moreover, the composition of this sector has companies with strong management and corporate governance. The valuations of companies in this sector that have a sustainable business model are reasonable. The prices do not reflect high investor expectations.

8.5.5 Health Care Sector

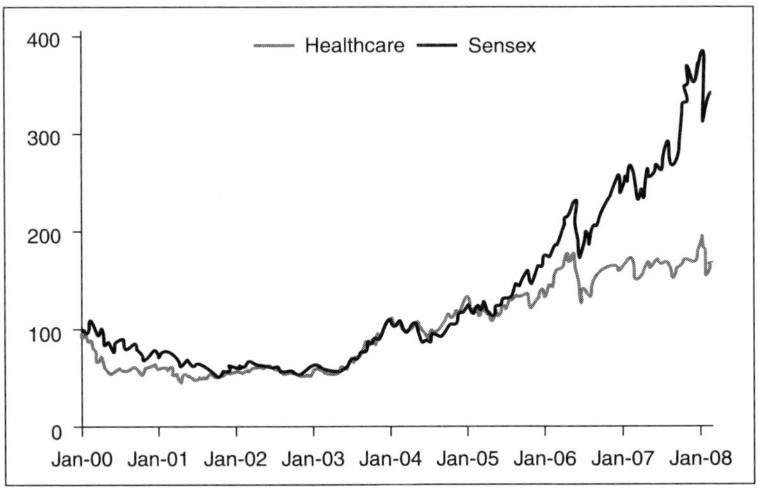

Figure 8.5 Performance of Healthcare Sector versus the Sensex

The BSE Health Care index was launched in August 1999, with a base period of February 1999. The base index value of 1,000 has gone up to 3,633.61 on February 2008, giving a return of 263.4 % over a period of nine years. The above chart (Figure 8.5) shows a steady rise in this sector, which is in line with the growth in the major indices, due to the sustained bull rallies that started in 2003. However, from 2006 it is evident that the sector is stagnating, indicating lack of investor interest.

The Sensex has been on an upward spree and the returns from the sector are lagging the Sensex.

Since inception, the sector PE was 20.59, and in February 2008 the sector PE has just inched up to 21.76, despite the bull run taking the Sensex from 3,000 to 21,000 in the same period. The sector has remained flat. Most of the companies are available below or near the average sector PE. It is a neglected sector and offers tremendous opportunities to long-term investors looking at good dividends and returns.

This sector comprises Indian as well as multinational companies with strong management. There has been a steady growth in this sector, but it was never a fancy of the investors. Since 2004, investors have been more attracted to fast-growing companies. They have been neglecting such steady sustainable businesses as exist in this sector. However, this sector holds good promise for future investment returns, and boasts of well-managed, innovative companies with strong research and development capabilities.

The companies in the sector are adequately valued and the prices do not reflect undue investor expectations. This sector has no investor interest or fancy.

8.5.6 Information Technology Sector

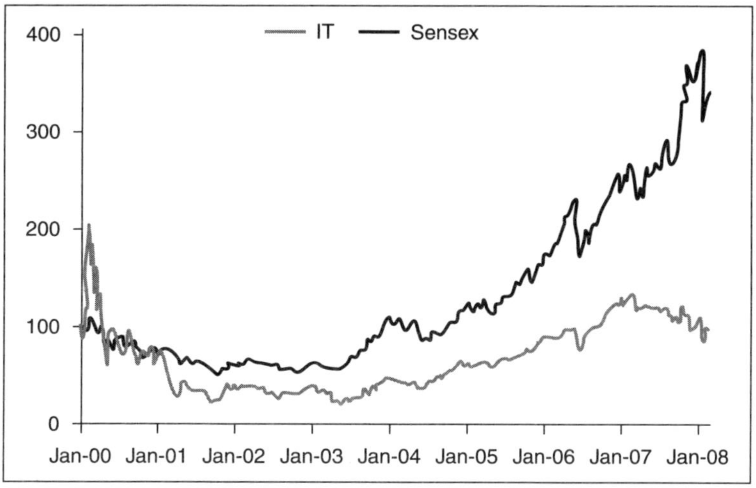

Figure 8.6 Performance of Information Technology Sector versus the Sensex

The BSE IT index was launched on 9th August 1999, with a base year starting 1st February 1999 with a value of 1,000. This launch was during the start of the dream IT bull run. The sector index was 3,843 in February 2008, giving an aggregate return of 284.3% over the decade. But if one looks at the chart above (Figure 8.6), one will find that most of the returns are due to the bubble period from 1999 to 2001. Thereafter, the sector stayed subdued for a couple of years, and showed some revival from 2003 due to improved market conditions. However, this sector has not been able to keep pace with the general stock market performance. In fact, it is evident that, from January 2007, the IT sector has been an under-performer to the market. This was due to the strengthening of the rupee against the dollar, which was expected to dent the profits of the technology companies. Most of them had dollar-denominated earnings from exports.

The IT sector PE at inception was just 4.31, and in February 2008 it has gone up to 20.97. It seems to have moved with the Sensex, but in reality, barring just two companies, the other companies are near or below the average PE. The two companies that create the distortion are Financial Technologies, commanding a PE of 135, and Aptech at a PE of 55. Even the market leader, Infosys, is available at a PE of 22. Other reputable companies, like Tata Consultancy Services, Mphasis BFL, Iflex, Wipro and Tech Mahindra, are available at a PE of 21 or less.

This sector exhibits no investor fancy and this is more evident after January 2007 when the export earnings started suffering due to the strong rupee.

This is a sector which has matured over time, having seen the excesses of the 2000–2001 bull market. With low built-in expectations and the sector growth stagnating, it offers good long-term returns.

8.5.7 Metals Sector

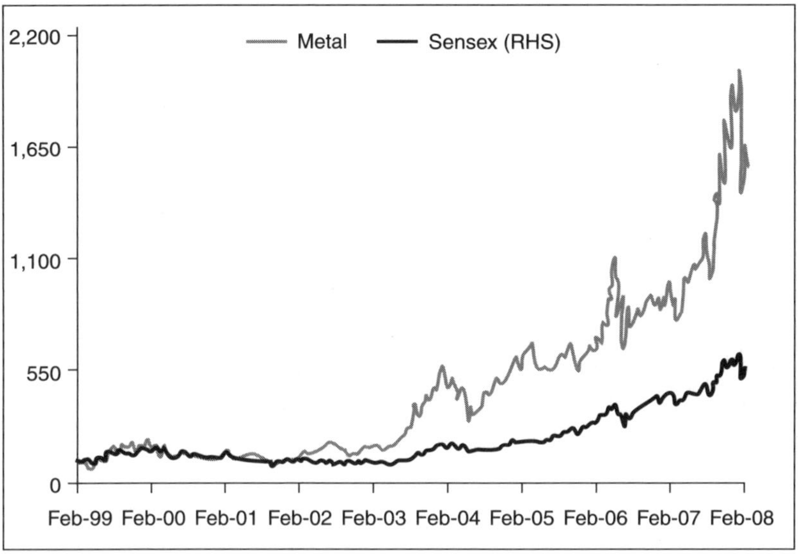

Figure 8.7 Performance of Metals Sector versus the Sensex

The BSE Metals Index was launched on 23rd August 2004, with a base period of 1st February 1999, and a value of 1,000. The BSE Metals Index touched a high of 20,494 on 4th January 2008, showing an aggregate return of 1,949%. This is one of the best-performing sectors over the last five years.

What explains this stellar performance from the Metals Index? The answer lies in understanding the nature of the commodity business. Unlike companies in the FMCG, consumer durables and healthcare sectors, which witness a consistent demand for their products, the demand for commodities is very sensitive to the overall expansion and contraction of the economic status of the world. During the last five years, the world has witnessed an expansion of the world economy, leading to a sudden spurt in the demand for metals. One of the prime reasons has been the emergence of China as a net importer of metals. The prices of commodities have seen an upward trend, resulting in a bonanza for commodity companies.

The optimism surrounding commodity companies during the late-2007 period is evident from the chart above (Figure 8.7), with a sudden spurt in the Metals Index due to the increasing commodity prices.

As Warren Buffet famously observed, one pays a very high price in the stock market for cheery consensus, people did pay a huge price for the high optimism as the Metals sector lost around 35-40% from its high of 20,494 in January 2008, by correcting to around 13,000 levels during the recent correction from 21,000 to 15,000 levels.

As an investor, one would do well to tread cautiously while investing in the Metals sector. All the talk about a 10-15 year extended commodity bull market will be belied once the world economy slows down. We are already seeing signs of such slow-down.

8.5.8 Oil and Gas Sector

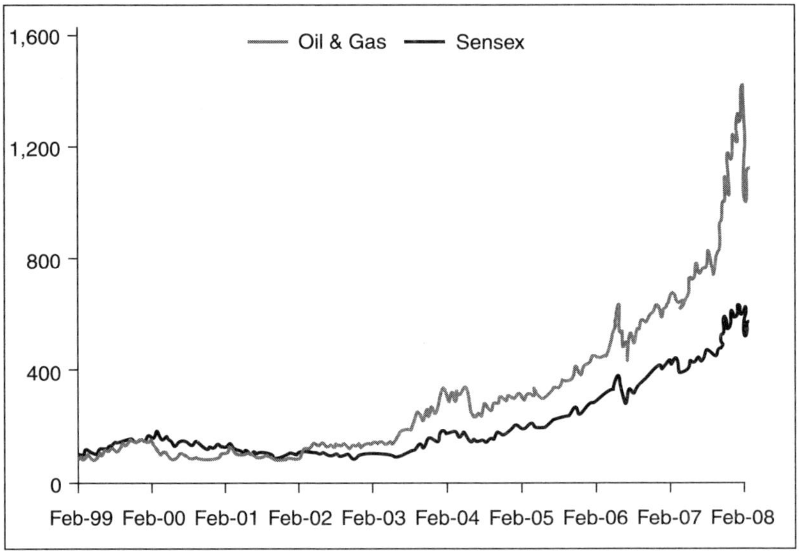

Figure 8.8 Performance of Oil and Gas Sector versus the Sensex

With a base period of 1st February 1999, and a value of 1,000 the BSE Oil and Gas Index was launched on 23rd August 2004. As of February 2008 the total value was 10,638, giving an aggregate return of 963%. With the improved market conditions, the sector has moved with the markets. However, mid-2007 we see a steep rise (Figure 8.8). However, there is no sign of a bubble in the sector. This steep rise is due to two highly speculative stocks, Essar Oil and Reliance Natural Resources, that went way up. This was an abnormal, speculative movement.

At the start of the bull run in 2003 the sector PE was 9.19 and the same has moved to 25.37 in February 2008. This is in line with the market's upward movement. The distortion in the PE valuation is evident from the high PE multiples of just three companies. As of February 2008, Reliance Natural Resources had a PE of over 628, Essar Oil 175 and Aban Lloyd 91; while other sector companies were well below the market average. Only Reliance Industries was a shade above the market average.

A bubble is evident in individual stocks, rather than the sector, although the chart shows a steep rise in spite of the downward Sensex. Investor irrationality and speculative manipulation is evident.

8.5.9 Power Sector

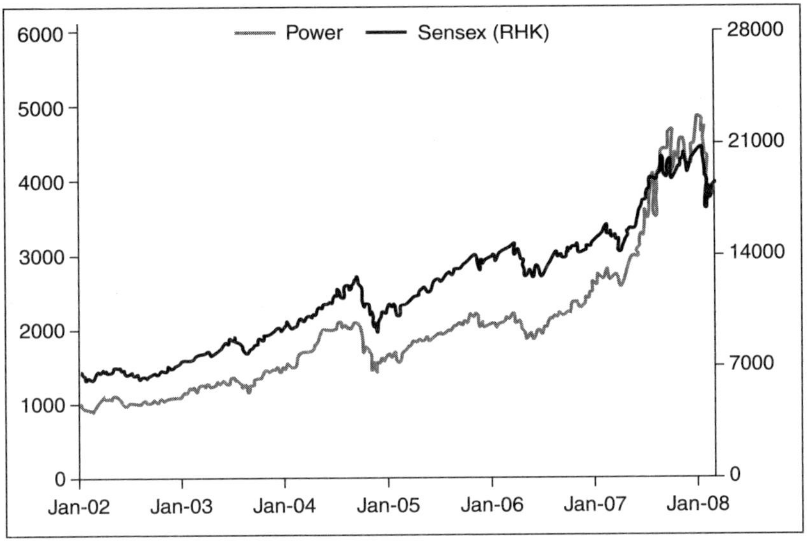

Figure 8.9 Performance of Power Sector versus the Sensex

With a base year of January 2005 and a value of 1,000 the BSE Power Index was launched on 9th November 2007. Power was a hot sector and hence the need arose to have a power index. This is evident from the fact that the aggregate returns have been 273.6 %. The value of the index stood at 3,736 in February 2008. The index has been cruising steadily in line with the BSE Sensex (Figure 8.9). However, in the later part of 2007, we see a big spurt. The power index starts beating the Sensex. This signifies build up of euphoria.

The power index stock comprises very good companies, both Indian and multinational, which have been favorites amongst investors. The sector includes companies in power generation and transmission, as well as power equipment manufacturers. The PE of the power sector in 2005 was 46.04, which has come down to 33.77 in February 2008. This could be due to the new companies entering after 2005. The years 2005 and

2006 saw the markets growing very fast and the infrastructure, power and power equipment sectors were very hot. New companies entered and commanded huge valuations. Over time this euphoria died and the valuations fell from their irrational peak.

This sector is still a fancy of the markets and we can see much more euphoria in the sector. Investor fancy was evident in the subscriptions received by Reliance Power on its debut. However, the listing saw investors losing, as the stock listed at less than the issue price. Gains on the listing of Reliance Power could have created a bubble-like situation, as the stock would have had a very large market capitalization and would have entered the BSE Sensex and the Nifty.

Power equipment manufacturers command higher valuations than the power generators, as the latter fall in to the category of utility companies. Moreover, power generation does have controls over pricing. Thus we have a mixed bag in this sector. Consequently, Reliance Power's over confidence of high valuations from the market was belied.

The sector bubble built up could be difficult, but as we saw with Reliance Power, we could have individual stock bubbles by companies selling dreams to investors.

8.5.10 Real Estate

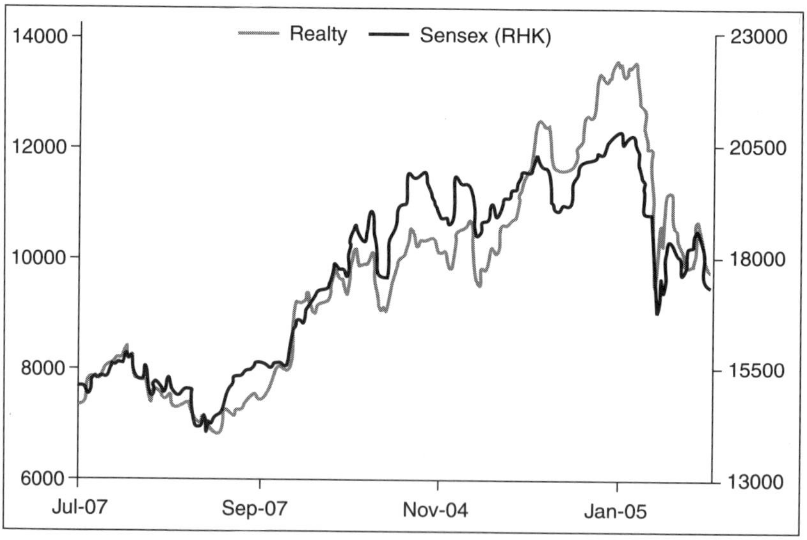

Figure 8.10 Performance of Real Estate Sector versus the Sensex

The BSE Realty Index with a base year of 2005 and a value of 1,000 was launched on 9th July 2007. As of February 2008 the value is 9,783.85, giving an aggregate return of 878.3% within a span of just three years. Since its launch, it has beaten the index by a large margin. However, even with the entry of new players, this index is showing an irrational upward trend.

PE in this sector is quite irrelevant as investors buy in to real estate companies based on the land bank concept. However, observing the PE trend gives us some startling insights of irrational human behavior. The PE at the launch was 50.12 and currently, in February 2008, it is 56.72. Some of the companies are quoting way above the average PE and some are way below. A company like India Bulls Realty is quoting at a PE above 850 and DLF, a market leader and part of the Sensex, is quoting at a PE of 67, while Parsvanath Developers is quoting at just around 14.54 and Ansal Developers at just 8. There is no sanity in valuations. In fact, although this is a very hot sector and a bubble-like situation is evident, the IPO of Emmar Holdings had to be called off when it opened for subscription in February 2008.

Long-term investors would be wary of getting in to the real estate sector due to the opaque nature of transactions. A great deal of unaccounted money changes hands in real estate deals. Moreover, development permissions and various clearances often come in by way of bribes to politicians and government authorities. Corporate governance is a big issue in this sector. Hence, we find that it has become the turf only of speculators and short-term traders.

8.6 SECTOR GROWTH EFFECT

When the stock markets are strong and a sector is showing growth and immense potential, entrepreneurs see it as an opportunity to expand existing capacities or to make fresh entry in the sector. A growing sector attracts investors and entrepreneurs eager to raise capital. Investors are attracted by their greed to make fast money in a growing sector and the raisers of capital are also attracted by their greed to raise resources at fancy prices as the investors are greedy enough to pay. In a situation like this, companies tend to over-price their issues, and the investment bankers appointed by the companies tend to aggressively sell these overpriced securities to the investors. Gray market operations start flourishing. Brokers start tracking the hot sectors, as they are easier to sell to the investors, enabling them to increase their business and income. Content is provided to the various print and electronic media in the form of news on the sector, corporate plans, mergers and acquisitions, research reports, analysts' interviews, etc. It keeps the TV channels busy and in turn attracts advertisement revenues. A new sector offers new marketing gimmicks to asset management companies. Sector-specific funds find their way to the market. It is the right time to increase money-under-management. No one gives two hoots if this strategy is against investor interest. As it is, public memory is quite short and a wrong done by all becomes a right. When the sector is growing, companies tend to bring out huge public issues, as it is easy to get subscriptions. Listing at fancy prices increases the market capitalization and this gets them entry into the Index. This ensures credibility for the management and the company. As will be seen in the chapter on index investing, entry to the index is dependent on the market capitalization and has nothing to do with the quality of the company or the management.

We have identified two hot bubble-like sectors in our sector analysis and I wish to bring out the behavioral traits of the various participants and the heuristic traps that endanger investors.

At the height of the power sector bubble, we saw the success of the initial public offering of Reliance Power Ltd., the mother of all issues. I have chosen Reliance Power Ltd. (RPL) as a case study because it brings out how sector growth worked for the company, as well as how the growth trap worked against the company and the investors.

8.6.1 Reliance Power IPO: Behavioral Traits

This is an interesting case study because it shows how greed can become a graveyard for even a strong brand like "Reliance". My idea is to study the various behavioral traits of the issue, rather than to be a critic of the company. Evidence has shown that the power sector was the hottest sector in 2007. It was showing signs of a bubble. However, everything changed in February 2008.

Management of RPL

Although the promoter had another listed company, Reliance Energy, they chose to float RPL as a separate company. Maybe the wild sector growth prompted him to get into the growth trap. There were certain transfers of contracts from Reliance Energy, and capital structuring and financing questions with RPL; but that is not the subject of our discussion. In short this action on the part of the promoter signifies greed.

RPL, a new company with a profit of merely Rs.16 lakhs, planned to enter the markets at around Rs.450 per share for a face value of Rs.10. This is again greed and the overconfidence in the Reliance brand. Overconfidence bias was so strong that one hardly saw any banners or advertisements of the issue details. Most of the advertisements were linked to the India growth story and powering India. No doubt, the issue was heavily oversubscribed and made a record to be called the mother of all issues. The brand name had worked.

Investment Bankers appointed by RPL

The job of the investment bankers is to advise the company on pricing the issue and to create a win-win situation for both the company and the investors. However, when brand Reliance is scouting for investment bankers there is a mad rush to be in the list. The advisory role takes a back seat and they all become selling agents. Their goal is to please the company and to sell the company's shares at the price the company wants. Professional wisdom takes a back seat and greed dominates. Greed to earn huge fees and greed to be associated with brand Reliance. The issue was oversubscribed and they all celebrated. Each one took pride in their collections to the issue. But no one knows how much of his or her own money he or she invested in the issue.

What made the issue a success?

1. Strong sector growth and fancy attracted the investors.
2. Brand Reliance under the leadership of the late Dhirubhai Ambani, the father of equity investing in India, had never let down those who invested in his company. RPL was an "Anil Dhirubhai Ambani Group" company. Representative heuristic was at work.
3. Bullish market conditions prevailing at the time.
4. Greed of the investors.
5. Aggressive selling strategy of investment bankers and gray market premium.

Behavioral Traits that Worked in Marketing

Availability Bias: There was this theme of "powering India". RPL was the answer. This was linked to the India growth story. Everyone believed in the India growth story and, thus, started believing in the RPL story of powering India. Moreover, it was the strong brand of Reliance that was vivid in everyone's mind.

Power was a hot subject in the stock markets. So all available information on the power sector was positive.

Representative Thinking: Since the power sector was hot, all the power companies' stocks were quoting at high PE multiples. Investors had seen the prices of these companies going up. There were also visible listing gains in companies like Powergrid and NTPC. This made investors see RPL as a representative of a good power stock, from which they would make money on listing.

Gray Market Premium Manipulation: Let us go back a decade, when there was a gray market premium for the close-ended mutual fund launched by Morgan Stanley. It was a classic case of investor insanity and brute manipulation. Investors got trapped and lost money. The reputation of Morgan Stanley was tarnished and, to date, they have not ventured to bring another mutual fund to the markets. There was a gray market premium of around Rs.400 to 500 in RPL. Investors got trapped with two heuristics: availability heuristic, where available information of a market price on listing assured profits; and representative heuristic, where RPL stock was representative of a price equal to the issue price plus the gray market premium. In short, a stock available at 50% discount to the expected market price. Over-zealous investment bankers capitalized.

Greater Fool Theory: The investors also understood that the stock offering price of around Rs.430 to 450 was expensive, but all were confident that they would sell their stock on listing and make a clean profit. There were broker reports recommending subscription to the issue with an exit on listing. The greater fool theory was at work. Surprisingly, even the qualified institutional investors were also thinking on the same lines.

Herd Mentality: Everybody wanted to sell on listing and the stock tumbled. It was the herd at work. The same herd had made the issue a mother of all issues just a fortnight back. This is how crowd behavior works.

Lesson to be Learnt: Only 10% of shares were issued to the public. The main promoters Anil Ambani and Reliance Energy Ltd. held 45% each. They had offered themselves each share at Rs.10, while the public was offered the same shares at Rs. 430–Rs. 450 per share. This was a blatant display of overconfidence and greed.

Wisdom Ignored: An issue price of Rs. 250–300 would have changed the situation drastically. The decrease in resource mobilization would have been more than offset by the goodwill of the investors gained. Brand Reliance would have become much stronger. This is what Mr. Dhirubhai Ambani would have done. He understood the psychology of markets and the investors. That's how he created brand Reliance and became known as the father of equity investing in India. Group IPOs in the pipeline would have been cake-walks. Anil Ambani would be the richest man in India and would have beaten brother Mukesh's market capitalization. Greed, together with biased advisors, evaded wisdom.

8.7 LESSONS FOR INVESTORS

Investors get trapped in the Growth Trap when they invest in sectors that are hot and fancy in the markets.

1. Investors end up paying crazy valuations for stocks when they chase stocks in the current hot sectors. This affects their long-term returns. This could also lead to capital depreciation.
2. When a sector is hot, new companies taking advantage of the market conditions enter the market with initial public offerings to cash in on the investor fancy. This leads to investors paying fancy prices for mediocre companies. Beware of IPOs.
3. Investment bankers try to cash in on the fancy sector by selling sub-par paper to the investors.
4. Be careful of the information fed to you by the media. Be wary of your favorite stock market TV shows. Carefully scan various buy recommendations from intermediaries.
5. Rapid growth in a sector does not mean good investment returns for the investors. In fact, the inverse is true. Investor returns are dependent on the right acquisition price.
6. A sector changes slowly, but companies' fortunes can change very rapidly. Misguided portfolio allocations based on sector growth can lead to acquisition of mispriced securities.

7. Sector bubbles are a warning to investors to reduce their allocation to the sector. We saw the IT sector bubble in 1999–2000. A similar bubble is evident in the real estate sector. Such sectors are not for the long-term investor.
8. A deflated sector, like FMCG or healthcare, offers good investment opportunities for long-term returns. The companies in these sectors are also available at reasonable PE multiples.
9. Do not buy what others are also buying. Long-term returns are a function of buying what others are not buying. It is here that you get the price advantage.

8.8 CONCLUSION

Sector investing is also akin to stock investing. You need not buy what is popular. You need not buy what all are buying, as that has already become expensive. You need not buy a hot sector, as the stocks in that sector are all expensive on representative thinking. Moreover, when a sector is doing well, an investor is more likely to get into the growth trap because the choice of a company in the sector may be wrong. Alternatively, when a sector does well, unscrupulous managements enter the sector with weak business models, as a result of which investors pay high valuations based on the sector. Companies would often change names representing the current hot sector to attract investor attention.

Judging by our past discussions, it really does make sense to look at a sector with sustainable economic characteristics, which is doing poorly due to lack of investor interest. However, the challenge would be to identify the right company in the sector. Companies in out-of-favor sectors can result in healthy investor returns.

Forging is a very dull sector per se. It has no charisma of technology innovation or a fancy of a growth. In the early-1980s, it was a neglected sector and not many companies would like to be in such a sector. With the exodus of companies from the sector due to uneconomic scales, only a few companies stayed in the sector. One such company was Bharat Forge. Its management concentrated on what it did best and improved its efficiency. When the sector did not have the fancy of investors, it did not have much competition. This gave it a lead to build an impressive moat around it. It did a mediocre business very efficiently and gave handsome returns to its shareholders. It has returned, on an average, over 31% compounded returns to its investors from 1979 to date. Returns are calculated based on reinvested dividends. At that time, the forging sector as well as the company were obscure names.

Similarly, at present FMCG is a neglected sector. However, the underlying business is sustainable despite weak economic conditions. Companies with a strong brand and a wide distribution network in this sector offer good investment opportunities. So is the case with a neglected sector like technology. Oracle invested in IFlex Solutions at Rs.2,100 a share. This stock is available at half the price at Rs.980. Can you go wrong? The sector is neglected and so is this great company.

NINE 9

INITIAL PUBLIC OFFERINGS

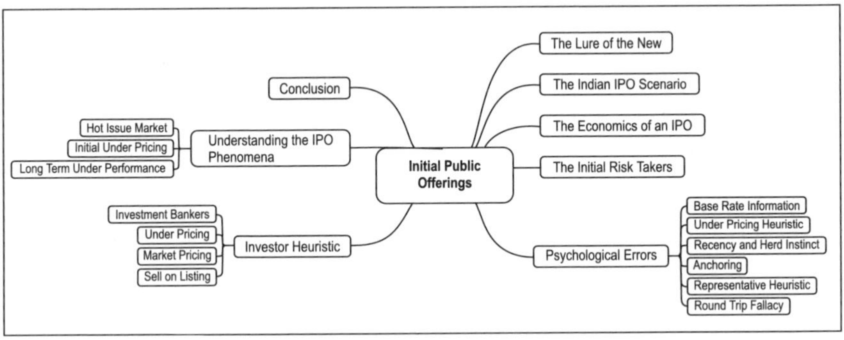

9.1 THE LURE OF THE NEW

We are always excited by the newness of a thing. Even when it comes to decisions as regards buying clothes, shoes, house, car, etc., we are excited to own something new and discard the old. In so doing, we end up getting poorer because we end up paying more for the new. Go to a car dealer offering you a new car and agreeing to buy back your old car. See the price differential. It's huge. You don't get a good price for a car you have maintained so well. Your leather seats are worthless and you paid a fortune when you fitted them. In the new car, you are again paying a bomb for the leather seats. It is our tendency to go for the new, as it satisfies our ego and also the belief that the new is better than the old.

When it comes to investing we are excited by the new. Be it a new growth industry, be it a new technology company or even a new initial public offering (IPO) of shares.

Even when it comes to investing we are excited by the new. Be it a new growth industry, be it a new technology company or even a new initial public offering (IPO) of shares. When we are thinking of a sound wealth-building strategy, we have to understand the pitfalls that besiege us in the stock markets. All through this book we have tried to understand various behavioral traits that affect our decision-making in investing. We will discuss in this chapter one such vehicle for investing, namely IPOs.

A lot of investors have made huge gains in stocks bought through IPOs. However, evidence suggests that such winners are very few and are far outnumbered by the losers.

In stock markets, you make money in some and lose in others, depending on your choice of stocks. However, in reality, most of the profits and losses arise out of emotional buying and selling. Chasing the new and the fads and fancies of the market are more out of following crowd behavior. If one has to buy clothes, jewelry, cars and items of personal consumption, it makes sense to be in tune with the latest trends and fashion.

However, in investing, it is not necessarily the right thing to do. Your returns get affected in the long run.

9.2 THE INDIAN IPO SCENARIO

Companies come out with public issues for a host of reasons. The need for external funds to reduce the burden of debt and reduce the interest cost prompt promoters to take the IPO route of financing. To fund huge expansion plans, promoters float IPOs. The promoters of the companies prefer to dilute their stake in the company when they are hopeful of getting a handsome price for their shares due to bullish market conditions. Unscrupulous managements come with IPOs to cash in on the current IPO boom in a bubble period—like the one we saw during the technology boom in 1999–2000, when a company had only to affix "dotcom" after its name to have investors willing to pay crazy valuations. IPO-mushrooming is very common in bull markets.

> **In stock markets, most of the profits and losses arise out of emotional buying and selling.**

India enjoyed a major boom of IPOs in the mid-1990s. This hot IPO period came to an end in 1995-96 with a fall in the stock market and a downturn in the economy. Investors who subscribed at the height of the boom suffered significant losses, and the primary market recovered from this debacle as late as 2004–5. With economic growth improving, we saw the start of a bull phase in 2003. However, this rise was with subdued optimism, and the primary market was lackluster. It picked up steam in 2006, with sectors like infrastructure, telecom, power and real estate doing exceedingly well. Investor interest soared. This led to a host of issues hitting the capital markets to take advantage of this frenzy. The bunching of IPOs was indicative of a bubble in the making.

In the late-1990s, the Indian corporate sector was in the midst of a structural transformation with the old economy companies' stocks doing badly in the face of global competition, while software companies delivered outstanding financial results. The stock market also rewarded the new economy stocks with high valuations. In this environment, it was difficult for most old economy companies to come to the market even with a credible business plan.

While the primary market has become an important source of mobilizing funds for Indian issuers since the commencement of the economic reform process in 1991–92, the ability of the primary market to provide resources to issuers has varied. The amount raised from the primary market increased from Rs.6,214.84 crores in 1991–92 to Rs.27,632.50 crores in 1994–95.

Investors like to always talk about their winning sprees rather than about their losses.

The primary market remained dull in 1995–96 and 1996–97 and the funds raised from the primary market declined to Rs.20,803.63 crores in 1995–96 and further declined to Rs.14,284.31 crores in 1996–97. In addition to the general economic and investment environment, the size of the issue has also depended on the eligibility criteria and disclosure norms, which have been made more stringent over the years, to ensure the availability of quality paper.

9.3 THE ECONOMICS OF AN IPO

A company intending to raise resources for expansion and acquisitions would like to go for an IPO. Or a group of initial investors desiring an exit would also like to go for an IPO. Or a company having plans for a new product or service would like to raise capital from the public, as no other mode of financing is available.

When the company is selling shares to the public it would want the maximum possible price. The higher the price, the more money it gets for its original investors and risk-takers.

When will it get the maximum price? In bull markets when people are willing to pay any price for owning stocks. So most of these IPOs are timed with bull markets, when prices are high. Therefore, as an investor, you buy such stocks at high prices. What are the chances of your earning healthy returns when you buy stocks at higher prices? Not much, unless you are very lucky.

Why do not many IPOs come in bear markets? Because in bear markets prices are depressed and the companies believe that their shares are more valuable than the price the market is willing to pay. So, in a bull market they are able to sell you the shares at a much higher value than the fair value.

We believe that we can make money by investing in the new. Some even consider it a sound strategy to invest in the new as, in a dynamic economy, creative destruction paves the way for the new. Hope it was correct and true as it sounds.

Looking back, during the 1994–1995 financial sector boom, we had a host of old as well as newly-floated finance firms entering the market to raise capital. The liberalization of the financial markets had begun and it was assumed that the growth in the sector would be fuelled by the entry of a vast number of players. There was a mad rush of IPOs in the financial sector. Every one of these had plans to set up a non-banking finance company and provide various services. This was also followed by IPOs in the plantations sector, which had all of a sudden become a hot sector and a fancy of the investors. Investors lost fortunes in both these phases. Most of these companies do not even exist today. All of these IPOs were oversubscribed many times and all had opened at a premium on listing. However, this hot period lasted for a short time only, after which the stocks started losing in value. (These hot periods are typical of IPOs and we shall discuss this in detail in the later part of this chapter.)

Most people base their judgment about risk and return on 'singular' information that is very readily and easily available, such as recent events.

Then. in the late 1990s, we had the technology boom and again a host of IPOs entered the market. This time, it was the hype of the new economy emerging and the death of the 'brick and mortar' business. Everyone talked about the new economy. But nobody understood whether the new economy was for real. It was the herd mentality at work. Everyone started believing in the new economy and everyone started buying such stocks and made a beeline to grab a piece of the IPOs. The argument went thus: Even if one out of ten of your new investments paid off, it was enough to take care of the losses in the remaining ones and you could still come out a winner. What gave them this confidence? It was the crazy valuations the listed stocks were enjoying. Visual Software reached a peak of Rs.10,000 for a Rs.10 face value, to come to a low of Rs.80 when the party ended. It was a favorite and highly recommended by one of the leading broker cum merchant bankers. The story does not end here. You have a long list of such heavy losers, like Himachal Futuristic, Software Solutions Ltd, DSQ Software and Pentafour Media to name a few.

Only one company, Infosys, has immensely rewarded its shareholders. However, it did not come with an IPO in the technology-boom bull market. It came much before that, in 1992, and its issue had a tough time getting subscribed. It came with an IPO with a genuine need to finance its expansion and growth. There was no intention to capitalize on the market boom, as none existed then. The intention being noble, the management has amply rewarded the shareholders with consistent growth in profits and earnings. It has done exceedingly well and is at present the market leader. During the technology boom when everyone was buying technology stocks or IPOs they were thinking that they were buying the next Infosys.

"Those who cannot remember the past are condemned to repeat it." *George Santayana*

The notion that the IPO is for the benefit of the investor to make money on listing is a big mental heuristic.

The year 2006–2007 saw another frenzy in the financial and real estate sectors. Sector growth was fueled by additions of new companies to the market. The financial sector boom was fueled by the entry and listing of financial brokerage services. The real estate sector boom was fueled by the entry of real estate developers and builders.

The ET Realty Index has lost 47% since the beginning of 2008, as on March 18th 2008. Of the 11 real estate companies that got listed since December 2006, seven companies were quoting at 40% below their listed price while the rest were just hovering around the issue price.

Mumbai-based developer HDIL's IPO came at an offer price of Rs.500 in July 2007. Within six months of listing, the stock touched Rs.1,432, and by March 2008 it was trading at Rs.538—marginally above listing price.

Similarly, little-known real estate companies, like Kolte Patil, which came to cash in on the investor euphoria got listed in late-2007, saw an all time high of Rs.272, and then crashed to Rs.92 in March 2008. Another company, Brigade Enterprises, touched an all-time high of Rs.428 in January 2008 and then crashed to Rs.173 in March 2008.

The only companies that provided an upside to IPO investors are relatively smaller companies like Orbit Corporation, trading at 300% above the issue price, and Akruti City, trading at 46% above the issue price, in March 2008.

Among financial services and brokerages, Motilal Oswal Financial Services, which made its debut in September 2007, saw its stock double in just three months. It touched a high of Rs.2,200 in January 2008, to crash to Rs.590 in March 2008, considerably below its issue price of Rs.825. Similarly, Edelweiss Capital, which got listed on the bourses in December 2007 at an issue price of Rs.825, went up to touch a high of Rs.1,800 in January 2008 to crash to Rs.611, way below the issue price.

What does this mean for the investors? Although there were a few winners, there were far too many losers. Most of the IPO investors have lagged the market returns.

Investors are always looking at benefiting from the new. A new breakthrough technology, a new product or an idea, a new business model, etc. Identifying companies promoting such innovations, and investing in them, is assumed to make good money for the investors. Such companies come to the market through the IPO route and investors make a mad rush to acquire these, even at higher prices. When all the investors are thinking this way, there is a demand-supply mismatch and the price goes up. Anything that becomes a fancy commands a fancy price. Investors thus lose out on their returns in the long run as they pay a fancy price.

It is not that such creativity and innovation do not benefit the investor. They do; but this space is reserved for the early investors who really took the risk when there was uncertainty. But IPOs come to the market when there is certainty, and it is only in such times that the investors are willing to pay a higher price. This willingness to pay the higher price benefits the initial investors who were the risk-takers.

Innovation and creativity do benefit the inventor. There have been so many millionaires who made it because of their innovations.

9.4 THE INITIAL RISK-TAKERS

In the chapter on index investing we will see that the returns on the laggards have far exceeded the returns on the newcomers. Here, too, we find that the IPOs, supposedly representing the new, underperform in the long run. One could conclude that it is best to stick with the old, and ask why one would venture to innovate, be creative and take risks if one is not ably rewarded. Initial risk-takers and the innovative and creative people do get rewarded, and that too immensely. Otherwise we would not have any innovations.

We need to understand how this wealth-creating process actually works. The inventor starts his company and has a unique product or service in mind. He requires capital and in comes the angel investors. The company grows and requires more capital. In come the venture capitalists and the private equity firms. The company grows further and, when the time comes for the initial investors to exit, they do it by way of an IPO, and that too when the market is bullish. This enables them to get good valuations. They are rewarded because they have been with the early stages of the company and taken big risks. The markets do reward the innovators and they make huge money on their products and services. If that were not the case, we would not have any innovations taking place. The early risk-takers, like the angel investors, venture capitalists and private equity investors also get rewarded because they were long-term investors. This, again, goes to prove that investing is all about holding for the long run.

Now when they need to exit they need to also price the issue properly, so that some money is left on the table for the IPO investors to make money. However, this initial listing euphoria is short-lived because of the hot issue markets, which we will discuss later.

9.5 PSYCHOLOGICAL ERRORS

9.5.1 Base Rate Information

Base rate information is typically abstract and not readily available. Historical statistics constitute examples of base rate information. Most people base their judgment about risk and return on information that is very readily and easily available, such as recent events. This type of information is called singular information. People who over-weigh recent events are prone to extrapolating recent trends while making forecasts and decisions based on these forecasts. That is why, in bull markets, people expect higher returns from stocks, and in bear markets they expect lower returns. When such extrapolation is unwarranted, then the resulting bias is called extrapolation bias. It is for this reason that people have invested blindly in the recent IPOs in bull markets and shunned them in the bear markets. In bull markets, people rely on singular information of how investors in IPOs have made money, without taking into consideration the base information or the historical statistics. This also makes them borrow from banks to subscribe for IPOs.

Moreover, investors like to always talk about their winning sprees rather than about their losses. So, even if a minority of IPOs has rewarded the investors, the available information being strong, it aids the recall value and investors believe that IPOs are the next best thing to happen in the capital markets.

9.5.2 Under-pricing Heuristic

It is assumed that a company under-prices its IPO and leaves some money on the table. Willful under-pricing is unlikely; the fact that stocks rise on listing usually signifies managers' and investment bankers' inability to judge market sentiment. It is also out of fear of the IPO failing that management believes in initial under-pricing.

However, the notional loss from under-pricing is more than offset by the gain from the management's current stake appreciating in value due to a higher stock price on listing.

Of course, we cannot generalize the under-pricing phenomenon, as there are some good managements which believe in giving adequate returns to new investors. A classical example is that of TCS, from the house of TATA, when it came out with its IPO. It was cheaply priced with money kept on the table for the investors. Such management does exist.

Nevertheless, greed and the endowment effect play a very important role in IPOs. In February 2008, Emaar Holdings entered the market with an overpriced issue which was rejected by investors. The company withdrew the issue. This itself signifies that the company was only interested in capitalizing on the boom conditions by selling stock to investors at ridiculous valuations, and not in raising resources for the business. Overpricing and withdrawal of the issue raises doubts on the credibility of the management and the concerned investment bankers.

However, stock markets are known for the fickle-minded behavior of investors, and as soon as the sentiment changes, they will chase the same company and investment banker.

9.5.3 Recency and Herd Instinct

IPOs make noise during their launch with big advertisement campaigns. Dreams are sold to the investors. Then there comes a gray market premium. Investors get carried away by all the news on the IPO and this recency effect makes them invest in the company.

When the news on the company is so vivid and eye-catching, every type of investor joins the bandwagon. The herd instinct takes over and investors start competing with each other to get a piece of the pie.

This was so very evident in the launch of the Morgan Stanley Mutual Fund in the early-1990s. The fund was supposed to collect money from the public and invest in the stock market. Considering the expenses involved, the net asset value could never be more than the issue price of Rs.10 per unit. However, there was a gray market premium of Rs.8 to Rs.15. The fund launch received immense support from investors. The recency effect was played by the reputed name of Morgan Stanley and the gray market premium instigating the greed of the investors. This recency effect led to a strong herd behavior by investors. When the listing took place, the reality dawned. The investors felt cheated. The company collected the money, their asset management company became profitable, and the investment banker made a fortune.

9.5.4 Anchoring

Initially in India we had a Controller of Capital Issues, who would decide the pricing of IPOs. This made subscription to IPOs very profitable and investors in the past have made handsome returns. However, today the office of the Controller of Capital Issues has been abolished and SEBI, the regulator, oversees IPOs. Today, IPOs have to be priced at market rates. So, technically, IPOs are like any other stock listed in the market and it should not be something really sought after where people feel that a lucky allotment would make them good money. However, investors are so anchored to the past that they are unable to see the reality as it exists today. They blindly chase IPOs.

This heuristic-driven IPO craze works so well on the psychology of the investors that even reputed mutual fund houses started marketing their new schemes as New Fund Offering (NFOs). Investors would chase such offerings thinking that a new offering is available at par. Not the right thing expected of professionals from such an industry. But when it becomes a standard practice followed by all it becomes the right thing.

9.5.5 Representative Heuristic

If investors have made money in a couple of IPOs then other IPOs become representative of profitable IPOs. Investors blindly chase IPOs. This herd mentality creates huge demand and the IPOs tend to get oversubscribed. This demand-supply mismatch creates a profit for the investors on listing. Investors start believing that investing in IPOs is the sure way to profits, and the IPO craze starts. Managements start looking at opportunities to capitalize on this investor craze and, thus, one sees a bunching of IPOs.

The year 2006 saw 75 IPOs entering the market, of which 54 were at a premium on listing. This set the basis for the IPO boom. Investors got attracted by the listing gains and chased every IPO. Banks freely lent money for the same. The year 2007 saw 96 listings, of which 61 were at a premium on listing. The premium listing performance was lower, at 63%, than the 72% observed in 2006. More investors entering had got more companies trying to capitalize on the IPO craze.

This downward trend got vitiated in early-2008, when investors lost in the most steeply-priced and hyped issue of RPL. The greed of the management and the investment bankers had pricked the IPO bubble. Issues like Wockhardt failed to get investor support in February 2008 and another hyped and overpriced issue of Emmaar Holdings had to be called off. IPOs once representative of profits turned representatives of losses.

9.5.6 Round Trip Fallacy

Consider the following statement, '*All successful people are hard workers.*' Could it be inferred that all hard workers are successful people. Not really. Hard work is of course one of the integral attributes behind successful people but it is not the singular attribute.

Similarly, most of the cheap stocks generally have low or moderate PE ratios and only in exceptional cases have high PE ratio. By believing that all low P/E stocks would necessarily be cheap stocks, one is succumbing to the 'round trip fallacy'.

Similar thing happens when investors rush for IPOs. The initial premium on listing makes investors believe that all IPOs will result in listing gains. Thus, investors rush for any IPO, and even go to the extent of borrowing money from the banks to participate in the IPO boom. This is how the IPO bubble is formed.

Listed companies act as a very good anchor for the new IPOs in a similar industry. IPO management and investment bankers price their issues below the comparable industry listed company PEs. This makes the IPO attractive, and investors use this yardstick for allocating resources to the IPOs. All companies are different and it is a fallacy to use the PE heuristic to make investment decisions.

9.6 INVESTOR HEURISTIC

Investors take shortcuts in processing information. They do not process the full information. This leads to certain biases in their decision-making. If they are able to understand the following realities, less fortunes will be lost in this mad rush for IPOs.

9.6.1 Investment Bankers

In case of a company wishing to come out with an IPO, it has to appoint an investment banker to market the IPO. The investment banker, over and above the fixed fees, is also given a percentage of sales as success fees, which acts as an incentive to price the IPO as high as possible. The investment banker, acting as the company's agent, helps it to get the maximum price. Those investing in the IPO rely on the information provided by the investment banker, and make investment decisions based on the research report prepared by the investment banker and/or their associates. In bull markets, investors blindly follow the investment bankers, relying on their recent successes. And in bull markets all have a past success record. This heuristic-driven mentality of the investors makes them prone to losing money when they try to choose the newest of the new.

RPL is a very good example. It had appointed the top investment bankers to advise the company. Investors relied on what these bankers said over television, newspapers and the media. They trusted these bankers, not in the least realizing that they were selling agents for the company. After the issue was sold, the rug got pulled and the stock quoted at a discount on listing. Investors lost, but the investment bankers collected their fees.

Another case of an investment banker developing cold feet and withdrawing is the IPO of Emmaar Holdings.

If Investment Bankers were to underwrite the issue before taking it public, then we would not have seen issues being overpriced and withdrawn. It was a mockery of the system and the investors. These are just a few recent cases in the long list.

9.6.2 Under-Pricing

The most basic problem of IPO under-pricing is the presence of both "good" and "bad" firms going public, together with asymmetric information between firms and investors. This is true of IPOs all over the world, and likely to be more relevant in India, where IPOs are marketed to retail investors who have very little knowledge. The possibility of informed investors capitalizing on their information is the driver of under-pricing. IPOs have to be under-priced on an average to compensate uninformed investors.

In a classic article, Rock (1986) explores the role of the "winner's curse" in IPO under-pricing. Rock's model has two kinds of investors, those who are perfectly informed about the true value of the firm and those who are completely uninformed about the true value of the firm. The number of shares being sold through an issue is fixed, and informed investors will only attempt to buy shares when an issue is relatively under-priced. Hence, uninformed investors, who do not know whether a given issue is under-priced or not, suffer from a winner's curse. They get all the shares they want of the poor issues, and they get a small allocation of the good issues. This sort of phenomenon is predominantly at work in India.

9.6.3 Market Pricing

Investors get unduly excited by the IPO phenomenon, and mistakenly believe that they are getting something cheap. IPOs are priced at the market price—a price that the investors are willing to pay. The market sentiment decides the price of an IPO. The investment banker prices the issue on behalf of the company and does so with the intention of getting the maximum price for the company. The price is never meant to be in favor of the investor. But still investors chase IPOs in the belief that they are good money-making opportunities. They follow this rule of thumb, which has no logic. On the contrary, evidence suggests that investing in IPOs is akin to buying a lottery ticket or betting on horse-racing.

The only difference is that, on listing, it can quote at a premium or a discount. It is this that makes investors chase IPOs in bull markets and shun them in bear markets.

9.6.4 Sell on Listing

Even if the investors are aware of all the facts mentioned above, it is their greed and the overconfidence in their ability, which makes them fall prey to IPO investing. This greed is so relentless that they also borrow at high interest rates to apply for IPOs.

Their overconfidence level is so high that they believe that, even though the issue is overpriced, they would be smart enough to get out of the stock, making a profit before the others do. However, the sad part is that all investors are also thinking on the same lines. Yes, this could work in some issues; but it is a risky business, as sentiments change overnight in the markets.

This was so very evident in the IPO of RPL. The IPO received overwhelming support and was heavily oversubscribed. Although the stock was priced at a hefty PE of around 5,000, investors were willing to stake a bet. They all understood the high valuations, but each one was thinking that he would sell on listing. Nobody really believed in the company or the sustainability of the stock price, but was confident of making a profit by selling on listing. It was a false hope that the price would be maintained and that there would be buyers for the stock at an even higher price. When all were thinking of selling on listing, they all came together and the stock price plunged.

One would think that such behavior would come from a lay investor who is ignorant and uneducated to understand the intricacies of the stock market. However, even the most sophisticated and qualified investors like the mutual fund managers and institutional money managers were also investors in the RPL IPO, and they also invested thinking of selling on listing. Why pay them such huge salaries when they also behave like a man on the street? Is it right to entrust them with such large amounts of public money?

9.7 UNDERSTANDING THE IPO PHENOMENA

9.7.1 Hot Issue Market

A hot issue market is when the demand for new issues is very high. Bull markets and irrational behavior of investors enable hot issue markets. A company intending to raise resources for its expansion and acquisition would like to get the maximum amount of money by giving a minimum amount of shares to the public. Or a group of initial investors desiring an exit would also like to get the maximum price for their stocks. Or a company having plans for a new product or service would like to raise capital from the public as no other mode of financing is available. In a bull market, when investors are greedy for buying stocks, such IPOs find their way to the hot issue market. In fact, bunching of such IPOs signifies the build-up of a bubble.

Revisiting 1993–1994, there is evidence of a bull market due to the liberalization of the economy. This led to a hot issues market, and the year 1993–94 saw more than 600 IPOs hitting the market. Most of these companies do not even exist today. In the absence of a regulator, all kinds of paper entered the market only to leave the investor poorer.

This was again followed by the technology boom in 1999–2000, when we saw many technology companies or internet or 'dot com' companies coming out with IPOs. However, this hot period was restricted to the IT sector. Investors lost heavily in most of these highly-priced companies when the bust came. Of all the IPOs that entered the capital markets in 2000 only 48% exist as of today. The rest have vanished. In the year 2000, 79% of the IPOs were by technology companies as that was the hot sector. Of these IT companies, 90% have been delisted or have disappeared altogether. This is enough evidence to support the view that hot sector IPOs are against investor interest. The sad part is that the investment bankers who got these issues to the market laughed their way to the bank, leaving the investors a poorer lot.

The year 2006 was when the IPO markets saw some movement and one had a choice of different companies in the hot sectors entering the markets. The stock markets were also going up on the strength of a strong GDP growth and foreign institutional investors making aggressive purchases in the market. Growth in the economy would lead to rise in infrastructure spending and thus lead to a growth of the construction and real estate companies. Along with this growth, the liberalization of the financial sector was already creating an impetus for the banking and the financial services companies. The healthy stock markets again made the financial services sector a favorite of the investors.

In 2006 we had 75 IPOs and 72% of these gave handsome listing gains to the investors. This was enough for the bankers to get in to lend money for investing in IPOs. The signs of an emerging hot market were evident.

In the year 2007 we had 96 IPOs and 61 of them made their debut with a premium on listing. We had 16 IPOs from the construction sector alone, raising around Rs.154.5 billion. The largest issue was that of DLF, raising Rs. 92 billion.

Following construction, we had nine IPOs from the banking and the financial services sectors, garnering around Rs.105 billion.

This was followed by 11 IPOs from the IT sector, raising just Rs.14.2 billion. These were relatively small issues.

Since the overall sentiment was good we did have issues across sectors; but the bunching of issues was evident in construction, banking and financial services.

At the end of 2007 there was evidence of increased activity in the power sector. Power Grid was listed at a handsome listing gain of 93%. Such utility companies with regulatory price controls were quoting at high PE multiples. Tata Power, NTPC and Power Grid were all quoting at PEs above 28. The hot IPO market was evident. One had only to wait for the excesses to happen and the sentiment would change.

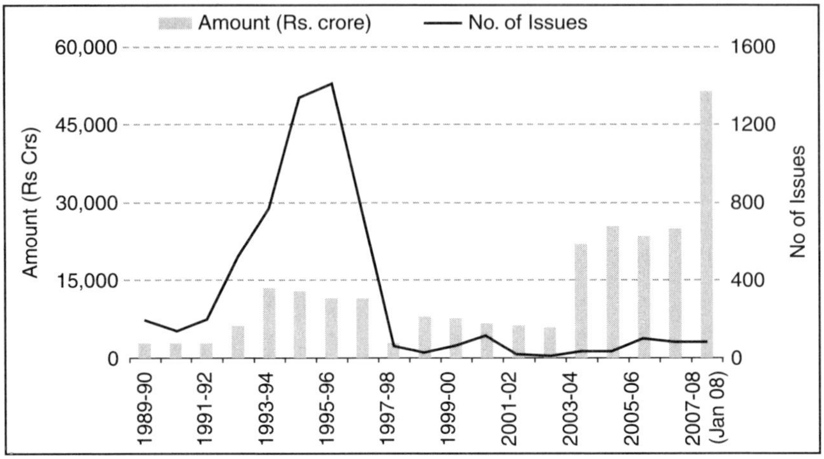

Figure 9.1 Number and Value of IPOs from 1989 to 2008

The chart (Figure 9.1) depicts the IPO boom from 1993 to 1996 due to the liberalization of the Indian economy. We had a record number of public issues entering the market to cash in on the hot IPO market. Thereafter, we had the hot IT sector in 1999–2000, when we saw a host of IT and 'dot com' companies cashing in on the investor frenzy. Thereafter, the markets were very subdued, and IPO activity nearly dried up until 2004. The only IPOs that entered during the dry period were those of PSU banks and some others which were due to government stake sales. From 2004 onwards, IPO activity gathered momentum and, more than the number of issues, the size of issues was significant. Resource mobilization of more than Rs.50,000 crores was leading to excesses.

9.7.2 Initial Under-Pricing

The notion that the IPO is for the benefit of the investor to make money on listing is a big mental heuristic. Why does one go for an IPO? To raise resources; and to do that, one does so in a hot market, so that the maximum price is obtained. Moreover, during such times investors become irrational, and in their greed to make money they invest in almost anything. Although managers in charge of raising resources try to price the issue appropriately, they find on the day of the listing that they made a mistake in under-pricing the issue as the listing price is way above the issue price.

One would think that the managers and the investment bankers had under-priced the issue to benefit new investors. But such things do not happen in finance, and that too in bull markets. The difference is in valuing the stock. The issue price could be more than the fair value the managers thought, but it could be well below the expectations of the market. When expectations are high—and rightly so in bull markets—you have the phenomenon of initial under-pricing. It is more due to the behavior of the investors. Most IPOs quote at a heavy premium on listing but soon the premium vanishes.

Very few companies are able to maintain the initial listing gains. The table below shows the start of the IPO boom in 2004. In 2001 38% of the companies gave a negative listing return, and a further 13% gave negative listing returns in 2002. The revival of the stock markets in 2003, although with fewer new issues, shows no negative listing gains. The years 2004, 2005 and 2006 witnessed positive listing gains by over 95% of the companies.

Table 9.1 Listing Gains from IPOs, 2001 to 2007

Year	Negative	0%–20%	20%–50%	50%–100%	>100%
2001	38%	38%	9%	15%	
2002	13%	50%	37%		
2003		22%	33%	23%	22%
2004	4%	20%	32%	28%	16%
2005	4%	33%	38%	20%	5%
2006	5%	45%	36%	12%	2%
2007	20%	36%	17%	27%	

However, these initial listing gains soon vanished, as the initial euphoria of the new vanishes. No longer does it command a fancy in the markets, except if the company comes out with extraordinary reasons for change of fortunes or some good corporate news. This is amply evident in the next table, which shows returns after one month of listing.

Table 9.2 Gains One Month after IPO Listings, 2001 to 2007

Year	Negative	0%–20%	20%–50%	50%–100%	>100%
2001	85%		7%		8%
2002	49%		38%	13%	
2003	11%	33%	12%	33%	11%
2004	16%	12%	36%	20%	16%
2005	15%	20%	22%	27%	16%
2006	39%	20%	17%	16%	8%
2007	43%	11%	19%	10%	17%

These initial listing gains have vanished despite a strong bull market extending up to 2008. No doubt, there have been certain stocks which, even after one month, have given more than the listing gains. However, this could be attributed to the bull market conditions and the specific sector fancies like real estate, infrastructure and capital goods, power and financial services sectors.

Our basic argument is that, if one is lucky, one can come across a few IPOs where one can reap immense benefits. However, there are too many IPOs where one can get trapped and that can take away the gains of the winners. It's all about paying the right price for an investment, to reap long-term, healthy returns.

The losses to investors in the earlier IPO boom of 1993–1996 were particularly unfortunate, as the IPO bust was followed by a prolonged bear market. We consider that situation in the following topic on long-term under-performance.

9.7.3 Long-Term Under-Performance

New issues earn lower returns for the investors than comparable stocks. Those buying the stocks on first day listing tend to lose in a big way. Since new issues tend to come when the appetite for stocks is strong, two things happen. Strong demand leads to higher pricing. Returns, as we have discussed earlier in the book, are always subject buying an asset at the right price. If a higher price is paid for an asset, the returns suffer. This is what happens to investors in IPOs.

Good investment opportunities in IPOs come in bear markets, as we saw with Infosys in 1992. Although the issue received a very lukewarm response, long- term investors have reaped handsome returns. Had the IPO come in 1999–2000, I am sure the returns for the investors would have been negative, as it would have been over-valued due to the bullish conditions at that time. However, the issue would have got heavily oversubscribed. During the technology boom, the price of Infosys' stock was more than 200 times its earnings. Investors who bought the stock at such high rates are still nursing their wounds. These multiples are not sustainable in the long run. Similar excesses in IPOs have been happening in 2007–2008. Investors are willing to pay excessive multiples. They are sure to lose in the long run.

The biggest losses come to investors when they buy IPOs on listing, as they were not lucky enough to get the initial allotment. They are caught in the winners' curse trap. When they are not lucky enough to get it on allotment, they try to buy it on listing at whatever the opening price. The goal of buying the investment at the right price is forgotten. The goal changes to being the proud acquirer of the stock. Yes, the stock is acquired; but at great financial distress in the long run.

Evidence shows that investors have lost money most of the time when they have bought IPOs at the offer price. Can you imagine the plight of investors who buy on listing? They always end up paying a much higher price on listing because of the initial investor euphoria in the price discovering process. Moreover, the gray market premium fluctuations also distort the prices on listing. Normally, for an IPO after the initial first listing, the hot market lasts for about six to nine months and, after that, the cold period starts, where you have a gradual drift in stock price, signifying loss of interest by investors.

A long-term performance analysis of the IPOs since 1991 shows a very disappointing picture. A sample of 1,540 IPOs that were listed between 1991 and 2000, has been taken. Out of the 3,122 IPOs for which we managed to collect data from the CMIE Prowess database, only 1,540 continued to be listed up to November 2006. This, in itself, shows that 50% of these companies got delisted, merged or vanished.

Investors lost a lot of money in these so-called new and growing companies. The 1,540 companies still being traded also do not give a very good picture. A performance analysis of these companies and their comparison with the market index (BSE Sensex) is summarized in the following table. The poor performance of these IPOs can easily be seen from the fact that more than 56% of these IPOs gave negative long-term returns, thus eroding investors' wealth. Only about 15% of the IPOs managed to give more returns than the Sensex. In the years 1993–1996, the maximum number (4,000) of IPOs came to the market. The performance of IPOs that came out during these most active years has been very poor. Investors would have lost their hard-earned money by investing in these IPOs with the thought of investing in the new. The extent of the loss can be judged from the fact that more than 50% of these companies have been merged (very small number), delisted or vanished. Note that in the table, (1) the average annual returns have been calculated from the monthly closing prices (average annual returns = average monthly returns × 12); (2) the returns have been calculated from the month of listing to November 2006; and (3) the excess returns have been calculated by subtracting the Sensex returns from the stock returns for the same period.

Table 9.3 Performance Analysis of IPOs from 1991–2000

Year	No. of IPOs	IPOs with Positive Annual Returns	%	Excess Returns than the Sensex	%	IPOs with Negative Annual Returns	%
1991	25	16	64.0	7	28.0	9	36.0
1992	63	29	46.0	11	17.5	34	54.0
1993	160	71	44.4	29	18.1	89	55.6
1994	397	159	40.1	49	12.3	238	59.9
1995	529	221	41.8	60	11.3	308	58.2
1996	232	118	50.9	49	21.1	114	49.1
1997	30	17	56.7	5	16.7	13	43.3
1998	12	10	83.3	6	50.0	2	16.7
1999	18	7	38.9	5	27.8	11	61.1
2000	74	26	35.1	13	17.6	48	64.9
Total	1,540	674	43.8	234	15.2	866	56.2

The next table shows the IPOs which outperformed the Sensex by a certain percentage. The maximum number of IPOs gave excess returns between 0% to 5%, only.

Of the 234 IPOs which gave excess returns as compared to the Sensex, 11% are from the banking and financial services sectors; 10% each are from metals and mining, and pharmaceutical and biotechnology sectors; and 9% each are from infrastructure and construction, and software sectors.

Table 9.4 Number of IPOs that Outperformed the Sensex

Excess Returns (%)	0–5	05–10	10–15	15–20	More than 20	Total
No. of IPOs	82	48	46	26	32	234

Of the 674 IPOs which gave positive annual returns, more than 50% gave only marginal returns in the range of 0% to 10%. The table below summarizes these IPOs according to the returns they gave.

Table 9.5 Number of IPOs that gave positive returns

Average Annual Returns (%)	0–10	10–20	20–30	Above 30	Total
No. of IPOs	364	164	86	60	674

9.8 CONCLUSION

It is safe to conclude that IPOs, which seem like a good investment vehicle are, in reality, not so. In fact an IPO is a product which is against investor interest, as it is mostly offered to investors when they are willing to pay a higher and outrageous valuation in boom times. It makes sense for the company and the investment banker to dump these stocks on the investors. IPOs only come to markets when the management feels that they will get a good price for unloading their stocks. Evidence has shown that out of the many IPOs that come to the markets only a very few reward shareholders. It makes sense for wise investors to wait for bear markets to pick up such investment opportunities. Of course, always avoid chasing these stocks on listing or during the hot IPO period. There are too many people who would be doing that and, when the losses come and their patience dies; these same people will offer you these stocks at tempting valuations. Do not be carried away by the newest of the new as you end up paying high prices only to take a hit on your returns.

TEN 10

INDEX INVESTING

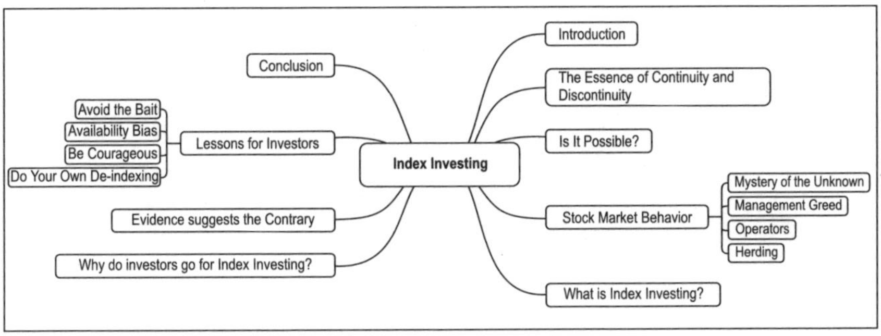

10.1 Introduction
10.2 The Essence of Continuity and Discontinuity
10.3 Is it Possible?
10.4 Stock Market Behavior
10.5 What is Index Investing?
10.6 Why do Investors go for Index Investing?
10.7 Evidence Suggests the Contrary
10.8 Lessons for Investors
10.9 Conclusion

10.1 INTRODUCTION

> **A company gets into the index not because it is good, but because it has a high market capitalization.**

The other day, I was with a client whose money we were managing for the last four years. We had done exceedingly well on his portfolio, with spectacular returns. I will not take any credit for the returns, as everyone in the Indian markets has done well, especially if you were lucky enough to get the money in 2003 as we did. I will take the credit for having invested his money in the right wealth-enhancing assets and walked our talk of having a long-term investing strategy. Our churn rate on the portfolio was negligible. We had beaten the Sensex by around 2% and the Nifty by around 1%, while ensuring that the downside was protected. The client, though pleased with the performance did not show any enthusiasm, as he believed that he would have also been better off had he just invested in the Index. Why was he going through all this when passive investing works so well? My immediate answer to him was that beating the index by 2% was not a small feat and if one were to compound the same for the next 5 to 10 years it would make a big difference to his portfolio. This argument also did not go down well with him, and I left it at that as I thought that this could be his way of bargaining to bring down the fees.

However, this got me thinking. Here we were making all efforts to do some value investing by spending time and energy identifying the right long-term stocks, and there you have a very passive form of investing that gives you nearly the same returns.

Who was I to argue when there was a track record of the most successful Vanguard Funds, which had pioneered the concept of Index Funds? On more introspection I concluded that their popularity soared from two distinct human behavioral traits.

One was the offer of lower fees as compared to the more actively-managed funds. Psychologically, it was a big positive, as it indirectly conveyed the message that lower fees added to the overall returns to the investor. Moreover, investors were quite dismayed by the fees that asset management companies charged, irrespective of the profits or losses made by them.

The other trait that worked was the psychological solace that one was with the crowd. If the markets went up, one would gain, and if they went down, one would lose. There being no benchmark to the Index but the index itself, there would be no regret-aversion in case of fairing poorly. People wouldn't mind losing if everybody was losing. As long as they had company they were comfortable.

> **Investing is a difficult game and there are a very few seasoned investors in the world who have done exceedingly well in the markets.**

Was "The Law of the Farm" being vindicated? Can such passive investing score over the efforts of identifying value and mispriced stocks? Being a firm believer in behavioral finance, it is my strong belief that the majority of market participants display crowd behavior that leads to irrational choices. This gives rise to mispriced opportunities. Index investing was also, in a sense, copying that crowd behavior. There was nothing contrarian about it. If it was that simple, can it benefit the investor? This called for some real soul-searching and, thus, started the research on index investing.

10.2 THE ESSENCE OF CONTINUITY AND DISCONTINUITY

Corporations are built on the assumption of continuity, and their focus is on operations. Capital markets are built on the assumption of discontinuity, and their focus is on creation and destruction. The market encourages rapid and extensive creation and, hence, greater wealth-building. It is less tolerant than the corporation is of long-term underperformance.

Why do people prefer passive investing like the index or the index funds? Most investors prefer to avoid the ups and downs of the markets and the rigmarole of choosing individual stocks and, thus, shun active investing. They believe that the best way to beat individual active investing is to put money in index stocks. There is this conventional wisdom, which says that index investing will beat individual stock-picking for the following reason.

Individual stocks have their life cycles. In the initial phase, the entrepreneur is filled with passion and works on intuition. When passion rules, information and analysis are ignored in the name of vision. The company keeps on growing and, over time, bureaucracy starts building up. The company does well, and passions cool down and are replaced by rational decision-making: the codification of what worked in the past. This causes a cultural lock-in and the company is unable to reinvent itself. This leads to the company's decline.

However, markets are very different. They lack culture and leadership. They do not experience the bursts of desperation, depression, denial and hope that the corporations face. They have no institutional memories, nor do they have any mental models. The markets allow weaker companies to be put up for sale or to exit and pave way for entry of the new. They help creative disruption to happen.

It was based on this hypothesis that indices were formed. It was to facilitate continuity by aiding the discontinuity of individual corporations, and helping the new ones to take their place. It was to be a representative of the markets.

It requires not only intelligence but also the emotional strength to be a good investor.

10.3 IS IT POSSIBLE?

In theory, it sounds very good; but when put to practice there are a few grave misgivings. How does one judge whether a company is good or bad? A lull (like the FMCG sector during the IT boom) or strong growth (the one we saw in 1999–2000 with the technology sector stocks) could be temporary phenomena. How does one identify a good or a bad company? Sales? Profits? Earnings growth? These are all variable factors. Again, indices have to deal with creative destruction; but how does one decide which companies are dying and which new companies are the right replacements? So many questions remain unanswered and the best way in this situation is to adopt the most non-controversial and the most ineffective. Market capitalization was the answer. Entry to indices was facilitated by the size of market capitalization the company enjoys. Judging quality being difficult, quality gave way to quantity. In new growth sectors, companies with large market capitalization found their way to the index.

Reliance Communications Ltd. got listed on 6th March 2006 and, due to a huge market capitalization, found its way to the BSE Sensex on 12th June 2006, with just three months of listing track record.

10.4 STOCK MARKET BEHAVIOR

We have discussed earlier that the markets aid creative destruction. However, in reality, the markets are not rational, especially in the short run. So the process of creative destruction does not happen as assumed. The markets comprise of people who have emotions, and most of the time their decisions are made from the heart rather than from the mind. Such decisions may not be rational. Stocks quoted on stock exchanges do not necessarily quote at their fair value. Their prices are dependent on various factors, like the market sentiments, the demand and supply mismatch, investors expectations, management interest in stock price, operators' manipulation, interest of institutional investors, entry into international indices, stock options trading, optimism and pessimism.

A company gets into the index not because it is good, but because it has a high market capitalization. This is a function of the stock being a fancy of investors and being a part of the latest frenzy of a growth sector. Investors end up paying hefty valuations for such a stock . This price increases the market capitalization and the same is reflected in the index. The index goes up because the price of the stock in the index goes up. Investor returns are directly connected to the price they pay for the stock. When investors pay a high price for a stock or an index, their returns over the long run suffer.

DLF Ltd. is a classic example of this. It had a tough time getting SEBI approval to enter the markets with an IPO in view of certain pending litigations with the minority shareholders of the company. However, after much delay, when the IPO hit the market it received good investor response as the real estate market was hot. It was the biggest issue in 2007 and garnered Rs. 92 billion from the market. The market capitalization of the company was substantial, and within three months it found a place in the index. It had an image makeover and a strong following of qualified institutional investors. None of them would ever be able to value the land bank the company claimed to own. However, since it was a large capitalization stock and an index representative, it was assumed to be a good company.

That is why we saw many big issues entering the market in 2006–2007. Although the number of issues was small, their size was so large that we had record resource mobilization in these years. In 2007 alone, we had a mobilization of Rs. 442 billion with just 96 IPOs.

Management's concentration has shifted from running businesses to managing market capitalization. Stock options act as a great incentive for them to do so. Behavioral anomalies responsible for the undue stress on market capitalization and its effect on the index are discussed in the following sections.

10.4.1 Mystery of the Unknown

Investors are always willing to pay more for the value of a mystery. So, in times when a new industry or a sector is in the offing, investors are excited by the promise of the unknown. So is the case with the advent of a new technology or a breakthrough invention. New ideas and new technologies supposedly are expected to change the rules of the game and expected to make money for the investors. It is on this basis that investors are willing to pay fancy prices to have a piece of the action. When such fancies are chased by the investors, their prices start going up and this increases their market capitalization. They start becoming big with their stock prices appreciating.

> **Successful investing is all about buying what others are selling and selling what others are buying.**

Remember the technology boom in the years 1999–2000? Technology companies commanded lofty valuations and this added to their market capitalization. Thus, we had so many companies finding a place in the index—not because they were really good businesses, but because they were popular with the investors who were willing to pay exorbitant prices to own them. During that time the technology sector had a weightage of over 25% in the BSE Sensex.

However, when the craze for the technology sector ended, all these stock prices crashed. Nothing had drastically gone wrong with the sector. Only investor sentiment changed. The hype died and so did the market capitalization of companies. Once the mystery unfolded, rationality prevailed. NIIT and HCL Technologies lost their places in the BSE Sensex.

10.4.2 Management Greed

When a company happens to be in the hot sector and its stock is chased by the investors, the management gets a false sense of security. The media reports about the rise in the net worth of the management and compares it with the peers. This comparison leads to overconfidence about ability. The management embarks upon huge expansion plans and acquisitions, leading to a further rise in stock prices and, ultimately, in market capitalization. The fear of slipping down in ranking makes them undertake risky business ventures. They become victims of the winner's curse. Over time, these ventures fail and the stock takes a beating. Dreams are shattered. In a highly competitive environment, it is difficult to keep up to high investor expectations. However, the lure created by media frenzy keeps the competition going.

Most corporate houses are in the market capitalization game. It gives them credibility and market following. The media cover them. It is a new-found craze. Envy and greed fuel this fire.

This is very much evident with Ambani brothers after the split of the Reliance empire. Both are so engrossed in the market capitalization game that every other day one hears about an announcement of some merger, acquisition, a private equity investment, a gas discovery, a government contract for building an airport or a SEZ, or a strategic alliance. Rather than concentrating on business, energy is diverted to increasing market capitalization. That is how Reliance Communications came in to the BSE Sensex, and, soon, so will RPL and Reliance Petroleum.

It just requires a little courage to go against the crowd and act in a contrarian way. Evidence has shown that going against the popular thinking pays in the long run.

It is this market capitalization that helps companies to grow exponentially, and the stock market helps such companies to raise huge resources.

10.4.3 Operators

A bull market gets many types of operators willing to pay the piper. If one is famous for some past successful bets, he becomes the mover of markets. Investors follow such operators blindly. The media also make them heroes by giving them extensive exposure. For the media, it is hot content catching eyeballs. Managements wanting to increase their stock prices approach such operators to rig their stocks. A higher stock price has many advantages for the management. They can raise more money from the capital markets, they get high media exposure, bankers are willing to extend credit, paper profits give them social standing, investment bankers and brokers chase them, and they become 'page three' regulars. This intoxication makes them glued to the stock price and they are always looking at keeping the stock price high. The operator handles the job. This operator can be an individual, a broker, or another investment banker. The game is, again, high market capitalization.

Investors need to be wary of such high PE stocks in spite of all the operators recommending the same. The technology boom had many such stories, like the K10 stocks which eroded investor wealth enormously. Every bull market has such manipulators, which we realize only after the bust. For investors, it is important to understand that some high market capitalization stocks command high PEs and investing in them is a sure way of taking a hit on the returns.

10.4.4 Herding

Why do the above manipulations succeed? Investors are always aware of such happenings but they invariably fall prey to them. It is the tendency of investors to go with the popular thinking. It is like following the herd. If everyone is doing something, even if it is wrong, it will become right eventually. The solace is in numbers. This following creates reflexivity in the stocks and they go up, reinforcing the reflexivity. It becomes self-professing and investors start believing in the rise, thinking it is for real. The initial profits make each one of them a salesman for the stock and this creates a bigger herd chasing it. This is how, in a bull market, the herd mentality creates a demand for a stock, which leads to a surge in its market capitalization. The stock can thus enter the index.

10.5 WHAT IS INDEX INVESTING?

The most popular and the oldest index is the BSE Sensex, which is regarded as the barometer of the Indian stock market. It is a basket of 30 stocks representing various sectors, on the Bombay Stock Exchange. These companies account for around one-fifth of the market capitalization of the BSE. The Sensex is calculated on the basis of free-float market capitalization, which is a globally-accepted method. Its base value is 100 and the base year is 1978–79.

The guidelines for a stock to find its way into the Sensex are as follows.

- **Listing History**

The stock should have a listing history of at least three months at the BSE. Exceptions may be considered if full market capitalization of a newly-listed company ranks among the top 10 in the list of BSE stocks. In case a company is listed as a result of a merger or demerger or amalgamation, a minimum listing history is not required.

- **Trading Frequency**

The stock should have been traded on each and every trading day in the last three months. Exceptions can be made for extreme reasons like stock suspension.

- **Fiscal Ranks**

The stock should figure in the top 100 companies listed by final rank. The final rank is arrived at by assigning 75% weightage to the rank on the basis of three-month average full market capitalization and 25% weightage to the liquidity rank based on three-month average daily turnover and three-month average impact cost.

- **Market Capitalization Weightage**

The weightage of each stock in the Sensex, based on three-month average free-float market capitalization, should be at least 0.5% of the index.

- **Industry Representation**

Stock selection would generally take into account a balanced representation of the listed companies in the universe of BSE.

- **Track Record**

In the opinion of the Committee appointed by the stock exchange for this, the company should have an acceptable track record.

On careful analysis of the above factors, we can see that market capitalization has been given maximum importance. Market capitalization is calculated by multiplying the number of shares issued with the current market price of the stock. Thus, in bullish times there are high chances of companies from the current hot sectors finding a place in the index.

From the above list, the first and the foremost factor clearly states that, even if the company is not listed for more than three months, should its full market capitalization rank in the top 10 in BSE, the stock shall be added to the index. The third point states that the stock should be in the top 100 companies listed by final rank. To calculate the rank, 75% weightage is given to the average three-month market capitalization. Finally, the three-month average free float market capitalization of the stock should be 0.5% of the index. All these factors mean that larger the market capitalization, the better the chances of finding a place in the index. Quality of management, sustainability of business model, earnings potential and growth, which usually are important factors when one judges a company, do not play any significant part. This means a newly listed, hyped-up company with an overvalued share price will find a place in the index, while a well-managed, dividend-paying company with a sustainable business model may not make it to the index if it does not have a large enough market capitalization. Moreover, such companies may be removed from the index if other large capitalization company comes. This is what happened when Tata Power—a consistent dividend-paying company, well-managed and with a sustainable business model—was replaced by Reliance Communications, which had a huge market capitalization but no track record. But telecommunications was a hot sector. Companies in the currently favored sectors have an easy chance to get in the Sensex. 'Hot sector' is generally a sector witnessing rapid growth. For instance, during the IT boom, Satyam Computers found itself in the Sensex at the cost of Tata Chemicals.

Index-based investing is merely investing in the stocks which form the index. It includes buying or holding all the stocks in the index in the same proportions as the index. It also requires buying a stock when it is added to the index and selling it when it is removed. It is assumed that the market forces aid creative destruction and so the index is representative of dynamic firms only. It would be a good idea if such a thing could be done. But we do not exist in efficient markets nor do investors make rational decisions. It is because of the behavioral anomalies of investors that we will never be able to distinguish between the performers and the laggards beforehand. It will always be in hindsight.

To satisfy the demand and the appetite of big institutional investors, the focus shifts to size and depth, that is, the liquidity in the stocks. Qualitative standards give way to quantitative standards.

That is how index investing was born— yet another invention of the financial markets.

10.6 WHY DO INVESTORS GO FOR INDEX INVESTING?

In behavioral finance, we have this concept of "heuristics". It is the shortcut the brain takes to process information. It does not process the full information and this leads to certain biases. Or, in other words, investors take their decisions by following a set line of thinking or a rule of thumb. Index investing is also a heuristic.

Stock markets the world over are gaining prominence, and investing has become a must for retail as well as institutional investors. Rightly so, as equities have been rewarding investors very handsomely over the last three years. Investing is a difficult game and there are a very few seasoned investors in the world who have done exceedingly well in the markets. One of them is the most admired Mr. Warren Buffet. It requires not only intelligence but also the emotional strength to be a good investor. Fortunately, Warren Buffet has both these traits.

Investing requires hard work and discipline. It is the nature of human beings to go for short cuts. If stock investing is so difficult and there are only a few successful investors is it possible to earn higher returns by passively investing in to an index? I wish money-making was that simple.

But most of the institutional investors also believe in, as well as practice, index investing. One reason for doing this is their suffering from the availability bias. The available information on index investing as a safe form of investing is so strong that they have started believing it to be a fact. Why is it so? Because there is no benchmark to judge it against.

Moreover, the big fund houses create this availability heuristic by offering index funds with very low fees. Every fund house would have an index fund and their advertising campaigns create a strong information flow on the virtues of index investing. If everyone is talking about it, it has to be good. Investors make decisions based on this most recent recall value. Moreover, they also suffer from affect heuristic; they rely on memory or instinct without a formal valuation analysis.

The most important lesson I have learned is that stock returns soar when the price paid for a stock is much less than the built-in expectations of the investors. In other words, neglected and out-of-favor companies give better long-term returns than the hot favorites. Index investing is again buying hot favorites.

How can investors be better off investing in the index? Let us see what hard core evidence suggests.

10.7 EVIDENCE SUGGESTS THE CONTRARY

10.7.1 The Study

The study we conducted includes comparing the returns when a stock is added to the index with the returns from the stock it replaced. It is assumed that 100 shares of both these stocks are bought at the then prevailing market prices and held until the incoming stock moves out of the index. During the holding period, any dividend is reinvested in the respective stocks and rights issues, if any, are subscribed to. The return is calculated from the day the replacement takes place.

For instance, the first replacement in the Sensex was on 1st April 1982 when Zenith Ltd.—which had a larger market capitalization, being in the steel sector, a very hot sector at the time—replaced Bharat Forge Ltd. One hundred shares of each of these companies are bought at the respective market prices. The yearly dividend is reinvested and rights issues are subscribed. Over the next decade, the fortunes of the respective industries and the companies changed. On 3rd August 1992, Bharat Forge in turn replaced Zenith, as Zenith lost favor and its market capitalization suffered. The returns of Bharat Forge from 1982 to 1992 are 50.5%, and returns from Zenith over the same period are 9.8%. This means that if you had bought 100 shares of Bharat Forge at Rs.28.50 per share on 1st April 1982, you would have 740 shares at Rs. 240 per share on 3rd August 1992, after adjusting for dividends, bonus and rights issues. Investment of Rs. 2,850 in Bharat Forge has grown to Rs. 1,77,600 in 10 years. At the same time, 100 share of Zenith have grown to 354 shares, and the price per share dropped from Rs. 45 to Rs. 33.50 during the same period (Table 10.1).

Table 10.1 Comparison of Returns from Bharat Forge and Zenith Ltd.

	Bharat Forge Ltd.			Zenith Ltd.		
Date	Number of Shares	Price per Share	Total Invest-ment	Number of Shares	Price per Share	Total Invest-ment
01 April 1982	100	28.5	2,850	100	45	4,500
03 August 1992	740	240	1,77,600	354	33.5	11,859
Returns (%)		50.5%			9.8%	

In 1986, Peico (Philips India), Voltas, Premier Auto and GE Shipping replaced Asian Cables, Bombay Burmah, Crompton Greaves and Scindia, respectively. Peico, Voltas and Premier Auto remained in the index till 1996. A comparative analysis of these three companies vis-à-vis Asian Cables, Bombay Burmah and Crompton Greaves shows that Peico and Asian Cables have given returns of 5.20% and -3.13%, respectively; Voltas and Bombay Burmah gave 12.83% and 26.24%, respectively; and Premier Auto and Crompton Greaves gave 9.23% and 33.1%, respectively. GE Shipping moved out in 1998 and its return for 12 years was 22.84%, against 10.58% for Scindia. Peico has outperformed the outgoing Asian Cables by a thin margin. However, GE Shipping (the newcomer) did exceedingly well over the replaced Scindia. The outgoing stocks—Bombay Burmah and Crompton Greaves—did much better than the incoming stocks—Voltas and Premier Auto.

The year 1996 witnessed the maximum number of replacements in the Index, with 15 companies being replaced in that year. Bharat Forge, which came back in the index in 1992, replacing Zenith Ltd., was out in 1996, making way for Bajaj Auto. In 1996, with a market price of Rs. 972.50 and paid-up capital of Rs.79.59 crores, Bajaj Auto's market capitalization stood at Rs. 7,740 crores, compared to a market capitalization of Rs. 482 crores for Bharat Forge. The market capitalization factor got Bajaj Auto in the index. However, an investor who is guided by the conventional thinking that entrants to the index are better companies, would have sold Bharat Forge and bought Bajaj

Auto. In so doing, he would have lost out on his returns. Bajaj Auto continued to be in the index till 31 December 2005. In this ten-year period, Bharat Forge returned 38.87% whereas Bajaj Auto returned a measly 15.20%; that is, less than half of Bharat Forge.

Bombay Dyeing was replaced by BHEL. Bombay Dyeing returned 13.16% as against 28.19% for BHEL. Textiles was a dying industry, and BHEL was a PSU with a strong engineering presence in the market. Similarly, BSES (now Reliance Energy), a company representing the promising new power sector, replaced Ceat Tyres to return 15.85%, as compared to 2.54% returns from the outgoing stocks, Ceat. Fundamentals played their part in both these scenarios.

From Table 10.2, it is seen that, out of 15 replacements in 1996, six outgoingstocks have outperformed the incoming stocks with a success rate of 40%.

Table 10.2 Comparative Performance of Outgoing and Incoming Stocks in 1996

Date of Replacement	Remained till	Outgoing Stocks	Returns of Outgoing Stocks (%)	Incoming Stocks	Returns of Incoming Stocks (%)
19-08-1996	30-12-2005	Peico, Philips	2.34	Ranbaxy Lab	17.2
19-08-1996	16-11-1998	Ballarpur Industries	-41.98	Arvind Mills	-41.23
19-08-1996	30-12-2005	Bharat Forge	38.87	Bajaj Auto	15.2
19-08-1996	30-12-2005	Bombay Dyeing	13.16	BHEL	28.19
19-08-1996	10-04-2000	Voltas	36.96	Tata Chemicals	-26.71
19-08-1996	30-12-2005	Ceat Ltd	2.54	BSES (Reliance Energy)	15.85
19-08-1996	10-11-2003	Century Textiles	-5.23	Colgate	-5.58
19-08-1996	30-12-2005	Premier Auto	-15.77	State Bank of India	16.37

(Contd.)

Table 10.2 (Contd.)

Date of Replacement	Remained till	Outgoing Stocks	Returns of Outgoing Stocks (%)	Incoming Stocks	Returns of Incoming Stocks (%)
19-08-1996	30-12-2005	GSFC	4.04	Guj. Ambuja Cement	18.67
19-08-1996	06-06-2005	Hindustan Motors	17.51	HPCL	-23.12
19-08-1996	31-05-2002	Indian Organics	10.87	ICICI Bank Ltd	20.37
19-08-1996	10-04-2000	Indian Rayon	-30.91	IDBI Bank	-19.36
19-08-1996	16-11-1998	Kirloskar Cummins	-10.66	IPCL	-29.09
19-08-1996	27-09-2004	Mukund	-30.33	MTNL	-2.24
19-08-1996	16-11-1998	Siemens	-39.84	SAIL	-47.71

In the late 1990s, IT stocks were hot favorites of the market. Any company with a "tech" or a "dot com" attached to its name caught the attention of the masses. Many IT stocks started replacing old economy stocks in the index. The weightage of IT stocks in the index reached a high of over 25% during that time.

In 2000, Tata Chemicals, an old economy company, was replaced by Satyam Computers. Satyam remained in the index until December 2005. Tata Chemicals was trading at Rs.53.35 per share and Satyam at Rs.3,907.35 the day it entered the index. Had one bought 100 shares of each company and held on till 31 December 2005, one would be holding 160 shares of Tata Chemicals and 527 shares of Satyam.

Table 10.3 Comparison of Returns from Tata Chemicals and Satyam

	TATA Chemicals			Satyam		
Date	**Number of Shares**	**Price per Share**	**Total Invest-ment**	**Number of Shares**	**Price per Share**	**Total Invest-ment**
10 April 2000	100	53.35	5335	100	3907.35	390735

(Contd.)

Table 10.3 (Contd.)

	TATA Chemicals			Satyam		
Date	Number of Shares	Price per Share	Total Invest-ment	Number of Shares	Price per Share	Total Invest-ment
31 December 2005	160	234.65	37492.12	527	737.8	388517
Returns (%)		31.47			-0.10	

Satyam's returns have been abysmally low, despite a five-fold increase in the number of shares, from 100 to 527 shares. Returns suffered because Satyam was a hyped stock and people paid a higher price for it on that account.

Dr Reddy, Zee Telefilms, Hero Honda, ONGC and Maruti Udyog were hot stocks when they entered the index. Table 10.4 tells the story.

Table 10.4 Comparison of Returns between Stocks that Exited and Entered the Index

Date of Replace-ment	Remained till	Outgoing Stocks	Returns of Outgoing Stocks (%)	Incoming Stocks	Returns of Incoming Stocks (%)
10-04-2000	30-12-2005	IBDI	35.14	Dr. Reddy	3.79
10-04-2000	06-06-2005	Tata Power	46.57	Zee Telefilms	-30.18
07-01-2002	30-12-2005	M & M	123.78	Hero Honda Motors	37.43
10-11-2003	30-12-2005	Glaxo India	173.96	ONGC	37.28
19-05-2004	30-12-2005	L & T	147.75	Maruti Udyog Ltd.	21.86

It is interesting to note that, out of the above five replacements three outgoing stocks have returned in excess of 100%—way above returns from the incoming stocks. These three stocks, viz., M&M, Glaxo and L&T were, undoubtedly, dark horses. I do not doubt the fundamentals of Hero Honda, ONGC and Maruti; but their returns are insignificant when compared to the outgoing firms. Their returns took a beating because investors paid a high price for them, as they were considered hot stocks. As against this, the outgoing stocks lost favor with the markets and, thus, lost value. But their business models were unchanged, and the market thus offered an opportunity to buy good businesses at a good price. Investors who bought these stocks earned phenomenal returns because they bought good businesses at a bargain price. The returns of IDBI and Tata Power are also phenomenal when compared to the incoming stocks, Dr Reddy and Zee Telefilms.

Table 10.5 shows all the replacements in the BSE Sensex from 1979, along with the returns up to 2005.

10.7.2 BSE Sensex

There were 42 replacements in the BSE Sensex from 1979 to 2005. Out of these, 21 laggard stocks have outperformed the replaced stocks, thus giving a success rate of 50%. The Sensex, which follows free float market capitalization, a globally recognized practice, has not aided the concept of creative destruction for which it is meant. Investors who blindly follow this strategy need to rethink.

10.7.3 A Second Study

We went a step further in our analysis to find the strengths and weaknesses of index investing, and conducted another study.

1. Make a portfolio of laggard and replaced stocks
2. When a stock is moved out, it enters the laggard portfolio and the new stock enters the replaced stock portfolio
3. Invest Rs.10,000 in each of the laggard and the replaced stock portfolios on the date of shake-up, and hold the investment until 31 December 2005. In cases where a company is delisted before 31 December 2005, the returns are calculated as on the last day of trading for making that comparison.
4. Calculate the respective returns up to 31 December 2005, and find the total value of the portfolio.

Table 10.5 Returns from Rs.10,000 Invested in Outgoing and Incoming Sensex Stocks

Date of Replacement	Outgoing Stocks	Returns of Laggards (%)	Value Realized in 2005 (Rs.)	Replaced Stocks	Returns of Replaced Stocks (%)	Value Realized in 2005 (Rs.)
01-04-1982	Bharat Forge	29.93	5037727	Zenith Ltd	2.2	16772
01-01-1986	Asian Cables	2.95	19891	Peico, Philips	3.47	19788
01-01-1986	Bombay Burmah	17.19	238989	Voltas	23.55	688034
01-01-1986	Crompton Greaves	23.14	643763	Premier Auto	3.45	19712
01-01-1986	SCI India	-8.77	1594	GE Shipping	26.58	1117232
03-08-1992	Zenith	-11.58	1918	Bharat Forge	24.07	180582
19-08-1996	Peico, Philips	2.34	12420	Ranbaxy Lab	17.2	44243
19-08-1996	Ballarpur Industries	7.1	19016	Arvind Mills	4.39	14957
19-08-1996	Bharat Forge	38.87	216881	Bajaj Auto	15.2	37653
19-08-1996	Bombay Dyeing	13.16	31848	BHEL	28.19	102465
19-08-1996	Voltas	36.96	190486.72	Tata Chemicals	9.12	22654
19-08-1996	Ceat Ltd	2.54	12649	BSES	15.85	39691

(Contd.)

Table 10.5 (Contd.)

Date of Replacement	Outgoing Stocks	Returns of Laggards (%)	Value Realized in 2005 (Rs.)	Replaced Stocks	Returns of Replaced Stocks (%)	Value Realized in 2005 (Rs.)
19-08-1996	Century Textiles	7.35	19436	Colgate	3.91	14324
19-08-1996	Premier Auto	-0.92	9170	State Bank of India	16.37	41392
19-08-1996	GSFC	8.6	21663	Guj. Ambuja Cement	18.67	49723
19-08-1996	Hindustan Motors	14.57	35767	HPCL	9.36	23125
19-08-1996	Indian Organics	18.06	47379	ICICI Bank Ltd	22.54	67166
19-08-1996	Indian Rayon	14.07	34331	IDBI Bank	10.48	25442
19-08-1996	Kirloskar Cummins	10.49	25464	IPCL	10.59	25680
19-08-1996	Mukund	9.97	24363	MTNL	-0.13	9878
19-08-1996	Siemens	24.23	76364	SAIL	9.43	23264
16-11-1998	Arvind Mills	23.21	44253	Castrol	1.21	10894
16-11-1998	IPCL	26.94	54732	NIIT	-13.16	3658
16-11-1998	GE 50. Shipping	50.27	182136	Infosys Technologies	53.5	211940
16-11-1998	SAIL	40.64	113612	Novartis	6.81	15991

(Contd.)

Table 10.5 (Contd.)

Date of Replacement	Outgoing Stocks	Returns of Laggards (%)	Value Realized in 2005 (Rs.)	Replaced Stocks	Returns of Replaced Stocks (%)	Value Realized in 2005 (Rs.)
10-04-2000	Tata Chemicals	31.47	47907	Satyam Computers	-0.1	9942
10-04-2000	Indian Hotels	32.14	49332	Reliance Petroleum	5.92	13900
10-04-2000	IDBI	35.14	56088	Dr. Reddy	3.79	12373
10-04-2000	Tata Power	44.48	82236	Zee Telefilms	-27.01	1648
08-01-2001	Novartis	5.86	13277	Cipla Ltd.	15.95	20890
07-01-2002	NIIT	4.71	12010	HCL Technologies	18.34	19548
07-01-2002	M & M	123.78	246931	Hero Honda Motors	37.43	35455
10-08-2002	Reliance Petroleum	51.25	37971	HDFC Ltd.	56.69	42554
10-11-2003	Castrol	-21.11	6020	Bharti Televentures	93.65	41128
10-11-2003	Colgate	42.73	21410	HDFC Ltd.	48.27	23227
10-11-2003	Glaxo India	173.96	86403	ONGC	37.28	19698
10-11-2003	HCL Technologies	52	24496	Tata Power	29.49	17384
10-11-2003	Nestle Ltd.	31	17820	Wipro Ltd.	38.5	20075

(Contd.)

Table 10.5 (Contd.)

Date of Replacement	Outgoing Stocks	Returns of Laggards (%)	Value Realized in 2005 (Rs.)	Replaced Stocks	Returns of Replaced Stocks (%)	Value Realized in 2005 (Rs.)
19-04-2004	L & T	147.75	43340	Maruti Udyog Ltd.	21.86	13765
27-09-2004	MTNL	14.46	11851	L & T	84.5	21602
06-06-2005	HPCL	15.55	10854	NTPC	63.87	13232
06-06-2005	Zee Telefilms	-9.83	9430	TCS	66.57	13355
Total			78,91,232			31,66,054

It can be seen that, of the 42 replacements, 21 laggards have outperformed the incoming stocks and *vice versa*, giving a success rate of 50%. In the laggard portfolio, however, an investment of Rs.4,20,000 has grown to Rs. 78,91,232, whereas, in the replaced stocks portfolio a similar investment of Rs. 4,20,000 has grown to just Rs. 31,66,054. This is a phenomenal difference.

When a stock is announced to be a new entrant to the Sensex, it attracts investors and its price starts going up. There are some institutional investors who start rebalancing their portfolios to mirror the index. Thus, they sell outgoing stocks and buy the incoming ones. As the announcement about the replacement is made in advance by the stock exchanges, there is a lot of activity in the counters prior to stocks entering or exiting the index. Outgoing stocks are subject to unfavorable reaction from the investors, whereas the incoming stocks gain in value as they are sought by investors. These incoming stocks enter the index at a much higher valuation and, having a weightage in the index, the index also goes up. You thus pay a higher price for the stock when it enters the index, and at the same time, if you buy the index, you end up paying a higher price for it. When one pays a higher price one's returns always suffer in the long run. This is also evident from the above portfolios of the laggards and the newcomers (Table 10.5).

Although there is a 50% success rate, the returns from the laggards are phenomenally high as compared to the newcomers. These higher returns are a function of capitalizing on crowd psychology.

10.7.4 NSE Nifty

Startled by the above revelation, we applied the same process for examining the replacements made in Nifty. Table 10.6 shows the results that can be expected by investing Rs.10,000 in each of the stocks involved in the transfer, and staying invested until December 31, 2005. In some cases, where a stock has been delisted before December 31, 2005, the returns for that set of shake-ups has been calculated as on the last day of trading for the delisted stock.

From Table 10.6 we can see that, in 22 out of 35 instances, the laggards have generated better annualized returns than their

Table 10.6 Returns from Rs.10,000 Invested in Outgoing and Incoming Nifty Stocks

Date of Replacement	Laggard	Returns of Laggard Stocks (%)	Value Realized in 2005 (Rs.)	Replaced Stocks	Returns of Replaced Stocks	Value Realized in 2005 (Rs.)
18-Sep-96	APOLLO TYRE	19	28,096	EI HOTEL	7%	16,115
18-Sep-96	INDAL	1	10,380	GLAXO	20%	24,678
18-Sep-96	CHAMBAL FERT	28	35,820	ABB	24%	32,095
18-Sep-96	HERO HONDA	451	4,29,329	ASIAN PAINT	34%	41,796
18-Sep-96	MADRAS REFN	56	62,311	M&M	26%	33,733
18-Sep-96	NAGAR FERT	5	14,410	NESTLE	41%	47,941
14-May-97	DR REDDY	94	91,571	HIND PETRO	7%	16,400
24-Dec-97	ESSAR GUJ	21	26,688	BPCL	22%	27,842
07-Oct-98	ANDRA VALLY	-2	8,904	CIPLA	32%	33,337
07-Oct-98	THERMAX	246	1,88,124	BANK INDIA	89%	74,661
07-Oct-98	ASHOK LEY	189	1,46,566	HERO HONDA	111%	90,008
07-Oct-98	MRPL	-1	9,468	P&G	17%	22,299

(Contd.)

Table 10.6 (Contd.)

Date of Replacement	Laggard	Returns of Laggard Stocks (%)	Value Realized in 2005 (Rs.)	Replaced Stocks	Returns of Replaced Stocks	Value Realized in 2005 (Rs.)
07-Oct-98	BPCL	54	48,913	INFOSYS TECH	263%	2,00,520
26-May-99	ARVIND MILLS	29	28,912	DR REDDY	20%	23,472
26-May-99	GE SHIPPING	237	1,66,820	NOVARTIS	-4%	7,634
26-May-99	REL CAPITAL	13	14,848	RECK COLMAN	-14%	5,277
08-Sep-99	IFCI	-3	8,395	BRITANNIA	7%	14,283
08-Sep-99	IND RAYON	142	99,453	SATYAM COMP	51%	42,015
24-May-00	EI HOTEL	85	57,708	HCL-INSYS	65%	46,196
24-May-00	IDBI	75	51,837	ZEE TELE	-9%	4,759
01-Sep-00	BANK OF INDIA	106	66,667	DIGITAL EQP	9%	14,777
17-Jan-02	HCL-INSYS	317	135424	SUN PHARMA	82%	42394
17-Jan-02	COCHIN REFN	198	88,409	WIPRO	15%	15,979
25-Jan-02	RECK COLMAN	15	15,805	ICICI BANK	132%	62,072
28-Oct-02	ASIAN PAINT	110	44,941	HCL TECH	83%	36,423

(Contd.)

Table 10.6 (Contd.)

Date of Replacement	Laggard	Returns of Laggard Stocks (%)	Value Realized in 2005 (Rs.)	Replaced Stocks	Returns of Replaced Stocks	Value Realized in 2005 (Rs.)
28-Oct-02	P&G	100	41,650	BPCL	51%	26,218
02-May-03	NOVARTIND	64	27,124	GAIL	86%	32,877
02-May-03	CASTROL	14	13,624	NATIONAL UM	71%	29,014
04-Aug-03	NESTLE	28	16,852	SAIL	52%	22,453
01-Mar-04	GSKCONS	66	22,131	BHARTI	61%	21,216
01-Mar-04	NIIT	-1	9,822	MARUTI	24%	14,361
24-May-04	L&T	196	41,475	PNB	45%	17,255
10-Dec-04	BRITANNIA	67	17,094	L&T	111%	21,707
25-Feb-05	IND HOTEL	83	16,999	TCS	30%	12,581
26-Sep-05	COLGATE	37	10,962	JET AIRWAYS	10%	10,257
Total			**20,97,533**			**11,84,641**

replacements. In terms of total portfolio size, the laggards portfolio has turned Rs. 3,50,000 invested in 35 stocks, which were taken out of the index, into Rs. 20,97,533. On the other hand, the Rs. 3,50,000 invested in the 35 stocks that were introduced into the NSE Nifty, only managed to convert Rs. 3,50,000 into Rs. 11,84,641—a huge difference of Rs. 9,12,892.

The above study highlights the fact that an investor is bound to lose out on his returns when he is chasing a fancy. Chasing the index is akin to buying what others are buying, and ending up paying a higher price. Successful investing is all about buying what others are selling and selling what others are buying. In so doing one gets a better selling price and one purchases at a bargain price. Simply put, it generates healthy returns. You may call it contrarian investing or value investing.

10.8 LESSONS FOR INVESTORS

10.8.1 Avoid the Bait

Fund houses and their asset management companies come out with index funds and tempt the investors with lower fees. I wish life were so simple that you just pick up a basket of stocks and then just wait for the market to go on rewarding you. The goal of fund houses is to garner as much as money as possible. It is all about huge assets under management and the fees they can charge on it. Moreover, for them there is no benchmark to judge their performance. The index is representative of the market, and if the market goes down, so will the index. There is authority without responsibility. We are in a competitive world and this form of passive investing is definitely an idea whose time has gone. But its marketability is very strong because it is a very good and an effective way to exploit the behavioral bias of loss-aversion amongst investors.

Lower fees should not be the attraction to buy into index funds. Do we choose our doctor depending on the fees he charges? Definitely no. Our health is more important than his fees. Similarly, our wealth and its growth are more important than the measly fees we try to save.

10.8.2 Availability Bias

All the available information on index investing is so positive that investors assume it to be right. In the absence of a benchmark, we do not know whether index investing has worked or not. Moreover, the stock markets have been volatile and speculators have made and lost fortunes. They lost, not because equity as an investing class is bad, but they lost due to their greed and irrational behavior. This information is so vivid amongst investors as every bull and bear market has these examples. Investing and making returns is all about the price one pays for the value one receives.

10.8.3 Be Courageous

It just requires a little courage to go against the crowd and act in a contrarian way. Over time, it becomes a habit as one's self-esteem and confidence grow. Evidence has shown that going against the popular thinking pays in the long run. Have the courage to act on this approach. There are a lot of irrational people around willing to give you good opportunities in the market. Bide your time and you will be successful.

10.8.4 Do Your Own De-indexing

Investing is all about buying a stock with least investor expectations. You find such stocks when they go out of the index. We have shown you the evidence that such stocks do better for investor returns in the long run. Do a little homework and choose such good stocks that are moving out of the index. Or, if you do not want to do that, just buy the stocks moved out of the index and make your portfolio. We have shown how the laggards have performed. Evidence is with you. You need the courage to go against the herd. That is the test of investing success. Your courage needs to be borne out of your conviction.

10.9 CONCLUSION

Knowledge is something that changes by the end of the week. It is the trends that tell us a lot. Trends matter the most as they help us to know the direction and give us evidence. This is what we have done in the above studies.

Index investing is in no way better than active investing. On the contrary, looking at the difference in the returns between the laggards and the replaced stock portfolios it is safe to conclude that following the contrarian path in indexing works better. Call it "De-Indexing" if you like.

Ultimately, investor returns are a function of the price you pay for a stock that has the least inbuilt investor expectations. The ability to control your emotions and resist the pull of the crowd is your way to become a successful investor. Are you able to challenge the popular thinking? Go ahead. It is like taking the road least traveled. It is only after years of perseverance that you will know that it made all the difference.

ELEVEN 11

BUBBLE TRAP

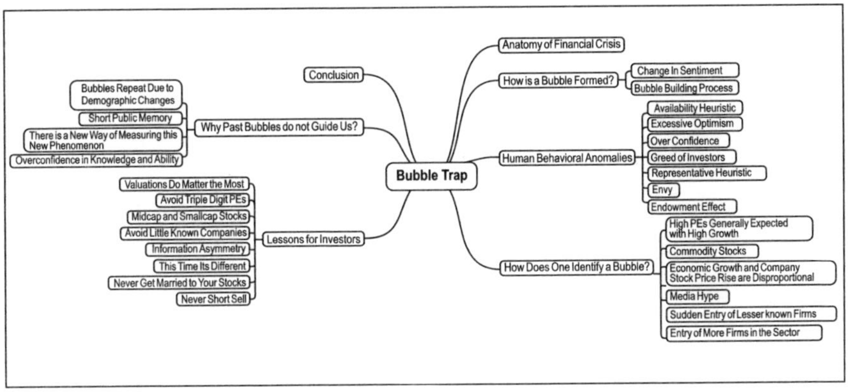

11.1 ANATOMY OF FINANCIAL CRISIS

About a century and a half ago, the philosopher, Santayana observed that those who do not learn from history are condemned to repeat it. Speculative excesses, referred to concisely as bubble or mania, and contraction from such excesses in the form of crash, crisis or panic, can be shown as, if not inevitable, at least historically common. It appears that the financial community as a whole does not seem to learn from the previous mistakes and continues to repeat these mistakes, in different forms, leading to the same painful end—financial crisis. The reason for this infrequent spurt of irrationality exhibited by otherwise rationally-acting crowds, will be discussed in this chapter.

Excessive optimism and overconfidence are the main causes of bubbles.

The word 'bubble' is used to connote a situation where people have lost touch with reality. In an economic sense, where it is assumed that participants strive towards their economic well-being and act as rational beings, is it appropriate to pronounce that a crowd, the sum of its individuals, can infrequently but inevitably lead to mass hysteria? If history is any guide, then mass hysteria, running contrary to economic belief, is real and not a myth. The IT bubble from the end of the last century and the more recent real estate and infrastructure bubbles provide interesting examples for our purpose.

In the light of evidence supporting the prevalence of manias in the financial world, it would be useful to understand the factors that lead to such a state of mass hysteria.

Excessive optimism and overconfidence are the main causes of bubbles. In such times, it is important that investors avoid getting into the bubble trap. There could be a bubble-like situation in the whole market, or there could be one in a sector as we witnessed in the internet bubble during 1999–2000. There could be a bubble in a particular stock. This could be due to the sector doing well as we saw in the case of the power and real estate sectors boom, where we saw stocks of Reliance Energy and India Bulls Real Estate hitting the roof. A bubble in a particular stock could also be due to some operator rigging, as we saw in the stock of Mazda Leasing during the Harshad Mehta boom in 1992–1993.

Investors need to avoid this bubble trap, and to do so, they need to understand what it takes to make a bubble. What sort of environment is conducive for bubble formation?

11.2 HOW IS A BUBBLE FORMED?

A bubble can only be formed when there are many greedy investors who are willing to allow someone to exploit their greed. This crowd goes on increasing in size, as other greedy investors join the bandwagon out of envy. This has a snowballing effect, leading to creation of an illusion in the form of a bubble.

11.2.1 Rational Individual vs. Crowd Psychology

One of the most important factors leading rational individuals, on being part of the crowd, to mass hysteria is that the underlying reason for the start of the optimistic wave is always a valid one. For example, the notion that proliferation of internet and IT products is going to change the way businesses operate was a valid one. Just that "any good idea taken too far leads to bad result" was in play here.

> **Investing is all about earning a reasonable rate of return on one's investment and that cannot happen if the company does not make profits.**

Similarly, the India growth story is here to stay and there will be a continuing demand for building infrastructure. Growth would help the real estate sector, and the increase in disposable incomes would lead to a spurt in demand for a host of other industries. The stock markets have a tendency to extrapolate a good idea too far, and this result in excesses.

In essence, manias are not castles *entirely* built on air, but have foundations (to make participants confident of better expectations and prospects from the future) upon which, instead of the initial capacity to support a 10-storey building, people in their optimism, bred on ignorance and the belief that 'trend is destiny', end up constructing a 20-storey building, leading to a weaker foundation for the whole structure which, sooner or later, succumbs under its own weight.

So, individuals who have every reason to be upbeat about the prospects and act as totally rational individuals, lose their composure as the outcomes of initial participants validate the assumption. This triggers the cycle of speculation from seeking consistent interest rates on capital, as in an investment, to going after additional gains in the form of capital appreciation.

11.2.2 Bandwagon Effect

> Every new bubble has a new story justifying how this time this is very different from the past bubble. However, the excesses are the same.

In the present context, after the initial hypothesis, of a shift in expectation is validated by a spurt in valuation, a whole new set of individuals is attracted towards the investment avenue. These investors might not be able to experience the same sort of success as the previous ones; but their success, relatively better than other opportunities, still validates the original hypothesis and attracts a new set of individuals, who are also drawn by envy of the success of their counterparts.

But with every new participant visiting the market place to reap the benefits from a finite source of wealth creation (which is what enterprises can do), the benefits flowing towards the incoming participant decreases. This is where the foundation of optimism deviates from economic reality to a point where optimism surrounds the objects of speculation; i.e., land, stocks, IPOs, junk bonds, etc. and becomes a self-sustaining mechanism until it eventually explodes.

11.2.3 Change in Sentiment

Sentiment plays an important role in the formation of a bubble. Along with sentiment, perception also changes. This new scenario is then extrapolated too much into the future. A change in the economic growth of a country, a change in the outlook of a sector, or a change in the fortunes of a company can be extrapolated to such an extent that irrational projections are expected to be real and excesses are committed based on these expectations.

The media play a very important role in the formation of a bubble. Through the media, information, rumors and stories make their way to the people. The media's job is to make all the current hot information available to the investors. Hence, when the economy is showing signs of improving, the media are quick to report it. Since that happens to be the recent hot topic, the media allocate a lot of time slot for such news. This is in the form of interviews with leading experts in the field, government officials, stock market experts' comments on the same, talk shows, round table discussions, and so on. The same procedure follows when there is an upswing in a sector or some great changes in the fortunes of a company. The current topics are so highlighted that they become the fads and fancies of the market. This, again, creates a larger following and leads to a bubble-like situation, with investor expectations running high. Stock market news dominates the TV channels 24 hours a day, and news providers become stock market advisors. Special shows and interviews with experts and analysts lure investors' eyeballs. An increase in advertisement demand further increases the frequency of such stock market programs, which in turn leads to more stock market tips and analysis.

The world over, stock markets are the barometer of the financial health of a country.

The lure of quick money invites more players to the market. Greed dominates and each one wants a piece of the pie faster than the neighbor. This results in the prices of stocks going up, as there are more buyers than sellers.

Greedy management looks at such opportunities to capitalize on the greed of the investors. Great expansion plans are laid out and huge resources get mobilized from the investors on the promise of making huge returns. IPOs hit the markets to take advantage of investor greed. These come with optimistic projections and thus dreams are sold to the investors. Greed again drives investor appetite for such offerings.

The markets need a pied piper to draw this huge crowd of investors. Such pied pipers come in the form of unscrupulous management, investment bankers, operators, brokers who weave vivid stories of growth and profit-making opportunities. They sell dreams of growth stocks, which cannot be valued by traditional valuation models. Investors chase such opportunities and, eventually, end up paying crazy valuations for such dream stocks.

Every government likes a bull market, as it is a sign of a growing economy. So, when stock market bubbles are being built up, the government is skeptical of pricking them, lest the sentiments turn negative and affect stock prices. Since identifying a bubble is difficult, the government's decision-making on it is paralyzed. By doing nothing, it encourages the bubble to be built up. Moreover, the feel-good factor is too much of an incentive to do nothing to check the bubble.

11.2.4 Bubble-Building Process

Bubbles usually form after long periods of financial prosperity and continuous flow of positive news. This usually starts with the news of the economy doing well and the GDP growth figures showing an upward trend. The year 2003 marked the end of the long bear market, when the BSE Sensex had touched a low of around 2,800, as we entered a phase of good economic growth. The liberalization process was bearing fruit. The economy was expanding quarter to quarter, but there was subdued optimism. The stock markets started going up; but, at every rise, investors sold. The memory of the long bearish market was very strong. The investors were so loss-averse that they sold at every rise. However, the economy was still growing, and the trend continued. This gave confidence to the investors and money started pouring into the stock markets. The trend turned bullish, as more and more investors entered the markets, and the stock prices started spiraling. Economic growth was a pointer to huge investments in infrastructure.

When investments start yielding profits due to a surge in the stock prices, investors tend to relate the success to their knowledge and ability.

With the positives on the economy being strong, we also had certain sectors benefitting from the improvement in the economy. Since the focus was on building a strong infrastructure, sectors like construction, power, engineering, and real estate attracted investor attention. These sectors became the market fancy and investors started chasing companies in these sectors. Investor expectations in these companies were so high that they were willing to pay higher prices to own stocks. The PEs of such companies started going up. However, since the demand was more than the supply the high PEs did not matter to the investors.

Internationally, commodity prices started rising and this gave a fillip to various commodity stocks in steel, aluminum, copper and cement. This also created a commodities boom scenario and stocks in the commodity sector started shooting up. This upward trend continued, and stocks also sustained their upward trend.

Overall, the Sensex went up from around 2,800 in 2003 to around 21,000 on 8th January 2008. This sustained period of good economic growth set the basis for investors' high expectations from equities.

The Greater Fool Theory was at work. As the market rises and investors get used to rising prices triggered by the recency effect, so does the number of investors or speculators ready to invest in a stock or a sector or anything for that matter, without considering the valuations attached to those, with the view of flipping it to somebody else hoping that the price will rise. This is akin to saying that I might be a fool in walking away from the conservative style of investing, but I would still make a profit, as a greater fool would emerge to buy off my stake at an even higher price.

This is nowhere more applicable than in investing in IPOs, where investors, in the later stages of a bull run, irrespective of the quality of the issue, subscribe blindly in the hope that at listing somebody else would be ready to buy off their stake at an even higher price. This cannot and does not go on forever and, at the end, most of the people indulging in such excesses bear the pain in the form of facing huge losses, wiping out their profits.

High built-in expectations from the power, real estate and infrastructure sectors led to certain stocks hitting record valuations. This was the beginning of the making of a bubble.

It started with good news on the economy, the beneficiaries of the good news were some sectors, and specific companies in these sectors attracted so much attention from investors that they reached crazy valuations.

11.3 HUMAN BEHAVIORAL ANOMALIES

Bubbles are formed due to irrational human behavior. History has shown that, when there is euphoria, people become irrational, and their decisions are more emotional than rational and practical. Remember the tulip mania: people were willing to pay ridiculous prices for tulip bulbs just because there was a fancy for owning these bulbs. People lost fortunes during this crazy phase. Such manias have existed in the world from time immemorial; the only difference is that there are new players repeating the same mistake. Stock markets are known for such bubbles.

Since these bubbles are due to irrational behavior, it makes sense for us to understand the various behavioral traps during a bubble phase. Understanding one's behavioral weakness is incomplete without understanding the behavioral deficiencies in the market and the environment. Various heuristics and behavioral anomalies affect decision-making in the markets. Understanding these is the key to becoming a successful investor. Control over one's emotions and understanding others' emotional behavior makes one a successful investor. Let us examine these in detail.

11.3.1 Availability Heuristic

People tend to make decisions based on recent events, which are vivid in their minds. When certain types of information hit you on a regular basis, you tend to be swayed by such information. Your decision-making process gets guided by this recently and regularly available information.

Media plays a very important role in the creation of a bubble. They are the vehicles for spreading ideas. These ideas may be in the form of the robustness of the economy, the huge investment flows from foreign institutional investors, the new hot emerging sectors, the new 10-bagger stocks, the new operator driven stocks, and so on.

In times of optimism in the markets, there is a lot of investor interest regarding company news, new offerings, new investment tips, etc. Companies see bullish markets as an opportune time to tap the capital markets. Advertisements highlighting their achievements find their way to the crowd through media. TV shows talk about the next hot sector and analysts appear on shows recommending their stock picks. The people keenly follow all information on the markets and they make decisions based on the information they get from the media. The media talk about the recent appreciating stocks and give data about their appreciation. Since such stocks are the movers due to their abnormal price behavior they become popular with the media. Investors start chasing such stocks in the belief that they are good investments.

Bullish conditions provide positive news on the economy, the stock markets and stock investments. The media are the vehicle to promote this news.

11.3.2 Excessive Optimism

In good times, people become excessively optimistic about the future. They believe that good times are permanent and refuse to see the darker side. They become more adventurous and tend to take more risks. Little success is assumed to be the stepping-stone to bigger success. All caution is thrown to the winds and people become reckless.

Investors become so optimistic that they tend to invest in any stocks in the hope that they will make money. Success in a couple of such stocks would make them optimistic about other stocks.

In times of excessive optimism, companies become very aggressive and come out with huge ambitious plans requiring huge capital outlays. They borrow excessively and approach the capital markets for funding. Excessively optimistic investors are always ready to take part in the action. The initial public offering of "Reliance Power Limited" (RPL) is a classic example of what excessively optimistic promoters and investors can do.

It is important to understand that nothing is permanent in life. Being equanimous is the key to success.

11.3.3 Overconfidence

Excessive optimism leads to the overconfidence. There is overconfidence in the knowledge and ability of oneself.

When one is fed with so much of information through the media, one tends to become overconfident of one's knowledge. However, more information is not knowledge. On the contrary, it can lead to information overload and confusion. Knowledge about a company is very different from information on a stock of a company. However investors tend to relate one with the other. We have seen in the markets that stock prices do not move in tandem with the fundamentals of a company.

Overconfidence in one's ability arises from one's success in investing. A string of a few successes in stocks, due to the general improvement in the stock market sentiment and a bit of luck, makes people overconfident of their ability. From 2003 onwards we have seen such a bull run that everyone who entered the stock markets has made money. However, this success is not related to one's ability alone.

When the sentiment changes and the tide turns, stock prices can just collapse even if the fundamentals of the company have not changed.

Being overconfident of one's knowledge and ability could lead one to make financial blunders, especially in a bubble phase.

11.3.4 Greed of Investors

No one can fool you if do not want to be fooled. It is up to you to fall for a bait or not. We always believe that if anything happens to us the problem is out there. In fact, we are the problem of all our misfortunes. Greed plays a very important part in our financial well-being. If we are greedy, then we provide ready material for someone to exploit our greed. Control of greed is so very important in the stock markets.

Why do smart people make big money mistakes? It is because of their greed. Let us visit the technology boom. So many stocks were quoting at ridiculously high valuations. We even had stocks of companies that did not have a business plan in place. But investors knowingly went for such stocks in their hope and greed that there would be something in it to make a fortune. That greed made people lose fortunes.

Why do companies try to raise resources from the market in bullish times? Because investors are greedy and are willing to pay fancy prices for such overpriced issues. Remember the plantations boom, the dot com boom, and the latest infrastructure and power boom. Investors have lost fortunes in the IPOs of such companies.

Your greed helps bankers to sell you loans at high interest rates to buy cars, two-wheelers, consumer goods and even your holidays. If you keep your needs under control and be disciplined it would be in your own interest.

Your greed to make a big fast buck helps your broker to sell you derivative products so that you can leverage yourself much more than you can afford. With your greed, you exceed your capacity and, thus, greed becomes your graveyard.

Your broker agrees to charge you wafer-thin commissions on your trades. You start day-trading and the broker earns more than he did when you were not a day-trader.

11.3.5 Representative Heuristic

Robust growth in the economy is representative of good times ahead for businesses and companies. Their stock prices start rising. Higher stock prices are representative of companies doing well and investors tend to chase stocks and are willing to pay any price for them. From 2003 to 2008, India's GDP grew from 6% to 9%, while the BSE Sensex grew seven-fold, from 2,800 to 21,000. The stocks had a much faster run than what the fundamentals of the economy justified. This is how representative thinking works.

It also happens in sectors. The steep increase in the demand for steel led to a change in the fortunes of the steel industry. Tata Steel comes out with excellent results and the stock goes up. Subsequently, all the stocks in the steel sector go up, irrespective of their performance. Representative thinking makes investors chase these stocks, as they believe that since they are representative of the steel industry they will also post good results. The same representative thinking was repeated in the infrastructure, power and real estate sectors, and we saw even mediocre stocks becoming a fancy of the investors.

When a bubble is in the making, and if a concept or a sector is a fancy, many companies enter the sector or change their names so as to be representative of that sector or industry. This gets them investor attention and the price of stock goes up. During the technology boom we had so many companies that affixed the words 'dot com' to their names and thereby attracted investor attention. These investors were willing to pay fancy price for such companies, as they were considered representative of the new emerging economy.

Reliance Energy had touched a high of Rs.2,700 in January 2008, but was down to Rs.1,300 in March 2008, even after announcing a buy back at Rs.1600. Representative thinking could change the perception of investors towards the company so the management announced that it was changing the name of Reliance Energy to Reliance Infrastructure.

Investors need to be aware of these traps of representative heuristic because the media plays a very important role in highlighting such representativeness.

11.3.6 Envy

It is a human tendency to talk about one's successes rather than failures. That is why you always hear about investors talking about how they have made a fortune in the stock markets. They narrate tales of how they had got into a stock at the lowest price and got out at the highest price. And you wonder how you are not as smart as he is. This can lead to envy and you try to buy what is hot in the market and indirectly become a part of the bubble-building process. Envy is the worst sin in the stock markets. Because you really do not know the facts. One could be only telling you of one's successes and not the failures. One could be taking a huge position and you feel he is making a killing. But do you know his price of acquisition? Do you know the amount of his leverage and the interest outgo?

There is so much of misinformation flowing that one must not rely on it. Again, the media plays a very big role. You hear analysts' talk shows, you have live roundtable conferences, successful investors, brokers and investment bankers. Operators appear on various TV shows and brag about how they made fortunes and start recommending stocks and strategies. You feel left out and become envious of such success. Greed overcomes you and you join the bandwagon. You help fuel the bubble.

Having faith in your own conservative thinking and wisdom is your path to investing success. Look for 'silent evidence'. Sherlock Holmes, in one of his famous stories, reasons that at the time of the murder, since the dog was present in the house and had not barked around the time the murder took place, the murderer must have been someone known to the victim. The moral of the above anecdote lies in noting how the detective looks for the hidden evidence rather than simply relying on the evidence available at the scene of the crime. Similarly, before investing in a company based on somebody else's recommendation or tip, or getting awed by someone's wealth-creating prowess, or someone's jet, or a mansion, or a BMW or a Lexus, always consider looking for the evidence that is discernible to any reasoning mind.

11.3.7 Endowment Effect

The value of a thing increases when it becomes a part of one's possessions. We tend to value more what we have than what others have. That is why when we want to sell what we have, we tend to ask for a higher price. When we go to buy, we are always looking at how cheaply we can buy. This is how the endowment effect works. The value of a thing increases when it becomes a part of one's endowment.

You are recommended a stock by a friend, an analyst, a broker, a fund manager or a financial advisor. The said stock is heavily tipped in the market and has been appreciating fast. Before just plunging in, ascertain if the endowment effect is at work. If all these people are recommending and also owning the stock they believe the stock is good because they own it. Endowment effect makes them salesmen for the stock and hence the strong recommendation. This is how stocks become a fancy and the bubble process gathers steam. Decide if you want to be a part of the process or wisely sit aside until the bubble bursts.

After the budget speech of the Finance Minister, the TV channels and the newspapers are busy interviewing a cross-section of people on what they feel. Every one has his own agenda and his own endowment effect guides his reaction to the budget. If a person happens to be an investor and the short-term capital gains tax is increased he is a critic. If sops are provided to pharmaceuticals, the industry applauds the budget. You have different reactions coming to you, depending on the endowment of the person interviewed. So, at the end, you really do not know if the budget in totality is good for the country or not.

Thus, endowment effect leads to information you really do not care about but you can get carried away.

11.4 HOW DOES ONE IDENTIFY A BUBBLE?

One identifies a bubble by observing the excesses created. When abnormal and irrational things happen, they are noticeable; but self-doubt questions our own intuition, leading to disbelief in our own selves. We, thereby, allow the environment to control us. However, if we have the courage to stand firm and trust our conventional wisdom we can save ourselves from the bubble trap.

Therefore it is easy to identify a bubble. Look around and observe the crazy things that are happening:

"This is the New Economy"

"This time it is different, this is the new world order"

"Profits don't matter; it is the eyeballs that matter"

"Look at the value of the land bank the company has, it cannot go wrong"

"Powering India, Reliance Power"

"High PE signifies high growth. In a growing economy high PE stocks are the sure winners"

"In the long run we are all dead, so why invest for the long run? Long-term investing is dead"

"You can't go wrong on real estate stocks"

"With the growth story intact, buy infrastructure stocks. They are still cheap. Conventional valuation models don't work any more."

These statements reflect insanity, especially when they are defying conventional wisdom. These are over-optimistic statements devoid of any rational thinking. The following guidelines would be suggestive of a bubble.

11.4.1 High PEs Generally Expected with High Growth

PEs are the short-cuts to assessing the expensiveness or the cheapness of a stock. However, when the market as a whole is willing to justify investments in high PE stocks based on the illusionary growth projections, it is a sign of caution. During a bubble, high PE stocks become the most chased after. Investors compete in buying such stocks. They forget the high valuations.

Responsible management would warn against such valuations. However, investors turn a deaf ear. Enthusiasm is so high that investors are willing to give ridiculous valuations to stocks.

Go back to the internet era. Stocks like Software Solutions Ltd (SSI) were quoted at outrageous valuations. They belonged to unknown managements who had a knack of being with the changing times. Investors lost fortunes investing in such companies, which were available at a PE of over 100. The same management having cashed out on the internet boom, went for a buy-back at a price around Rs.40. They were quick to embrace the real estate boom with a newborn SSI. All information on the company concentrated on the real estate business. Yes, they did not change the name to SSI real estate. However, they did capitalize on the new flavor of the markets and participated in the new real estate fad.

The internet era is the remembrance of the high PE stocks like Global Tele at 158 PE and, DSQ Software at 100 PE, where investors lost fortunes. Investors also lost in blue chip companies like Infosys if they bought the stock at 206 PE in 2000. Although it was a great, well-managed company, investors lost because they made the mistake of buying a stock which had high built-in expectations of investors. Anyone who bought Infosys in the year 2000 at ridiculous valuations is still a loser in 2008. Not because he bought a bad company but because he paid an excessively high price for the stock of a good company. This is enough evidence for an investor to understand that excessively high PEs of a stock are suggestive of a bubble pricing.

In the present scenario, on January 01, 2008, stocks of real estate companies—like India Bulls Real Estate available at a PE of 800 and the market leader, DLF Ltd, available at 450 PE—signify a bubble phase.

The power sector also has its share of high PE stocks like Reliance Energy at 62 PE and RPL at 900 PE. Incidentally, the original power players and fundamentally strong companies are Tata Power at a PE of 39, NTPC at a PE of 23. What do you call this difference? BUBBLE.

Reliance Natural Resources Ltd. (RNRL) a company with just an MOU with Reliance Industries Ltd to get gas at a concession rate, which is challenged in the court, is quoting at a PE of 601. It is a hope sold to the investors. However, the IPO of RPL from the same management has disappointed the investors with a below par listing, and is sure to hurt the investors of RNRL who have bought the bubble stock. It is a question of faith and trust.

Good reputed managements also get trapped in their own bubble stocks with their inability and lack of courage to warn the investors of the bubble pricing. The meteoric rise in their stock prices also blinds them to the reality and they get swayed in the bubble formation. In fact, they create an environment for the growth of the bubble where they get hurt the most.

The above have been examples of bubble stocks with hardly any track record but a lot of noise.

Credible managements would warn investors of such movements in their stocks by making a public statement or selling stocks in the market and making a public disclosure.

Excessively high PE stocks are the first sign of a bubble in the making.

11.4.2 Commodity Stocks

I am still not in terms as to how investors invest in commodity stocks. If one is to bet on commodities there exists a commodity market to place one's bet. However, when the prices of commodities start firming up, investors tend to chase commodity stocks. It would be much simpler to buy the commodities.

Commodity stocks command a set PE that ranges between 5 and 10. It is a simple business depending upon the price of the commodity and the management expertise of the company. There cannot be much deviation.

However, stock markets are known for their euphoria and even commodity companies start quoting at ridiculous valuations. This is more due to the higher and unreasonable expectations of the investors. This leads to overpricing of commodity stocks. This is a sure sign of investor irrational behavior.

Commodities also have their cycles. However, in times of a bullish cycle, commodities' stocks tend to be priced at ridiculous valuations, signifying high investor expectations. The same is corrected when the cycle turns bearish.

Investors need to be aware of ridiculous valuations of commodity stocks. It is a sure sign of a bubble.

11.4.3 Economic Growth and Company Stock Price Rise are Disproportional

Good news on the economy is discounted much faster in the markets than the fundamentals justify. Economic growth is time-testing and the benefits accrue over a period of time.

However, the stock markets are known for extrapolating too much into the future. They discount the future too fast. Hence, the stock markets are very quick to celebrate the success of economic growth. This over-optimism and enthusiasm lead to stock market indices going up at a faster rate than the economic growth justifies.

The Indian economy grew at 6% in 2003 and went up to 9% in 2008; however, the popular BSE Sensex rose from 2,800 in 2003 to 21,000 in 2008, a six-fold increase. The velocity of the rise in the stock markets showed signs of over-optimism. Such a fast rise signifies the build-up of a bubble.

This was in no way in conformity with the economic growth and needed to get corrected. It went down to a low of 16,000 in March 2008. The bubble was pricked and sanity restored amongst investors.

Investors should understand the impact of good news and its effect on the stock markets. If it is irrational, it is a sign of a bubble in the making.

11.4.4 Media Hype

What is the current flavor in the media? The current topics and happenings are so vividly highlighted by the media that they always have a fast recall value. This leads to everyone talking, discussing and believing in the same.

During the internet boom, the media played a very important role in disseminating information on the emergence of the new economy, as to how the bricks and mortar business was out and the internet-based business models would survive. No doubt, the internet was the best thing that was happening to the economy and has changed our lives drastically. But the way investors reacted by paying any price for the internet stocks was due to so much information flowing from the media. Easy recall value created the internet hype and investors acted on the same.

Remember the 'India Shining' story in 2003–2004? We all believed in the same. Everyone was talking and convinced of India shining. How did this happen? The media carried discussions by prominent businessmen, economists, industry leaders, and politicians on their views on India shining. Even those who had no knowledge of what was happening had to back up the India shining story, lest they were the odd ones out. Viewers believed what they heard from the media and they also started talking about it. We had everyone talking about it and the available information was so strong that it became the truth.

The reality dawned when the NDA government lost the elections, only to realize that India was shining only in the cities where the media had a strong presence and the propaganda worked.

The current media hype on economic growth, the foreign institutional investors' money flows to the market, and the high demand for Indian equities should be a signal to investors to not get swayed.

So is the case with the power, real estate and financial sectors. Observe the advertisements in the media. These sectors top the list. The money spent on advertisements gets them visibility in the media through invitations to give their expert comments, take part in roundtable conferences, express their expert opinions, etc. The viewer then acts on such information. Be wary of media hypes.

11.4.5 Sudden Entry of Less-known Firms

When less-known firms start entering the markets through IPOs and the indices, it is a sign of a bubble being formed. Companies enter the indices based on the market capitalization. Unfortunately, the track record of listing or profitability is no criteria for entry in the indices. It is the size that matters. Such entries of lesser-known firms take the sector weightage up. This is what happened during the internet boom. The IT sector weightage increased to over 24% in a very short time.

After the split of the Reliance empire, a less-known company Reliance Communications, got listed on the markets and entered the BSE Sensex within three months of listing. Its market capitalization enabled entry in the index. Telecommunications was a hot sector and started showing representation on the indices. This hype is evident from the fact that Reliance Communications was quoting at a PE of 60 in January 2008.

Real estate has a similar warning of a bubble. DLF Ltd came to the market with a mega-issue and, within three months of listing, found its place in the BSE Sensex. Its PE at the time of the listing was 218. The issue price was Rs.525 and within six months the price jumped to over Rs.1,250 in January 2008. However, the bubble was pricked and the price fell to Rs.630 in March 2008.

Similarly, another real estate company, Unitech Ltd., entered the Nifty in September 2007. Its PE was 46 at the time of listing.

11.4.6 Entry of More Firms in the Sector

A fast increase in a sector weightage with the entry of new firms is also a sign of a bubble formation. When a sector is hot, new firms enter the business, the existing firms come out with expansion plans, and we see a flood of IPOs.

The hot sectors like capital goods in the infrastructure space, real estate and power have seen a lot of new entrants to the market. The markets have been dominated by IPOs in these sectors.

A similar hype existed in the power sector. RPL came out with an IPO at a price band of Rs.430 to Rs.450, and was heavily oversubscribed.

Here, the bubble-like situation was evident when the IPO was announced. Investors were willing to pay Rs.430-450 per share for a Rs.1.8 crore profit-making company with promise of dream projects expected to be commissioned by 2014.

However, on listing the price dropped below the issue price. Had the sentiment not changed it would have been the largest capitalized stock to find a place in the index.

The real estate sector also saw many new entrants in the market with IPOs. DLF entered the market quoting at a PE of 218, India Bulls Realty (a stock market favorite) commanded a PE of over 390. Many other real estate developers also entered the market.

However, the sentiment changed in February 2008, and we saw the withdrawal of the IPO of Emmar Holdings, an internationally-reputed real estate developer. The pricing was too steep and investors were turning rational.

Although the markets have reacted sharply and the bubbles in the above sectors have been pricked, these examples provide evidence for investors to identify bubble-like situations.

11.5 LESSONS FOR INVESTORS

11.5.1 Valuations do Matter the Most

You cannot pay any price for growth or a new idea or a concept. Ultimately, it is the profits from an enterprise that matter. And for that stream of earnings there is a price to be paid. That is the value you attach to a stock. Paying high price for an expected future stream of earnings is a sure way to losses.

This is conventional wisdom. No new economy or the advent of any technology can change that. Remember the IT boom. The new adage was "eyeballs". How many hits a site generated made the company owning that site very valuable. People gave crazy valuations to such companies. Profits did not matter, as in the so-called new internet economy what mattered was eyeballs.

Investing is all about earning a reasonable rate of return on one's investment and that cannot happen if the company does not make profits. Such fads lasted for some time until wisdom dawned and the prices of such internet stocks came crashing down.

Most of the real estate, infrastructure and power stocks are highly expensive, but the India growth story is so hyped up that investors believe in paying higher prices for the growth they see in these sectors.

It is difficult to value the land bank of a real estate company. Moreover, in real estate deals, a lot of unaccounted money changes hands in the form of cash. There is a question of corporate governance. There being lack of transparency in dealings, it becomes difficult to value the company. But, in the hope of a boom in real estate prices and the India growth story, investors are willing to buy these stocks at ridiculous valuations.

Take the case of power companies. These companies should deserve the valuations of a commodity company. Moreover, pricing of the power is also subject to certain government controls. There is no way that, in a poor country like India which has a power deficit, the power companies will be able to make great profits to justify high valuations. But power being a hot sector the power stocks is a fancy and media-hyped.

Even on the infrastructure front, many capital goods companies and construction companies that will be direct beneficiaries of infrastructure growth, are commanding steep valuations. Investors ignoring the valuations are sure to get hit.

11.5.2 Avoid Triple Digit PEs

Another sure way to losses is chasing triple-digit PE stocks. In a bubble situation, the hype and the investor euphoria are so severe that investors pay any price to acquire certain hyped-up stocks. No doubt, sometimes a company comes out with an excellent performance due to a breakthrough technology or change in fortunes. However, the investors extrapolate this too far into the future. They are so excited about the salient event that they overreact. They assume that this will be repeated and will thus justify the high price they are paying. There is no way that such performance can be sustainable.

During the technology boom, we saw how even a company like Infosys was commanding a PE of over 100. It was an excellent company with a very good track record and management. However, such a high PE was unwarranted. There was too much of investor expectations implicit in the price. Any investor who bought this great company in the year 2000 would be losing on his investment. Not that the choice of the company was wrong, but the price paid was exorbitant. Even a long-term holding period of eight years could not undo the mistake of paying triple digit PEs.

Reliance is a strong brand in the Indian capital markets. However, some stocks like Reliance Natural Resources Ltd are quoting at a PE of over 700 Reliance Infrastructure is at a PE of over 190. Such valuations cannot be sustained in the long run, and investors are bound to get hurt.

Similarly, another real estate company India Bull Real Estate Co was at a PE of over 800 in January 2008. With the meltdown in the market in March 2008 it declined to trade at a PE of over 600. A dangerous PE at which to buy a stock. However, *The Economic Times* reported on 20th March that George Soros, the billionaire investor (speculator), had picked up 2.5% stake in the company at Rs.455.80. If one is investing, it is a dangerous thing to do. No wise investor would do this. This is speculation. Investors take the cue from such news and make investment decisions. It is on the assumption that George Soros knows all. However he is human and prone to make mistakes as much as you are. His speculation does not make the investment instrument any better. It still remains a triple-digit PE stock and investors need to avoid it.

In times of madness anything can happen. Even a public sector company, MMTC of India, was commanding a PE multiple of over 800. This soon crashed, to the dismay of greedy investors who paid such a lofty valuation.

11.5.3 Mid-Cap and Small-Cap Stocks

Once the highly capitalized stocks start getting expensive, the market is looking at identifying new opportunities. Thus, the focus shifts to the mid-cap and the small-cap stocks. The growth stories of the hot sectors are woven around these stocks.

There is nothing wrong in mid-cap or small-cap stocks, but the problem comes with representative thinking. In a market bubble. when the leaders go on becoming expensive, it is very easy to rig the mid- and small-cap stocks. Due to their lack of liquidity, their rise becomes fast and they become operator favorites. Unscrupulous management, operators and brokers take advantage of a bubble phase in certain stocks and sectors by rigging the mid-cap and the small-cap in these representative sectors.

During the IT boom, since IT stocks were doing very well, we found that many small and less-known companies attracted investor attention due to representative bias, and when the tide turned these stocks became worthless paper.

Examples of smaller companies affixing the words 'dot com' to their names became sought-after companies and investors paid a heavy price for chasing them.

Moreover, when the bull market ends the mid-cap and small-cap stocks become highly illiquid. In such a situation, they lose their value very fast in the absence of any buyers. After the Harshad Mehta boom in the early-1990s, when the financial sector liberalization started, we had a boom in the financial services industry. Any company having a financial services business was sought after. When the party ended in 1995, investors were left with worthless paper and the entrants in the industry without jobs.

Revisiting the real estate sector, we had new entrants in the mid-cap category entering the markets to take advantage of the boom. Akruti City was one such stock, commanding a lofty multiple of over 90. Similarly Mahindra Life Space Developer became an investor craze with the PE at over 160.

11.5.4 Avoid Large Little-known Companies

In a bubble phase, little-known companies tend to become large due to the market capitalization going up because of the price increase. Such companies attract media and investor attention. Analysts always want new ideas and thus are born such growth ideas around little-known companies. These companies being in the limelight, become famous and their recall value in the minds of the investor increases.

Visual Soft during the IT boom is a fine example of a little-known Hyderabad-based company which became large because its stock price went up to as high as Rs.10,000 for a Rs.10 face value. It was the talk of the town, recommended heavily by reputed investment bankers, brokers and analysts. Investors lost a fortune when the tide turned.

Financial Technology is another little-known company which came into the limelight due to its presence in the fast-growing financial sector and its knowledge-base of stock exchanges. It promoted the Multi Commodity Exchange of India. It is a very good company, with able promoters and a good business model. However the triple digit valuation of over 120 PE, in the mid-cap category makes it an unattractive investment idea. There are many such examples in the hot sectors like real estate and infrastructure.

11.5.5 Information Asymmetry

Beware of information asymmetry. Information travels in a channel, right from the people surrounding or involved in the situation to the ultimate recipients, the investor. The medium encapsulates various mediums and forms. Right from management updates to stock exchanges to business news channels to sources close to the company to your next-door neighbor who happens to know somebody in the company. When you are bombarded with information from various directions, always consider what part of the news reflects the ground reality and what part is somebody else's interpretation of that event. Be critical in your reaction to such news items, otherwise one might have to face seemingly reliable news turning out to be a hoax, resulting in losses and distress.

Moreover, one has to be aware at what step of the information ladder one is. If one is not at the second or third step of the information ladder, one is likely to be a loser. Availability heuristics create such information ladders. These are created through web sites, blogs, newspapers, business magazines and rumors. They also have geographical variants. Information in Mumbai city could be old and tenth on the information ladder, but in Ahmedabad the same could be brand new information and first or second on the ladder.

The initial investors become salesmen and spread the information more widely. It is only when such inside information becomes public news and many investors chase it that the stock price goes up and the initial investors exit. So avoid being an investor who would help the initial investors to exit. Always check how fast the stock has appreciated in the near past.

11.5.6 This Time it is Different

Every bubble phase has a new theme; however, the excesses are the same. Institutional memory of investors, though strong regarding the past mistakes in bubbles, fails to help them as they believe that "this time it is different".

Every bubble signifies excesses and irrational crowd behavior. This leads investors to buy expensive stocks, buy what others are buying, buy what is fancy in the markets and buy dreams.

However, every new bubble has a new story justifying how this time this is very different from the past bubble. These are just new ideas and fads to act upon the new mania.

During the technology boom did we not hear "this is the new economy emerging", "the old rules do not apply", and "bricks and mortar is dead"?

In recent past, the India growth story is leading to excesses in sectors like infrastructure, real estate and power. Stocks in these sectors have been investor favorites and available at expensive multiples. But over a longer period of time, the excesses will be corrected.

There are certain universal principles that do not change, irrespective of other changes: A company has to make a profit to reward its shareholders, to earn returns one has to buy at the right price, valuations matter the most, there are no short-cuts, and you cannot sow today and reap tomorrow. Irrespective of different times and circumstances prevailing, the universal principles do not change. The euphoria of markets makes one forget the conventional wisdom.

11.5.7 Never Get Married to your Stocks

One common mistake investors make is to fall in love with their stocks so much so that they are not willing to part with them. Yes, one could be lucky to make a fortune in a particular stock, as one was lucky enough to buy it at the right price. Now when the stock has risen and becomes expensive what must one do? There are chances of one getting into a decision paralysis mode.

One must undertake this small exercise:

1. Ascertain the profit you are making on the stock. How many times have you been lucky enough to make such money? Do

these opportunities come often? What can you do with this money? This will set the clarity for your decision-making process.

2. Thereafter, assume that you have money and need to invest. Ask yourself if you would buy the stock at this rate? If the answer is yes, don't sell. If the answer is no, sell your stocks and keep the cash handy to buy when the markets offer good buying opportunities.

Remember bull and bear markets follow each other. Cash is the king. Opportunities always come, but when they come you need to have the cash. This cash can come when you follow the basic tenets of investing: buy low and sell high. There are a lot of foolish people around who will give you such opportunities. So never get married to your stocks.

11.5.8 Never Short-Sell

After understanding the signs of a bubble one may become confident and think of short selling, the act of borrowing shares and selling them with the intention of buying them back when the price drops. This is one temptation which needs to be avoided, as a bubble can last longer than one imagines. A stock at a triple-digit PE of 100 may be overvalued, but the euphoria of the market can take it up to even 600. No one can judge how long the madness will last.

There is another danger in short-selling. If one buys a stock at a price one knows the maximum loss one can make. However, when one short-sells, one does not know how much the stock will go up. If one buys a stock at Rs.50 the maximum damage is Rs.50 if the stock goes down to zero. However, if one sells a stock at Rs.50 the loss is unlimited. The stock can go up to Rs.100, 500, 1,000. Or even Rs.10,000.

When one buys a stock, one can borrow the money from various sources to pay for the stock. However when one short-sells the stock, one needs to go to the owners of the stock to borrow. And these owners can demand any price. One's universe of borrowing is very small.

The stock market contract is thus heavily biased towards the buyer. Moreover, every government would like the markets to be moving up, as that signifies a healthy economy and good economic policies of the government. The world over, stock markets are the barometer of the financial health of a country. Whenever there is a crisis in the stock markets, the government comes to the rescue. Large government institutions step in to buy to support stock prices, the Finance Minister soothes the sentiment by announcing stimuli, the Reserve Bank brings down interest rates, etc. Now, in such a situation, a short-seller is never respected and is seen as unpatriotic. He cannot have any government sympathy, although he is only defying the market stupidity.

So it is best to watch the "fun" end and then buy your stocks at good valuations.

11.6 WHY DO PAST BUBBLES NOT GUIDE US?

The most important lesson for a human being is to learn from one's mistakes. It is not that people do not want to do that, but there is so much of information flowing in the stock markets that people tend to mistake this overload of information for knowledge. Based on this new knowledge, different mental models emerge. However, greed being the basic emotion, the mind convinces the person that this time is very different from the past bubble. Greed blinds the investor and, believing only what he wants to believe, he goes ahead to make the same mistakes.

Confirmation bias takes over and one only looks at advice or information that fits with one's line of thinking. Any other information that is contrary is ignored.

Moreover, crowd behavior drives individual behavior in the stock markets and, hence, investors get swayed by the most recent popular thinking.

11.6.1 Bubbles Repeat due to Demographic Changes

One would argue that the recent technology bust is just seven years old and how would investors make the same mistakes of buying junk stocks, paying ridiculous valuations and leveraging their positions. If the tide turns, investors are bound to get hurt.

However, demographic changes play a very important role. Every year, we have so many students graduating and looking forward to starting their careers. The new generation makes its way to stock markets in the form of employees, sub-brokers, day-traders, dealers, etc. If the markets are bullish then we have an exodus from other markets joining the stock markets. There is a new breed of players without any institutional memory

Where are the people with institutional memory? Bust follows the boom, so most of the people make losses and exit the market. Loss-aversion makes investors flee the markets to safety.

After the technology bust, investors had lost fortunes and they would have exited the markets. However, a new set of investors enters the market, bringing in new crazy ideas and concepts.

In the boom starting from 2003, we have seen so many new entrants in the markets. Most of them would not have seen the technology bust. They are without any experience of what a bear market can do. Hence, we have a new generation of investors who are fresh and they make the same old mistakes.

11.6.2 Short Public Memory

Seven years is too long a period in public memory. Investors who lost in the technology bust would readily make the same mistakes, as the recency effect has faded with the passage of time. Now the new concepts and fads do their work. This is the most recent information in their minds, and they tend to get swayed by the same.

The fact that we saw investor loss-aversion in 2001/2002/2003 demonstrates that the recent losses were fresh in their minds and they were loss-averse. Moreover there was no new idea or concept or fad to take their fancy. In 2004, as the India growth story started unfolding, investors started leaving the bad memories behind and once again joined the crowd.

Envy played an important role in such behavior. When people saw others making money in stocks they joined the herd.

11.6.3 There is a New Way of Measuring this New Phenomenon

Every bull phase has a new concept, a new story, a new fad and a new measurement tool. There was a time when earnings per share was popular, then we had the price to book value, followed by the cash flow per share, the replacement cost theory, the eyeballs and, lastly, infrastructure and the land bank concept. Stock markets are known for such fads.

Investors start becoming greedy and participate in the same excesses of buying the fancies according to the present valuation norms. As the markets go up, and the profits start flowing in, they start believing that this time it is very different and the new measurement tools are the order of the day. Conventional measurement tools are ignored.

To understand the fickle-minded behavior of the investors, let us go back to the year 2000, during the time of the technology boom. Bricks-and-mortar was dead and the internet was the answer to all business models. People paid huge multiples for internet- and web-based business models.

Now, eight years down the line, when the internet has stabilized, and broadband has arrived with the security systems and checks and balances in place, we find investors embracing the bricks-and-mortar business models. That is also one of the reasons for the rise in real estate prices.

Nowhere is this more evident than in the financial services sector. Most of the financial services firms are getting huge valuations, which are dependent on the number of branches they have. Financial firms, like Geojit Financial Services, Motilal Oswal Financial Services, ILFS Invest Smart and Emkay Finance, have become investor favorites where investors are willing to pay crazy valuations for a cyclical business dependent on the stock market boom. The new way of measurement is the number of branches a firm has. This is akin to the "eyeballs" measurement tool. Private equity players and qualified institutional investors are a dominant part of this herd.

On the contrary, internet-based models are an idea whose time has not only come but is here to stay. No more do we go to the travel agents for airline or hotel bookings. We do it through the internet. However, stock markets behave irrationally and give weight not to what is important, but to what is more popular and current.

11.6.4 Overconfidence of Knowledge and Ability

When investments start yielding profits due to a surge in the stock prices, investors tend to relate the success to their knowledge and ability. This newfound confidence leads one to be more aggressive in the quest for higher profits. One convinces oneself that the present is very different from the past, and one goes out and makes the same mistakes but in different ways.

Here is an example of my client who also has a couple of other brokers. During the technology boom, he had lost a sizeable amount through another broker, and every time he remembered his loss and blamed the broker. I explained to him that the reason for his losses was not the broker, but he himself as he became greedy and bought stocks which were fancies of the market and paid ridiculous prices to acquire them. He agreed with me, and vowed to be very careful in his future investing decisions. Thereafter, he used to deal with me and kept with my philosophy of value investing. That meant buying only when a good opportunity arose and thus less interaction with the broker. He was doing fine and one day in December 2007 he phoned me and complained regarding my or my firm's inability to give him good investment ideas. When I told him that we found everything expensive and would wait for a good buying opportunity he exploded and told me that other brokers were giving him so many tips everyday and the stocks were also going up. Why should he deal with me when I did not have the research and the expertise to identify winning stocks? Although he was in touch with me as we were family friends, he stopped doing business with me. Moreover, he claimed that his son was a reputed professional and with his contacts with the company management, he was able to get so many investment tips. I explained to him that he was losing his discipline and he would be sure to meet the same fate as in the technology bust. In one of my subsequent meetings he asked me about L&T stock. I told him that at Rs.4,000 it was an expensive stock at a PE of over 60. He argued with me that it was a very good stock and would still go up. I guessed that he had bought the stock and now he wanted confirmation from me that he had done the right thing. I told him that L&T was a great company but a bad stock at such a high PE. I am sure if he loses in L&T he will put the blame on the broker. This is how investors get swayed by their greed and envy. They never learn because they believe that this time "I am smart".

11.7 CONCLUSION

Investors would do better not only in investing, but also in all walks of life, if they keep in mind the behavioral biases that affect clarity in thinking. Money is good as long it is in the pocket. It becomes dangerous when it goes in the head. That is when we become irrational and start making blunders.

'House money effect' is used to denote the tendency common amongst gamblers playing in casinos, where they are ready to take more risk with money earned easily or unexpectedly, which is eventually what success in gambling means. This tendency is not limited to gamblers in the casinos; it is prevalent in the stock market as well, particularly during bull runs.

As the bull run moves from stage to stage, the money made during one stage is put at risk much more easily as the thrill and ease associated with making money in the market increases. Thus, just as an investor avoids taking risk before the onset of the bull run because he values his money more highly, he eventually becomes much more vulnerable to parting with his money, which has grown somewhat during the initial stages of the bull run. This, in part, explains what makes market valuation lose touch with economic reality.

Human beings have a tendency to credit their successes to themselves, whereas their failures are attributed to external variables. This bias is termed as 'attribution bias'. Money is made mainly backed by the overall increase in stock market levels because of increase in the demand for stocks. People start attributing their successes to themselves and become more and more confident about their ability and methods. But any event is a confluence of internal and external factors and the same is the case in investing.

Thus, when an investor makes money, he should reason his success by appreciating any unforeseen event, which led him to make money out of a trade and, accordingly, weigh his strengths against his weaknesses, rather than blindly attributing all the success to himself. If he fails to do so, he will cease to see the linkage between cause and effect and the result would not be favorable in the long run.

Imagine the confidence you will have if you are able to spot a bubble. Waiting for it to burst can open up a host of opportunities to make a fortune. But it requires courage and patience—rare attributes amongst humans accustomed to quick fixes and instant gratification.

TWELVE 12

INVESTOR BEHAVIOR BASED FINANCE

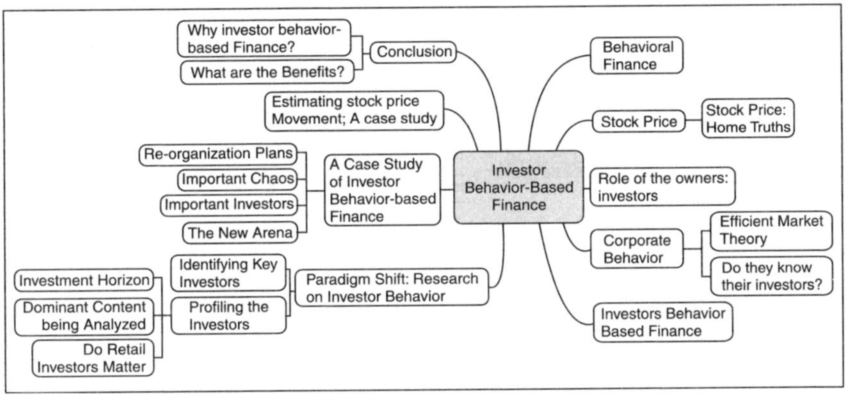

Throughout the book we have discussed about identifying a good company, verifying whether the stock is available at a good price, and how one could make money by following different investment strategies.

It was evident that most of the losses suffered by investors were due to their emotional indiscipline and their unwillingness to delay gratification. Stock markets offer good investment opportunities in the form of listed companies that are prone to sway between business cycles and bouts of human emotion. But, over the long run, investors can benefit from regular dividends and capital appreciation if the choice of the company and its business model has been right.

A lot of time, money and effort have been expended to study the companies listed on the stock markets. Brokerages, investment bankers, analysts and investors are always on the lookout for investment opportunities in companies capable of delivering above-average returns to make them immensely rich in a short time. This makes them look for technology breakthroughs, new business models, new markets, innovations, new products, changing business cycles, quality of management, economic growth, ability of companies to grow, competitive environment, etc. In efficient markets, if one takes the trouble to understand the companies and their competitive edge, it becomes easy to identify winners and investors would smile their way to the banks. However, the stock markets are inefficient especially in the short run and hence do not offer such opportunities.

Stock markets offer good investment opportunities in the form of listed companies that are prone to sway between business cycles and bouts of human emotion.

Stock prices fluctuate not according to the fundamentals of a company but according to what the investors think of those fundamentals. Different investors are governed by their own unique emotions and their decisions are subject to their emotional outbursts.In times of optimism, investors are willing to pay much higher prices for stocks, way above their intrinsic value, and in times of pessimism they are willing to sell the same stocks much below their true worth. When caught between greed and fear, investors behave in an irrational manner.

These same investors do research on companies, but make their decisions more out of emotional reactions rather than reasoning out of fundamental facts of the company. They play havoc with a company's stock price, getting in and out of a company stock at the slightest hint of discomfort.

Investors ask the management all sorts of questions regarding the progress of the company. They are the owners, and the management is responsible to them.

However, looking at the way investors make their decisions—out of greed, fear and short-term gratification—it is important for companies to research their investors. Knowing how different classes of investors behave, what matters to them, how each one is different and what information is important to them, is what companies need to research.

Let us try to understand the nature of the markets and its participants. The role of a corporation is to maximize shareholder value as epitomized by the stock price. This stock price fluctuates according to the whims and fancies of different types of investors, who get swayed between bouts of fear and greed. Investors do research on companies and make a buy or sell decision.

However, do companies research their investors?

These investors form an important constituent of any corporation. They are the owners and, at the same time, their fickle-minded behavior can play havoc with stock prices.

> **The stock price is never a true reflection of the true worth of the corporation. It is a function of the perceptions of the investors.**

12.1 BEHAVIORAL FINANCE

Flawed Thinking

General thought process is governed by the concept of traditional economic theory that says that markets are efficient and that people make rational decisions to maximize profits.In short, traditional finance may be represented as '1+1 = 2'.

However, the new school of thought as propounded by behavioral economic theory believes that, while traditional economic theory may hold true in the long run, in the short run markets are not efficient and people do not make rational decisions. People have a mind and a heart, but people do not always make decisions only out of their mind. When decisions are made from the heart, they are emotional decisions and may not be rational. People donating to charities or celebrating their birthdays are examples of action driven by emotions, which do not possess the motive of profit maximization. Behavioral finance may be represented as '1+1+emotion=2 or 8 or 50 or 0'.

12.2 STOCK PRICE

The goal of a corporation is to maximize shareholder value as epitomized by the stock price. The stock price becomes important as it reflects the true state of affairs of a corporation. If the corporation is doing very well, its stock price goes up. In times of adversity, the stock price is down.

12.2.1 Stock Price: Home Truths

The stock price is never a true reflection of the true worth of the corporation. If that were so the stock markets would be very dull and boring. The stock price is a function of the perceptions of the investors who are governed by their emotions of greed and fear. The uncertainty of the markets coupled with unpredictable investor behavior causes stock volatility. This investor behavior causes a big disparity between the true worth of the company and the stock price in the markets.

> **Unpredictable investor behavior causes a big disparity between the true worth of the company and the stock price in the markets.**

In times of prosperity and boom conditions, the stock price is more than the true worth, as investors are willing to pay a higher price, expecting good times to continue. In times of depressed conditions, stocks are available at less than their true worth, as investors are bearish on the future. So, it is all a function of sentiments and perceptions. This can change overnight and that is why we have bull and bear markets that follow each other.

The stock price is the fulcrum around which a lot of things happen. A host of decisions affecting the corporation are made based on the stock price. It is the yardstick to judge the performance of a company. Stock price has become so crucial that it can make or break a company.

A good stock price is able to attract investors, as it signifies good times for the company. It signifies investor interest and this leads to more investors investing in the company. This demand leads to the stock price going up further. Such stocks become media favorites and receive attention and become popular.

This is good for the company as it helps it to undertake expansion plans without having to worry about resources. There are investors waiting to invest. So is the case when the company is going for mergers and acquisitions. A good stock price not only helps to get more investors willing to invest, but also helps the company in bargaining a favorable share swap deals in the case of mergers.

A good stock price also keeps the creditors and the bankers happy. Bankers are willing to lend to such companies at more favorable interest rates, as well as to participate in expansion plans. The company's credit rating is high. This helps the company to pursue long term investment plans at lower interest rates.

We are in a financial jungle where the rules are very different and corporates need to learn how to play by the new rules.

A good stock price helps the company to attract talent and retain top performing employees. Stock options issued by the company have a significant meaning and impact employee morale if the stock price is good and fancied in the stock market.

In short, a good stock price reflects an optimistic future for the company.

On the other hand, a depressed stock price reflects pessimism and a gloomy future for the company. The business model and the opportunities and the profits may be good for the company but lack of investor interest resulting in a depressed stock price does not auger well for the company on many fronts.

There are grave organizational consequences of a depressed stock price. The ability of the company to attract talent is considerably reduced. Retaining employees becomes hard, as employees like to go where the future is bright and rosy. A depressed stock price signifies a pessimistic future. In such a situation, stock options have no meaning or attraction to the employees.

A depressed stock price can make an acquirer company an acquiree. We saw that in the case of Great Eastern Realty. A great business with a depressed stock price saw Mr. Abhishek Dalmia, an investor, acquiring stocks at a depressed price, only to enable the company to be acquired by Mahindra Realty and thus unlock the hidden value of the company. A depressed stock price and the complacency of the management made the Sheths lose control of the company.

Depressed stock prices also do not find favor with bankers and creditors, which can derail a company's long term plans as it will fail to get loans at favorable interest rates. This can jeopardize the future expansion plans and new initiatives.

Investors' interest also wanes in companies whose stock prices are depressed. It becomes very difficult for such companies to access the capital markets for their expansion plans. Rights offers and IPOs become very difficult for such managements.

> **Companies should concentrate on the four constituents: employees, customers, suppliers and investors.**

It has, thus, become very important for the management to ensure that its stock price reflect the underlying fundamentals of the business. However, it is the most difficult thing to do. This stock price changes at the whims of its owners who are the investors and also the shareholders. Is it not surprising that the owners of a company are the ones who play havoc with their own company's stock price and have the ability to put the company in a fix?

This is the nature of the markets where such stocks are listed. They are full of transient investors. These investors do not have any conscience. They become owners to benefit from the movements in the stock price. It is their profits and losses that are important and these are again the outcome of their emotional outbursts of greed and fear. Let us understand these investors.

12.3 ROLE OF THE OWNERS: INVESTORS

We need to change the paradigm of ownership when we look at investors in the stock markets. Can owners play havoc with their own companies? Conventional wisdom would say no. But the realities of the stock markets are very different. When stocks are listed, investors can get in and out of a stock with the click of a button. Thus, ownership changes in seconds. How can we hope to have any loyalty from transient owners? Although these same investors, during their tenure, have every authority over the management of the company, they have no responsibility towards the same company that they own.

Let us understand these investors and their behavior.

1. These investors help the company to grow and flourish by providing resources in the form of capital. This comes in many ways, like subscriptions to an IPO, subscription to a rights offer or investing in a private placement. Had it not been for this entrepreneurial spirit of investors we would not have had such a vibrant capital market.
2. These are the investors who do research on companies. They keep the management on alert. They pose all sorts of questions to management regarding the healthy functioning of the company. They study the business model, the markets, the technology adopted by the company, the corporate governance, the human resources policy, etc., to judge the quality of the company.
3. They help companies in their expansion plans and mergers and acquisitions efforts by providing capital in times of such needs. This form of financing is fast and does not involve the procedural delays of the banks and financial institutions.
4. Investors help in determining the valuation of a company's stock. It is their perception and their optimism or pessimism that decides the stock valuation, which is then reflected in the stock price.
5. These same investors also create volatility in stock prices by moving in and out of a stock at the slightest hint of uncertainty. Investor greed and fear create this volatility.
6. In so doing these same investors can make or break a company.

This is the fickle-minded behavior of the investors who are supposedly the owners. At one time they are in love with their company and at other times they become so repulsed that they play havoc with the stock price.

Why does this happen? There are two very strong destabilizing changes that have happened with equity ownership. The growth of mutual funds has led to institutional ownership going up. This has led to the rise of professional money managers whose job is to make money from the markets from equities at any cost. Secondly they are dealing with other people's money and hence their risk-aversion is very minimal. With such a trend the concept of ownership and responsibility no longer exists. We are in a financial jungle where the rules are very different and corporates need to learn how to play by the new rules.

12.4 CORPORATE BEHAVIOR

12.4.1 Efficient Market Theory

Corporate managers follow the efficient market theory assuming that the management's job is to concentrate on developing strategies for creating shareholder value and explain the rationale to the investors.

They assume that investors make rational decisions based on a rational analysis of the company and its long-term financial performance.

This assumption makes them believe that if some investors exit the company, there are other potential investors who will step in to replace the sellers.

The managers' job is to run the company efficiently without being bothered about any external factors.

In so doing, they want to concentrate on the conventional wisdom, which says that the employees, the customers and the suppliers are the most important constituents of a company.

Every effort, time and money is spent on the employees. There are various employee-retention and loyalty schemes to reward the employees. You have a Human Resource Development (HRD) division to make the employees comfortable. Stock option schemes are there for employee retention.

Then again we have the customers. "The customer is king" goes the popular saying. Corporate managers do everything possible to please the customers in order to retain their loyalty. Huge amounts are spent on customer market surveys, loyalty reward programs and studies of customer behavior and spending patterns.

Lastly, the suppliers are also very important to the corporate managers. They play an important role in charting the company's expansion plans, delivery schedules and the research and development efforts. Corporate managers take good care to make the suppliers happy and, in turn, loyal to the company.

Companies follow the traditional model of focusing on what they want to say rather than understanding what investors wish to know. They believe that everyone is on the same wavelength and, thus, they come out with communication packages for all types of investors. There is no effort made to understand what the investor is looking at. There could be some investors who look at a company from its strategic position, while others may look at it from its organizational capabilities. Feeding both these types of investors the same information can lead to different reactions from them. Understanding investor behavior, the information one looks for, while making an investment decision and the investing timeframe one has in mind are important aspects a company should know when communicating with investors.

Analysts' meet, followed by cocktails and dinner along with specific communication package is the routine followed by companies.

The sad part is that corporate managers ignore the most important aspect, and that is the complex behavior of investors. No effort is made to study the behavior of the investors.

12.4.2 Do they Know their Investors?

You ask a company who are its investors, and they will give you a long list of shareholders at a particular date and tell you that these are the investors. This is where the problem begins. For a listed company every investor in the market place is its investor. He may not be in the current list of shareholders but with a click of a button he becomes a shareholder. The stock markets make that happen and technology facilitates that within seconds.

With institutional ownership going up, it is important for the company to understand the professional fund-managers, who are investors. Their behavior and their perceptions on the company need to be monitored regularly. Efforts need to be made to understand these investors. Their behavior is very complex as, although they are owners, they can exit as owners within seconds. Moreover, they are investing other people's money. These two criteria make it important for the company to take pains to understand the complex behavior of these investors.

These are the investors who can play havoc with stock prices. They can make or break a company. They do research on the company. But do the companies research their investors? This is an idea whose time has come.

Companies should concentrate on all the four constituents: employees, customers, suppliers and investors.

12.5 INVESTOR BEHAVIOR-BASED FINANCE

> **Investor do research on companies. Do companies research their Investors?**

Investors do research on companies but do companies research their investors?

Looking at the way the investors play havoc with stock prices by buying and selling on the slightest market noise it is important that corporations understand the profile of its investors.

To start with, one needs to outline a basic framework for profiling investors. This is done by identifying the key investors and ascertaining their investment horizons. Thereafter, one needs to understand their analytical process, which drives their decision making. This would help the corporation to know the type of investors it has.

To study investor behavior in detail, it is important to obtain investor finances and trading patterns. This enables a corporation to predict and gauge the potential impact of investor decisions on stock prices.

Stock volatility is a function of the investor community rather than of specific investors of a corporation. If communication from corporations is made available to like-minded investors, it can go a long way in building a strong network of loyal investors. Hence, investor mapping and tailor-made communication to match investor perceptions is the need of the hour.

12.6 PARADIGM SHIFT: RESEARCH ON INVESTOR BEHAVIOR

This calls for a paradigm shift in the way companies look at their investors. Understanding investor behavior can only be done by profiling and mapping the investors. The first step would be to profile the investors by identifying the key investors and their reasons for investing. The second step would be to map the investors with reference to the content they analyze for making investment decisions and also their horizon of investment.

12.6.1 Identifying Key Investors

When given the task of identifying the key investors, one would naturally conclude that the largest investors would be the key investors. However, this may not be true if we are looking at investors who play havoc with stock prices. These large investors could be passive as they could have invested in the company because it happens to be a part of the index or it could be because the investor needs a certain amount of exposure in the particular sector and so on.

However, it is the active traders who really influence the stock prices. Now these could be large shareholders or past shareholders who suddenly become active due to the change of fortunes of the company, revival of the sector in which the company is, or change in management following an acquisition or a merger. This news can make the existing small investors active as well as attract new investors who could influence the price. So, medium to small traders do play a very important role when we identify the key investors.

It is also important to know the organizational safeguards imposed on such active influential investors or fund managers. The organization could have its set of guidelines for not exceeding a certain percentage in a particular stock or an industry, the regulatory controls, and the fund managers' own limits on stock and industry exposure. Liquidity concerns also affect investor trading decisions. Knowledge of all these is important for the company to understand its investors.

12.6.2 Profiling the Investors

After the key investors have been identified, it becomes necessary to profile them. How does one profile the investors? Understanding the investment time horizon and the dominant content analyzed helps us in profiling the investors and thus communicating with them on their specific interests.

Investment Horizon

Long Term: Most long-term investors base their decisions on the long-term growth projections stretching over a period of five years or more. They follow the discounted cash flow model to judge whether a stock is worthy of investment. They look at the long-term prospects of the business and the quality of management. Investors like Warren Buffett fall into this category.

They follow the fundamental long-term approach to investing and, thus, are known as fundamental analysts. However, their investing behavior can be very different from their fundamental approach. Say a stock is bought based on fundamental analysis, but the price moves up very steeply, the fundamental analyst can become a short-term trader. Therefore, a fundamental analyst need not necessarily be a long-term investor. My experience has also shown that most of the big institutional investors talk about long-term investment strategies but their trading pattern depicts short-term behavior. Therefore, most of the professional investors are not long-term fundamental investors.

Medium Term: The time horizon of these investors ranges from 12 to 18 months. They are looking at certain news that could affect the company in the medium-term. Such news could be in the form of a turnaround in the company, the effect of a new product in the market, etc. A majority of the large active traders falls into this category. These types of medium-term investors could be termed as 'news forecasters'. They are the ones who are most influential price movers in the medium-term.

Short Term: These investors are smaller than the long- and the medium-term investors, but they can be in the top 100 and are a formidable force to reckon with. Their time horizon is short and it ranges from a week to a couple of months. They move in and out of a stock fast and they closely follow different corporate actions. Their buying and selling takes place ahead of specific news such as earnings predictions, a technology breakthrough announcement, outcome of a major contract or a bonus announcement. These investors are busy buying on rumors and selling on news. Large, as well as retail investors, form a part of these short-term investors. Since they are looking at events to unfold we can term them as 'event bettors'. Their behavior is well described by the famous saying, 'Buy on the rumor and sell on the news.'

There is also a great deal of overlapping when we attempt to map and identify investor behavior. Biotechnology is a long-term business, as most of the value that companies create from its products will not be realized for more than a decade. As a result, one might expect the fundamental analysts to dominate the shareholders' register and, therefore, the share price.

But the opposite is happening: 90% of the investors in this segment are news forecasters or event bettors. They make decisions based on short-term events such as clinical trials.

So there are no hard and fast rules but the trend and the patterns of behavior from trading data serve as useful guide posts.

Dominant Content Being Analyzed

Different investors have different yardsticks to measure a company's performance and the business outlook. Investors like Warren Buffett would invest in companies whose business he understands. On the other hand, there could be investors who look at the organizational structure of a company, and there could be still others for whom organizational structure is irrelevant but product innovation and technology are very important. Thus we can map investors with the content they analyze.

1. **Organization watchers**

They lay more stress on organizational issues when making investment decisions. Organizational changes make them active and they buy or sell a stock based on such changes.

Relevant data

They look at organizational changes with great interest. They believe that as long as a good business is run with good organizational capabilities, its ability to be profitable and reward the shareholders is guaranteed.

Such organizational capabilities could be due to a strong leader in the form of a successful entrepreneur (Dhirubhai Ambani) or an efficient CEO (Narayana Murthy or a Nandan Nilekani). It could also be due to good corporate governance systems and values (TATA Group).

A big reshuffle or an exodus of senior management would make such organizational mavens active. Organizational takeovers, mergers and acquisitions would also call for activity by the mavens.

Conditions that make them active

- Change in organizational structure. This could be due to restructuring, downsizing, merger or an acquisition.
- Appointment or firing of a CEO.
- Changes in senior management cadres.
- Exodus of star performers from the company.
- Regulatory inquiry in the affairs of the organization.
- Death of the entrepreneur or a CEO with an impeccable track record.

2. **Strategy followers**

They look at important business strategies a company adopts. They give more importance to such issues when making their buy and sell decisions.

Relevant data

- A change in the business model of a company.
- A different marketing and sales strategy. For example, a consumer goods industry adopting an aggressive marketing strategy earmarking a huge resource outlay to capture market share.
- A takeover of a company and thus increased customer acquisition and market penetration.
- Selling off existing loss-making divisions.
- Entering a new line of business and its implications on the current business.
- Introducing product innovations in the market.
- Growth through acquisitions.

Conditions that make them active

A change in the business model could have mixed reactions. These developments have to be viewed with market trends and the state of the stock markets. During the technology boom, many companies decided to get into the technology sector, considering the new potential. However the said strategy worked for some but not all.

An innovative sales and marketing strategy for market penetration would depend upon the resources available with the company and the strength of the competitors. These would have mixed reactions.

A takeover of a company for increase in customer base and market penetration would have a favorable impact with the investors. However, as discussed in an earlier chapter titled 'Sector Investing,' the price paid would be a subject of debate as the fear would be of the company getting trapped in the winner's curse.

Hiving off non-profitable businesses would be viewed favorably by the investors.

Entering a new line of business in a bull market would have favorable implications. However, in a bear market, investors would not be very excited.

Introducing product innovations would have initial favorable interest. This information will be viewed with the impact on profitability and the ability of market success.

Growth through acquisitions would be a favorable strategy in a bull market but a neutral one in a bear market. Moreover, the fear of winner's curse will always linger with the sophisticated investors.

3. **Financial addicts**

Looking at financial figures for investment decisions is one of the most important parameters. However, in current times, with the spread of day-traders and short-term punters, investor behavior has become very important when it comes to reacting to financial figures. And investors' behavior to financial figures is responsible for the volatility in the markets.

Volatility is increased with the disclosure of quarterly results by the companies. Investors get in and out of a stock depending on the quarterly results. Investors have been very brutal with companies not able to consistently post favorable financial figures. However the silver lining for long-term investors is that such an erratic and short-term view by a majority of the investors offers great buying opportunities.

Relevant data

The relevant data is all about the financial profit figures. It has nothing to do with the financial health of the company. The most important data for such investors is the quarterly results declared by a company. These need to match with investors expectations. And these expectations are formed by expecting growth over the past quarter. Other relevant pieces of information are the guidance given by the management, year-on-year profit growth of the company,the dividend payout of the company, and the issue of splits.

Conditions that make them active

- A company exceeding investors' expectations.
- A company not meeting investors' expectations.
- Management warning of a slow-down.
- Management unable to meet the guidance given.
- Quarterly results beat market expectations.
- Quarterly results disappoint.
- Stock split announcement.
- Dividend cut.
- Dividend payout raised.

4. **Management watchers**

These types of investors believe that as an investor you are entrusting your money to the management. Hence, the quality of the management is a very important parameter to them. They are very sensitive to management actions, both company-specific and personal.

Relevant data

- The track record of management's performance.
- The vision and the organizational capabilities of the management.
- The integrity and honesty of the management. Do they walk the talk?
- Are they dependable and trustworthy?
- What is the stake of the management in the company? Especially when the company is family-owned.
- Do they have the interests of the shareholders at heart?
- What is the management's contribution to the society?
- Are they manipulating their own stock prices?
- How are they managing the company's resources? Are they extravagant in their personal spending?
- Is the company's financial showing a true picture of the company?

- The reputation of the management.
- Succession plans and ability to retain talent.
- Do they give the right information on the company to its investors?
- Are they fair with all the stakeholders?
- Is the management conservative?
- Treatment of its own employees.
- Dealings with its business associates, like timely payment to suppliers and fair dealings with customers.

Conditions that make them active

- Management frequently misses its guidance.
- Management is involved in a scam.
- Regulatory or statutory proceedings against the management.
- Internal control problems and conflicts.
- The company skips dividends, but balance sheet shows abnormal and questionable expenses.
- Personal wealth created at the expense of the company, like huge salaries and allowances even when the company is not doing well.
- Consistently rewarding shareholders.
- Over-performing the guidance given.
- Get awards from business associations.
- Acknowledgements for services and contribution to society.

The above are just a few examples of how investors can be mapped. They could also be further mapped as sector followers, index stock watchers, innovation punters, market-trend bandwagons, etc. Once the investors are mapped with reference to their behavior, the content analyzed by them and the conditions that make them active, it becomes fairly easy to gauge their investment actions. Companies can benefit immensely from such analysis as they will be able to effectively communicate with the investors.

Do retail investors matter?

It may be easier to map and profile the big institutional investors, but at the retail level we need to separate them according to their velocity of trading.

High-velocity retail investors come in the form of day-traders. But their entry and exit in a stock is so fast that they really do not affect the stock prices unless the stock happens to be illiquid.

The low-velocity investors are the inheritors and the retired, who hold on to stocks for sentimental reasons or with an idea to benefit from the dividends and capital appreciation. They do not have any impact on stock price volatility.

The medium-velocity investors are the most important group which creates some impact on the stock price. They are the retail event bettors who trade at a medium velocity, generally holding stocks for a few months to a year.

12.7 A CASE STUDY OF INVESTOR BEHAVIOR-BASED FINANCE

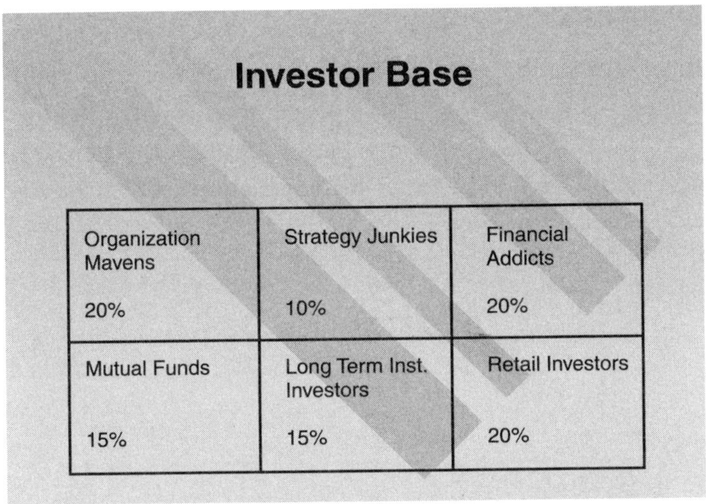

Figure 12.1 Distribution of the Investor Base

The company has done some research to map its investors (Figure 12.1) and it finds that 20% of the investors are organization mavens; i.e,. the dominant content they analyze constitutes organizational issues; 10% lay stress on strategies; and 20%, being financial addicts, concentrate on the financial figures. Financial institutions like pension funds hold 15% of the shares, and they are long-term passive investors. Mutual funds hold another 15%, and the remaining 20% are held by retail investors. This investor holding is the free float in the market and does not include the promoter holding.

12.7.1 Reorganization Plans

- Change Business Strategy
- Require organization structure revamp
- Adopt a vibrant new business model

The company intends going ahead with a restructuring plan, which would require it to change the business strategy and reorganize the organization structure. The new business model would enable it to improve its long-term profitability, but the short-term pains of having two bad quarters (earnings would drop by 25%) are the price to be paid.

12.7.2 Investor Chaos

Such an announcement would lead to chaos, and investors would react to such news (Figure 12.2). The company stock price could take a beating. However, the company being ready with the data on its investors, would be confident of bringing about the change without being unnecessarily worried.

Investor Chaos

Organization Mavens 20%	Strategy Junkies 10%	Financial Addicts 20% Selling
Mutual Funds 15% 5% Selling	Long Term Inst. Investors 15%	Retail Investors 20% Confusion 10% Selling

Figure 12.2 Distribution of Investor Reactions

Since the announcement is about the change in strategy and the organization revamp, which would increase the long-term health of the company, it would present the case favorably to the organization mavens, the strategy junkies and the long-term investors. They will be able to understand and will not be unduly perturbed by the temporary drop in profits for the first two quarters; thus, 45% of the investors would not panic and continue to hold on to the stock. The financial addicts are always the short-term traders, who base their decisions on events, and they would sell. The company expects all of them to sell, as the action of the company does not match their perception. This 20% of the investor base will sell their shares. Mutual funds hold 15%. Of these, the growth funds will stay invested. However, specific sector funds and balanced funds could sell. Hence, a selling of 5% is assumed. From the retail investors it is expected that 50% would sell. Hence, a 10% selling from them is expected. Overall, a total of 35% selling can be expected.

12.7.3 Important Investors

The next step is to identify the most important type of investors. They would be:

- Organization Mavens
- Strategy Junkies
- Long term Investors

The company then needs to position itself as a long-term investment opportunity, as it is changing its business strategy and revamping the organizational set-up. The current investors who believe in the new business model will not only increase their holding, but a whole new set of investors emerges, to whom the company can go and present itself. The company needs to make the existing investors its champions and present the new business model to prospective new investors.

12.7.4 The New Arena

This exercise enables the company to open itself to a whole new set of investors who would be willing to invest (Figure 12.3). The initial selling pressure could be absorbed by the new set of investors. The price drop could attract new financial addicts, as well as short-term traders willing to wait for the next six months. Doors open for event bettors to make a bet as well. Value investors may find the price attractive. A price drop

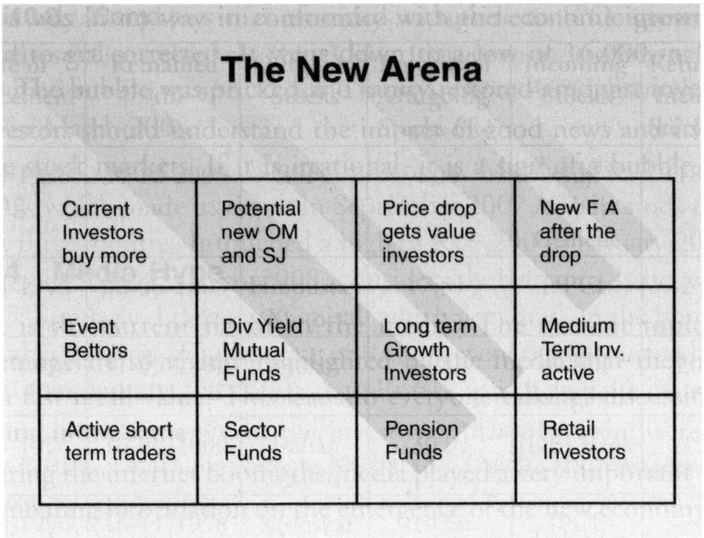

Figure 12.3 The Potential Investor Base

could make the dividend yield attractive and mutual funds with focus on dividend yields could be potential buyers.

This is just a simple way of depicting how investor behavior-based finance would work. Now, let us get into the details, to see how one can really study individual investors from their trading and past investment patterns after having mapped them and made a reasonable estimate as to how the stock price would be affected.

12.8 ESTIMATING STOCK PRICE MOVEMENT: A CASE STUDY

The Sun Corporation wants to acquire the Moon Corporation, which is one-third of its size. It wants to pay a 30% premium. The directors do not want the stock price to fall more than 10% as a result. The decision rests with 60 large active investors.

The investor base comprises the following.

Star Fund, the largest investor, holds 10 lakh shares. A fundamental analyst and a strategy junky hold 3% of Sun (below 5% official limit, but 5 times daily average volume as against the 4 times official limit). Cloud Fund, another significant investor holds five lakh shares, and is critical of the acquisition strategy, due to loss of jobs. During Sun's last acquisition, Cloud had sold four lakh shares. Cloud is a 'blaster'[1] .

Although Star Fund invests on the fundamentals of a company and understands and believes in the strategy of the company, it will not be able to increase its position, even if it likes the move of the company. It has not exceeded its limit of 5% prescribed by the organization. It is only holding 3%. However, the fund manager has exceeded the daily average limit of four times the average daily turnover. Last time, the fund manager had to obtain special permission from the board to exceed this limit. Reluctantly, the Board had agreed to the same. Hence, any additional investment coming from this fund was out of question. The company was reasonably confident that there would be no selling pressures either.

As against this, the Cloud Fund does not like acquisition strategies as it leads to loss of jobs and low morale. Its track record also shows that it becomes a seller on such acquisitions. So, this time the Star management can expect a sale of five lakh shares coming from Cloud. Since Cloud is a blaster, it can create a huge impact on the price. Because of this, the Star management feels that the dent in price could be a good opportunity for financial addicts and event bettors to enter.

- After mapping 60 investors, the company finds that15 investors would buy 25 lakh shares,
- 12 would maintain the status quo,
- 18 investors would sell 31 lakh shares, and
- 15 investors are difficult to predict.

This would be a rough estimate the company would reach. A regression analysis of the same would give the following results:

- Five to seven lakh shares would be sold, and
- The stock price is predicted to fall 6% to 8%

This being in tune with the thinking of the Star management, the Board would be confident to go ahead with the acquisition. This results in huge gains for the company, as it is able to build trust and faith with

[1] There are two types of sellers: blasters and bleeders. Blasters sell their stock at one go and create a temporary dent in the price. Bleeders on the other hand sell small lots of stocks every day for an extended period of time. This could see the stock stagnating for a long period and frustrate the existing holders

the investing community. It would also help in its strategy implementation, as the feedback of its action is measurable. Needless to say, such transparency with the investors will lead to less stock volatility. Such a proactive approach leads to better-informed decisions and investor-friendly strategies.

12.9 CONCLUSION

12.9.1 Why Investor Behavior-Based Finance?

Financial markets are growing all over the world. Every country needs to attract capital for its growth and what better route can there be than the stock markets? Borders are opening up and, with the use of new technologies such as the internet, information is available to all. Thus, financial markets have become very fluid. With the click of a button, transactions take place. This has led to growth of an investing class hungry for investing opportunities to make a fast buck. The chaos in the market along with the emotions of greed and fear have created investors who are very short-sighted and unpredictable.

It is important to understand the behavior of these investors so that we can manage their perceptions and, thereby, control the volatility in the stock prices due to their actions. They are the stakeholders of a corporation and understanding their behavior will help the corporation to manage its stock volatility.

12.9.2 What are the Benefits?

- Identifying and mapping investor behavior leads to better understanding of the investor base
- Being proactive leads to informed decisions
- Increase faith and trust with investors
- Transparency leads to investor-friendly strategies
- Make stock price less volatile
- Manage investor perceptions
- Create better understanding of the company
- Manage irrational behavior of investors
- Completes the missing link with employees, customers and suppliers

BIBLIOGRAPHY

Bernstein, Peter; ***Against the Gods: The Remarkable Story of Risk***; Wiley (August 31, 1998).

Bogle, John; ***Bogle on Mutual Funds: New Perspectives for the Intelligent Investor***; Dell (October 4, 1994).

Browne, Christopher; ***The Little Book of Value Investing***; Wiley (September 22, 2006).

Buffett, Warren; ***Letters to Shareholders of Berkshire Hathaway Inc.***;

http://www.berkshirehathaway.com/letters/letters.html

Buffett, Warren; ***The Super-investors of Graham and Doddsville***; Hermes, The Columbia Business School Magazine (April 1984).

Cialdini, Robert; ***Influence: The Psychology of Persuasion***; Collins Business, Revised edition (December 26, 2006).

Cunningham Lawrence; ***The Essays of Warren Buffett: Lessons for Corporate America***; Wiley, Revised and Updated Edition (April 9, 2002).

Daniel Kahneman, Paul Slovic, and Amos Tversky; ***Judgment under Uncertainty: Heuristics and Biases***; Cambridge University Press (April 30, 1982).

Dreman, David; ***Contrarian Investment Strategies in the Next Generation***; Simon & Schuster (May 18, 1998).

Ellis, Charles; ***Winning the Loser's Game: Timeless Strategies for Successful Investing***; McGraw-Hill, 4th edition (March 14, 2002).

Fisher, Philip; ***Common Stocks and Uncommon Profits and Other Writings***; Wiley (September 4, 2003).

Franklin, Benjamin; ***The Autobiography of Benjamin Franklin***; Touchstone (December 23, 2003).

Galbraith, John Kenneth; ***A Short History of Financial Euphoria***; Penguin (July 1, 1994).

Galbraith, John Kenneth; ***The Great Crash of 1929***; Mariner Books (April 30, 1997).

Graham, Benjamin and Dodd, David; ***Security Analysis: The Classic 1934 Edition***; McGraw-Hill (October 1, 1996).

Graham, Benjamin and Meredith, Spencer; ***The Interpretation of Financial Statements***; Collins Business (May 6, 1998).

Graham Benjamin; ***Intelligent Investor***; Collins Business, Revised edition (2003).

Greenblatt, Joel; ***The Little Book That Beats the Market***; Wiley (November 19, 2005).

Greenblatt, Joel; ***You Can Be a Stock Market Genius***; Fireside (February 25, 1999).

Greenwald, Bruce; ***Value Investing: From Graham to Buffett and Beyond***; Wiley (January 26, 2004).

Hagstrom, Robert; ***Latticework: The New Investing***; Texere (November 17, 2000).

Hagstrom, Robert; ***The Warren Buffett Portfolio: Mastering the Power of the Focus Investment Strategy***; Wiley (January 1, 1999).

Hagstrom, Robert; ***The Warren Buffett Way***; Wiley (October 4, 2005).

Kaufman, Michael; ***Soros: The Life and Times of a Messianic Billionaire***; Knopf (February 19, 2002).

Kaufman, Peter; ***Poor Charlie's Almanack: The Wit and Wisdom of Charles T. Munger***; Walsworth Publishing Company (2005).

Kindelberger, Charles; ***Manias, Panics, and Crashes: A History of Financial Crises***; Wiley, 5th edition (2005).

Klarman, Seth; ***Margin of Safety: Risk-Averse Value Investing Strategies for the Thoughtful Investor***; HarperCollins (October 1991).

Le Bon, Gustave; ***The Crowd***; Dover Publications (January 8, 2002).

Lefevre Edwin; ***Reminiscences of a Stock Operator***; Wiley; Revised edition (January 17, 2006).

Lowe, Janet; ***Benjamin Graham on Value Investing: Lessons from the Dean of Wall Street***; Penguin (Non-Classics) (March 1, 1996).

Lowe, Janet; ***The Rediscovered Benjamin Graham: Selected Writings of the Wall Street Legend***; Wiley (April 15, 1999).

Lowe, Janet; ***Warren Buffett Speaks: Wit and Wisdom from the World's Greatest Investor***; Wiley, 2nd edition (August 31, 2007).

Lowenstein Roger; ***When Genius Failed: The Rise and Fall of Long-Term Capital Management***; Random House (October 9, 2001).

Lowenstein, Roger; ***Buffett: The Making of an American Capitalist***; Random House (August 22 1995).

Lynch, Peter; ***Beating the Street***; Simon & Schuster; Revised edition (May 25, 1994).

Lynch, Peter; ***One up on Wall Street***; Simon & Schuster; 2nd edition (April 3, 2000).

Mackay, Charles; ***Extraordinary Popular Delusions and the Madness of Crowds***; Wiley (1995).

Malkiel, Burton; ***A Random Walk Down Wall Street: The Time-Tested Strategy for Successful Investing***; W. W. Norton, 9th edition (December 24, 2007).

Mauboussin, Michael; ***More Than You Know: Finding Financial Wisdom in Unconventional Places***; Columbia University Press (September 26, 2007).

Pabrai Mohnish; ***The Dhandho Investor: The Low-Risk Value Method to High Returns***; Wiley (April 6, 2007).

Rogers, Jim; ***Hot Commodities: How Anyone Can Invest Profitably in the World's Best Market***; Random House (March 27, 2007).

Schwed, Fred; ***Where Are the Customers' Yachts: A Good Hard Look at Wall Street***; Wiley 2006.

Siegel, Jeremy; ***Stocks for the Long Run***; McGraw-Hill; 4th edition (November 27, 2007).

Siegel, Jeremy; ***The Future for Investors: Why the Tried and the True Triumph Over the Bold and the New***; Crown Business (March 8, 2005).

Shefrin, Hersh; ***Beyond Greed and Fear: Understanding Behavioral Finance and the Psychology of Investing***; Oxford University Press, USA; 1st edition (May 16, 2007).

Smith Adam; ***Money Game***; Vintage (August 12, 1976).

Smith, Adam; ***Supermoney***; Wiley (May 26, 2006).

Soros George; ***The Alchemy of Finance***; Wiley (July 29, 2003).

Straker, David; ***Changing Minds: in Detail***; Syque Press (2008).

Surowiecki, James; ***The Wisdom of Crowds***; Anchor (August 16, 2005).

Taleb, Nassim Nicholas; ***Fooled by Randomness: The Hidden Role of Chance in Life and in the Markets***; Random House; 2nd Updated edition (August 23, 2005).

Taleb, Nassim Nicholas; ***The Black Swan: The Impact of the Highly Improbable***; Random House; 1st edition (April 17, 2007).

Tim Koller, Marc Goedhart, and David Wessels; ***Valuation: Measuring and Managing the Value of Companies***; Wiley; 4th edition (June 8, 2005).

Train, John; ***Money Masters of Our Time***; Collins Business (May 13, 2003).

Tweedy Browne Company LLC; ***What has worked in Investing.***

Whitman, Martin; ***The Aggressive Conservative Investor***; Wiley; Updated edition (November 4, 2005).

Williams, John Burr; ***The Theory of Investment Value***; Fraser Publishing Co. (June 1, 1997).

Zweig, Jason; ***Your Money and Your Brain: How the New Science of Neuroeconomics Can Help Make You Rich***; Simon & Schuster (August 1, 2007).

GLOSSARY

BEHAVIORAL FINANCE

Ambiguity Effect: When people make choices, sometimes they have a good understanding of the probability of something happening, while at other times the situation is ambiguous. In such situations, people are more likely to choose the former situation, preferring certainty over uncertainty. This is termed as ambiguity effect.

Example: Reasoning of a retail investor highlights ambiguity effect: 'I know that there is at best a moderate chance of my earning a moderate return by following the advice of my current investment advisor, whom I have known for a while. There is a possibility that the advisor recommended by my best friend is a far better investment adviser than the present one. But rather than 'risking it', I will just continue with my present adviser.'

Anchoring Heuristic: We tend to base estimates and decisions on known 'anchors' or familiar positions, with an adjustment relative to this starting point. We are better at *relative* thinking as compared to absolute thinking. This is referred to as anchoring heuristic.

Example: Say you own a stock and you have seen the price going up to Rs. 2000. However, when the price is Rs.1500, you get some bad news about the company and you are recommended to sell it. You are most unlikely to sell as in all probability you would be anchored to the high price of Rs. 2000. Had the stock not touched Rs. 2000 and would have been around Rs. 1500, you would have most likely sold it. The absence of the anchor makes decisions easier.

Availability Bias: We make a judgment based on what we can remember, rather than complete data. In particular, we use this for judging frequency or likelihood of events. Various factors can affect availability. Things which are easier to imagine, for example, if they are very vivid they make themselves more available. Things which are uncomfortable to think about can push people into denial, making these thoughts unavailable. This may be the reason why we seem sometimes egocentric because our own experiences are more available to us.

Example: We buy stocks, which are the current flavor of the markets, which are recommended by leading analysts and brokers and which we hear about in the news media. In such cases, availability heuristic is at play. We act on this readily available information, which is vividly displayed.

Belief Perseverance: Once we have our faith in something, we try to stick to it, even in the face of disconfirming evidence. In particular if other people are aware of our belief, it can be embarrassing when we fail to establish that assertion. It is also difficult to abandon a belief which has been woven into a wider web of belief, without disturbing those other beliefs.

Example: An IPO investor says to himself, 'All my friends know that I subscribed to Reliance Power IPO. Now if I sell it at a loss, everybody will think I made a mistake. I would rather wait for it to be quoted at above the issue price.'

Buyer's Remorse: After we commit our capital into something, self-doubt triggers of remorse or deep regret about having done something terribly wrong. In such times, until you have deep conviction in your stand and are ready to face the uncertainty, it becomes very difficult to hold on to that position.

Example: When people buy on tips, they are most susceptible to buyer's remorse and it is common to notice them shuffling their portfolios like a pack of cards because they lack the conviction to stick to their investments.

Bystander Effect: When there is an emergency and the more bystanders there are, the less likely it is that any of them will actually help. Mass ignorance is when they assume nothing is wrong because nobody else looks concerned.

Example: When all my friends are investing in the markets, I guess that investing in equity is not risky. May be they know something that is unknown to me. Let me try my luck at investing.

Cognitive Dissonance: Cognitive dissonance emerges when we believe something about ourselves and then do something against that belief feel the discomfort. This feeling of discomforting tension comes from holding two conflicting thoughts in the mind at the same time.

Example: Investors can find all kinds of reasons to explain away their mistakes because they cannot accept the alternative, which is to accept that they were simply ignorant or wrong.

Commitment Theory: A commitment is a public or private decision to act. If we make a commitment, we often feel bound to follow through with it, out of fear of social rejection. When we are committed to something, we will not change our minds very easily, especially if that commitment is known publicly.

Example: Investment bankers who volunteer to help an enterprise by raising capital from the markets are prone to over estimate the fair value of the business. In doing so, they keep up with their recommendation to buy even when the economics of the business behind the stock is falling.

Confirmation Bias: When we have made a decision or a hypothesis, we will actively seek things to confirm it and also avoid things which will disconfirm this. The alternative is to face the dissonance of being wrong. We use this approach both for searching for confirmation in our memory and in the external world.

Example: After buying a stock, some search for an expensive stock in the same sector to confirm that they have bought a bargain in the name of relative valuation.

Consistency Theory: When there is conflict between behavioral response that is consistent with our core belief systems and a response that is consistent with social norms, the potential threat of social exclusion sometimes leads us to go against our deeply held convictions and respond as is consistent with social setting, in spite of the significant discomfort it causes deep down. In social proof, there is an absence of knowledge about what is the right thing to do; however, as per consistency theory, inspite of indication that we might be wrong in following the crowd, we get influenced to conform to and persist with irrational behavior.

Example: If a friend recommends an outright by expensive stock, you will feel bad if you do not follow his advice. Hence, you end up investing in spite of evidence indicating a mistake in advance.

Contrast Effect: When we make decisions, we tend to do it by contrasting between the decision item and reference items. When two things appear close to each other, we will tend to evaluate them against each other more than against a fixed standard.

Example: If somebody recommends the most expensive stock in a fancy sector, people investing in a less expensive stock within the same sector convince themselves that they have got a good bargain to invest in it.

Control Theory: We have a deep need for control that itself, paradoxically, controls much of our lives. The endless effort to control can make us miserable as we fail in this impossible task of trying to control everything and everyone around us. The alternative is to see the world as a series of choices.

Example: We presume that we know our investments in and out. But, it is only on cross-checking from time to time while explaining it to the like-minded friends that we get an opportunity to realize how much do we actually know about it.

Endowment Effect: When we own something, we tend to value it more highly. Accordingly, if we have to sell it, we will probably ask for more than its real worth.

Example: How many times have you found yourself giving a higher limit to your broker to sell a stock and giving a lower limit to buy a stock? This is inspite of the broker informing you the price prevailing in the market. You want more for what you hold and are willing to pay less for what the other one owns.

External Justification: When we do something that causes discomforting cognitive dissonance, we tend to justify it by blaming it on external factors. This is opposed to internal justification, where in we attribute it to our character or some personal trait or belief.

Example: When you last had an investment loss, did you blame yourself? Or did you blame the investment adviser, broker, CNBC or somebody else?

False Consensus Effect: Human beings do not weigh information in total isolation from the situation. Their pre conceived notions influence how they come to perceive any given situation. In the absence of complete information and biased approach toward gathering and responding to information, it is only natural that our perception is subject to crude approximations. We approximate by drawing consensus through discounting the views held by our friends, acquaintainces and reading books. In the process, how strongly we want to substantiate something has an effect on how we weigh information while making decisions. This lopsidedness in reaching a consensus based on the assimilation of widespread information is known as false consensus effect.

Example: Optimism over an investment is high following the buy decision made by us. However, with the passage of time we realize that if we have missed discounting the key negatives. The sooner one gets over the cloud-nine effect, the better would it be to realize any mistakes and reduce the losses.

Framing Effect: A frame is a combination of beliefs, values, attitudes, and mental models, which we use to perceive a situation. We effectively look through this frame in the same way as we would look through tinted spectacles. The frame significantly affects how we infer from and understand the situation. Kahneman and Tversky define a decision frame as 'the decision-maker's conception of the act, outcomes, and contingencies associated with a particular choice.'

Example: I see a stock as a long-term investment opportunity. My friend sees it as a chance to make a good short-term speculative gain. My son sees it as a candidate for an arbitrage opportunity.

Fundamental Attribution Error: When we are trying to understand and explain what happens in social settings, we tend to view behavior as a particularly significant factor. We then tend to explain behavior in terms of internal disposition, such as personality traits, abilities, motives, etc., as opposed to external situational factors. This can be due to our focus on the person more than his/her situation, about which we may know very little. We also know little about how they interpret the situation.

When we are playing the role of an observer, we make this fundamental attribution error. When we are thinking about ourselves, however, we tend to make situational attributions.

Example: Taking credit for the investment successes and finding excuses for the losses incurred is a common behavioral trait among majority of the investors, financial advisors and fund managers.

Group Think: Groups sometimes falls into a line of thinking wherein the maintenance of the group's cohesion and togetherness becomes all-important and results in very bad decision making.

Group think happens most often when the group is already cohesive, and isolated from conflicting opinions, and the leader is open and gives directions. The lack of a formal decision making process is also common. Problem-solving and task-oriented groups are particularly susceptible to this problem. Resulting decisions are often based on incomplete information and don't take cognizance of alternatives and risks.

Example: The most conducive environment leading to group think is when no single person is to be held responsible for the mistakes made and also when performance in itself has little to do with the compensation of fund managers. A good example is the investment committees in government-controlled financial institutions.

Halo Effect: When we consider a person good (or bad) in one category, we are likely to make a similar evaluation of him/her in other categories. It seems as if we cannot easily separate categories. It can also be connected with tendency to avoid dissonance as making them good in one thing and bad in another would make an overall evaluation (which we do anyway) difficult.

Example: Just because somebody has invested a lot of his/her savings in equities, it does not mean that he has the competence to invest wisely or spot bargains in the markets. An investor having made a fortune in the bull market is not necessarily nor evidently a smart investor.

Herding: Herding is a tendency to get in groups to ensure safety. The common benefit to the group as a whole is more than the loss in terms of sharing the resources. This strikes as a selfless act but in reality it is a trade-off where safety and common sharing go hand in hand. The size of herd varies as the benefits and the costs associated change with the inclusion of new members.

Example: It is difficult for an investor to 'think out of the box' and stand outside the pack consistently for longer period of time. It requires an unflinching conviction in one's ability to withstand being called a failure until the culmination of the struggle. And this difficulty leads people to get together in mental herds, wherein everybody holds the same belief as most others around him. If everybody around you is wrong, you don't mind being wrong as long as you have company.

Hindsight Bias: It can be embarrassing when things happen unexpectedly. To cover up this embarrassment, we will tend to view things which have already happened as being relatively inevitable and predictable. This can be caused by the reconstructive nature of memory. We do not have a perfect memory and tend to 'fill in the gaps'. This is also known as the 'I-knew-it-all-along' effect, reflecting a common response to a surprise.

Example: During the technology boom, technology stocks were over priced. Everyone knew about it but kept holding on to the stocks. When the markets crashed and investors lost money, everyone blamed the excessive valuations. Did everyone not know about it?

Illusion of Personal Invulnerability: Human beings tend to overestimate their own abilities and underestimate other's competence. An extension of this tendency is a condition called 'illusion of personal invulnerability,' wherein people perceive less risk for themselves on the ground of their high estimate of their ability to control the situation.

Example: Fund managers MBAs from 1vy League shools and working in high positions in big multinational corporations hold this illusion of personal invulnerability. They miss out on the important point that in markets, it is experience that counts rather than educational qualifications and positions.

Information Bias: While taking a decision, we generally seek data on which to rationally base the choice. This goes wrong when we assume that all information is useful and 'more is better'. Sometimes, extra information adds no significant value, rather it simply serves to confuse.

Example: Fund managers listen to a lot of brokers and take information on stocks. They believe that more information is more knowledge. However, it leads to information overload and noise. This is done by them more to justify their decision should it go wrong. More information gives them the safety of numbers.

Information Cascades: Information cascade underlies a situation in which every subsequent factor, based on the observations of others, leads to the same choice without thinking. Sometimes, when the imitation involves a wrong anchor, the information cascade can lead to devastating results for the group as a whole.

Example: During the speculative excesses, a common behavior observed among investors shows an interesting example of information cascade. People seem to cease to reason on their own and simply imitate the actions of others believing that it is the easiest way to make money. When majority of the people get into this sort of behavior, information cascade results in bubbles wherein reality is in sharp contrast to the underlying fundamentals. Around 70% of all mutual funds portfolios in a similar category will have the same stocks.

Instant Gratification: When faced with the choice between realizing a benefit now and a better one far into the future, some people tend to choose the former option as they don't have the emotional discipline to withstand the curiosity and delay gratification.

Example: The allure of instant gratification plays an important part in investor stock preference. Growth stocks satisfy this impulse. This is also one of the reasons for momentum investing. Value investing does not find flavor because it requires patience.

Justification of Effort: People tend to work hard in order to be successful. This not only involves making enough money to stay alive and comfortable but also move up in the social hierarchy. How we are perceived by our colleagues and friends has a special bearing on self-perception. With such incentives, it is quite natural that the desire to justify our efforts to ourselves and our peers, as heading toward the right direction is deeply ingrained in our belief system. In the process, we tend to look for evidence to justify our effort.

Example: Some people find it hard to sell the under performing stocks just because it nullifies all the effort that had gone into making that investment. Analysts prepare long reports with a lot of charts and tables and historical data to show the amount of their efforts. This makes the research report attractive as a lot of efforts seem to have gone in.

Myopic Loss Aversion: The pain of a loss is three times more than the pleasure of an equal amount of gain. Investors are not risk-averse or else they would not enter the markets. But they are loss-averse. They will shy away from any opportunity where there is a potential loss. For any investment decision, one must weigh the risk–reward ratio and then take an investment decision. However, investors become loss-averse when even the slightest hint of a loss lurks in their minds.

Example: Investors hold on to losing investments knowing fully well their loss. They sell winners too fast. When the markets go down, investors flee the stock markets and go for fixed-income securities. These are all examples of myopic loss aversion.

Overconfidence Barrier: We tend to have too much confidence in the accuracy of our own judgments. As we find out more about a situation, the accuracy of our judgments may well not increase, but our confidence will, as we equate quantity with quality. Confidence also tends to increase if we are given incentives to perform well.

Example: If one has been lucky to have well performing stocks in one's portfolio due to the overall bullish conditions in the market, one tends to be overconfident about one's abilities. From 2003 onwards till some time ago, there has been a fantastic bull run with everyone investing in stocks and making money. This has created a band of investors, fund managers, and analysts overconfident about their abilities and knowledge.

Planning Fallacy: It is a fact that future is full of uncertainties. However, people in an organization working towards a common goal get rewarded for beating the odds and making the best-case scenario happen. Nobody takes *No* for an answer these days. With such incentives, it is pertinent that people portray future in the light of certainty. And right from planning a dinner for a family gathering to projecting the capital outlay for a new plant, this behavioral anomaly can lead us to mispredict the future probabilities and plan inappropriately. The planning fallacy will become clearer in the following example.

Example: Managements are very susceptible to planning fallacy while providing a timeline for their new projects coming on stream. It is no surprise to currently see most of the projects getting delayed and investors getting upset it. Managers are human beings and susceptible to mistakes as well. It does not make them out bad managers if sometimes things are out of their control. When making investment decisions based on such management claims, it is important to know that things may not turn out as planned.

Rationalization Trap: When acting to reduce dissonance, one can end up with as a whole set of justifications and rationalizations that lead to ridiculous or even immoral actions. Like Pinocchio's nose, one defense leads to another until we are all out of shape. The trick is to avoid unthinking reaction, and tolerate dissonance for long enough to be able to decide on a more appropriate action.

Example: When your friend tries to justify his investment in a hot sector or a much hyped IPO, try and see if his reasoning is sound or if he is simply rationalizing his stance by creating value out of thin air.

Recency Effect: Given a list of items to remember, we tend to remember the last few things more than the ones in the middle. This happens because we are not blessed with unlimited memory and recent experiences are easier to recall than the past hidden ones.

Example: We tend to be swayed by the recency factor. Hence, we buy stocks when we see a lot of brokers recommending the same and analysts talking about them on TV shows and the print media. This remains fresh in our minds and affects our decision making. There is so much of advertisement and noise before the launch of an IPO that creates the recency effect with investors flocking to buy such IPOs.

Regret Theory: As per the Prospect theory losses are three times more painful as compared to the pleasure experienced by a gain of similar magnitude. What is the reason behind this anomaly? The answer is that people hate regret and losses produce regret. Sometimes, with the sole view of insuring themselves against future loss and regret, people weigh only the negatives and let the potential of regret influence their decision-making process. As the old saying goes, 'nothing ventured, nothing gained,' one should learn to see the potential and chances of regret in light of the potential for gain while making decisions and not let the prospect of regret cloud their thinking.

Example: When some people decide to buy a stock, they are so terrified of buying a heap of junk that they read whatever they can on the company or ask lots of knowledgeable friends about the investment idea. And sometimes they simply listen to other people's advice rather than buying the stock, which they think is a great bet.

Representative Heuristic: People tend to judge the probability of an event by finding a 'comparable known' event and assuming that the probabilities are similar. As a part of drawing meaning from what we experience, we need to classify things. If something does not fit exactly into a known category, we will approximate with the nearest class available.

Example: If Tata Steel prforms extraordinarily, investors will rush to buy Essar Steel. Their representative thinking makes them believe that Essar Steel will perform similarily.

Round Trip Fallacy: Consider the following statement: "All successful people are hard workers." Should we thus conclude that all hard workers are successful people? Definitely not. Hard work is one of the most important attributes of successful people but it is not the single one.

Example: Most of the cheap stocks generally have low or moderate P/E ratios and high only in exceptional cases. However, while believing that all low P/E stocks would necessarily be cheap stocks, one exposes oneself to "Round Trip Fallacy".

Scarcity Principle: In our need to control our world, being able to choose is an important freedom. If something becomes scarce, we anticipate possible regret that we did not acquire it, and so we desire it more. This desire is increased further if we think that someone else might get it and hence gain social position that we might have had.

Example: The upper price circuit in stocks enforced by the stock exchanges creates the scarcity effect. On a particular day when there are more buyers than sellers, the stocks hit the upper price circuit and cannot go beyond it on that day. This illusion of scarcity leads to more buyers chasing the stock and next day it again gets frozen at still a higher upper circuit.

Investment bankers create scarcity while advertising IPOs. Is it not true that the stock will be available for investment post the listing of the stock on the stock exchange? Is it also not known that most of the IPOs tend to trade at a level below their issue price after the mania in the sector or the bull market ends?

Self-Fulfilling Prophecy: If a person thinks us clever or stupid, he/she will treat us accordingly. If we are thus treated we tend to act, and even become so. The person thus has had his/her prophecy about us fulfilled.

Example: When everybody is convinced that a particular sector is going to be the fancy of the stock market, the demand for stocks in that sector results in short-term speculative profits which, in turn, validates the stand taken by the public creating a self-fulfilling prophecy. It lasts until the whole bubble bursts under its own weight.

Self-Serving Bias: Self-serving bias is our tendency to take credit for success and deny any responsibility for failure. This protects our ego and enables us to confirm that we are meeting our goals. We will tend to be less self-serving if other factors interrupt, for example, public scrutiny.

Example: Investors buy good as well as bad stocks. But, they tend to take the credit for good stocks for themselves blame others for the bad stocks. Fund managers are known to take credit for their good performing stocks, while for the non-performing stocks they blame the brokers or the market conditions.

Social Contagion: Emotion can spread rapidly through large crowds, as the massive social proof leads us into extreme situations. This explains much of crowd behavior, whereby 'normal' people act in ways they may later deeply regret.

Example: Just watching people and friends around subscribing to over-priced IPOs leads hordes of people not even familiar with the equity investment process to open demat accounts and join the mad rush.

Sunk Cost Effect: When we put efforts into something, we are often reluctant to pull out fearing losses we might incur, even if continued refusal to jump off the ship will lead to even more loss. The potential dissonance of accepting a mistake ties us to blind hope.

Example: When technolgy stocks were sinking from their high point, sunk cost fallacy not only induced investors not to sell but also buy more at falling prices. Sunk cost effect makes investors average the cost of purchase.

Winner's Curse: When lot of people after a scare resource and also the real value of the resource is not precisely calculable, the winner of the race can end up over paying for that resource and making a bad investment.

Example: In a competitive bidding process, the winner always pays more. This is very evident in corporate takeovers. Tata Tea acquired Tetely of UK in December 1999 bidding 20% higher than the competitor. Satyam Infoway bought World Com at 2000 times the earnings, which led to huge losses in Sify over the next several years.

FINANCE

Asset Class: An asset class represents a group of securities that have the same underlying asset type, behave similarly in the marketplace, and are subject to the same laws and regulations. The three main asset classes are equities, fixed-income securities, and cash equivalents (money market instruments). In addition to these are real estate and commodities.

Bear Market: Bear markets are characterized by excessive pessimism, and loss of investor confidence resulting in downward trend in the stock prices. Investors' interest in stocks remains very low and they go after fixed-income securities.

Beta: Beta is a measure of the volatility of a stock or portfolio as compared to the rest of the financial market, which are the broader indices like Sensex or Nifty. A beta of greater than 1 indicates that the security's price has been more volatile than the market in the past and can be expected to be so in the future. For example, if a stock's beta is 1.2, it is theoretically 20% more volatile than the market.

Bull Market: Bull markets are characterized by all round investor optimism and positive expectations resulting in an upward trend in the prices of an asset class. Many a times, bull market happens to be a result of improvements in the corporate performance and the change in the economy resulting in optimism about the future. It can also be due to irrational investor behavior as it happened during the Harshad Mehta-driven 1992–1993 rally and the 1999–2000 technology bubble.

Capital Structure: Capital structure denotes the ratio of debt, common equity, and preferred equity in the overall capitalization of the firm. The capital structure helps understand how a firm finances its operations and growth by using different sources of funds. Usually, when people refer to capital structure, they refer to a firm's debt–equity ratio, which provides quick insights into how financially sound a company is.

Debt-Equity Ratio: Debt-Equity is a financial ratio used to map the leverage that an enterprise has in comparison to its equity. This ratio has two important implications for an equity investor. First, it indicates the financial strength of an enterprise. A low ratio indicates strong financial position of the enterprise as any possible business downturn could be dealt with comfortably. Second, a debt incurs a fixed interest cost to be paid from the earnings every year. In case of lower return of capital and assets resulting in lower profitability, the creditors eat into the share of equity shareholders' profits., i.e., dividends are often reduced or omitted when times are bad so as to continue the payment of interest to creditors.

Discounted Cash Flow: Discounted cash flow (DCF) is the most commonly used valuation method for calculating the intrinsic value of an enterprise. In DCF, the estimated future cash inflow and outflow from the business are taken into consideration, and the net cash flow are discounted using net present value calculations and an appropriate discount rate. As any other tool, DCF also has its disadvantages. It is only as good as the estimates and the assumptions used. As an investor, one would do well by using realistic and conservative estimates while using DCF.

Earnings before Interest and Tax: Earnings before interest and tax (EBIT) is used while comparing firms with different capital structures and tax outgo. The advantage of using EBIT instead of profit before tax (PBT) or profit after tax (PAT) is that it helps in a better understanding of the operational efficiency of an enterprise and its place within an industry. Also, in spite of the fact that interest costs and tax outgo are real cash expenses incurred in running the enterprise, they prevent an investor from developing a better understanding of how well the operations are carried out by the company as compared to its rivals. In effect, even though it does not serve as an indicator of cash earning and power of a firm, it is a useful tool to make comparative analysis of companies within an industry.

Earnings Per Share: As the name suggests, earnings per share (EPS) is the total profit divided by the total number of shares outstanding. It serves as a quick indicator of a company's profit accruing to equity holders.

Economic Moat: Economic moat denotes the competitive advantage enjoyed by an incumbent enterprise in its line of operations over any new entrants, who can turn out to be competitors. The economic moat can result from any of the following: having a well-known brand occupying a favorable place in consumers' mind, regulations acting as a barrier against the entry of new competitors, pricing power from low-cost structure, advantage of scale, etc.

Efficient Market Theory: Efficient market theory states that existing share prices always incorporate and reflect all the relevant information making it impossible to beat the market consistently. As per the theory stocks always trade around their fair value, making it impossible for investors to purchase undervalued stocks. However, it is rightly pointed out that 'experience is what happens when you are looking for something else'. Experience teaches us that efficient market theory does not work especially in the short run due to irrational investor behavior.

Enterprise Value: Just as market capitalization maps the current market value of the equity portion of an enterprise, the enterprise value is used to map the overall value of the enterprise. It is calculated by adding debt to market capitalization and subtracting excess cash and cash equivalents. Generally, while comparing companies, market capitalization is used more often but sometimes, when one company has large amounts of debt and the other is a debt-free company, it can turn out to be very misleading. At such times, enterprise value is a better guide.

FERA Companies: The Foreign Exchange Regulation Act (FERA) was enacted in 1970s and all foreign companies operating in India were asked to either list their shares on the Indian bourses or quit India. Some companies like Hindustan Lever, Nestle, Colgate obliged but others like Coca Cola quit. Indian shareholders for the first time had an opportunity to invest in the foreign companies. This was the beginning of a new era in equity investing in India, and all these companies, which got listed, were known as FERA companies. They soon became the stock market favorites and mostly all of them commanded high PEs.

Fixed-Income Securities: Fixed-income securities, as the name suggests are securities that provide periodic fixed returns in the form of interest income and the eventual return of principal upon maturity. In light of predictable fixed cash inflow and outflow from the securities, these are considered much less riskier than equities returns from which are unpredictable. However, safety comes at a cost, as the real returns are not attractive in the long run when inflation is taken into account. An example of fixed-income securities is Public Provident Funds, generally known as PPF.

Fundamental Analyst: A fundamental analyst is somebody who uses the trend of earnings, strength of the balance sheet, and future estimates of potential earnings while making an investment decision. The whole process is classified as fundamental analysis.

Gross Domestic Product: The Gross Domestic Product (GDP) is defined as the market value of the total output produced within the country in any given year. The main variables that have an impact on the GDP are consumption, investments, fiscal expenditure, and net exports by the country. A related but less-known figure is Gross National Product (GNP), which takes into consideration also the market value of the goods produced by domestic companies outside the national boundary.

Growth Trap: Growth trap is defined well by Benjamin Graham in the following quote: 'Obvious prospects for growth do not translate into obvious profits for investors.' An investment decision should not only take into consideration the hot initial growth of a company but also factors like how much growth is already expected by the market participants as is reflected in the market price and how much capital would be required to achieve that growth. Many a times, the high expectations of investing community from a company or an industry renders the growth meaningless and sometimes the businesses require continuous capital outlays to register growth resulting in sub-optimal use of capital. This leads to investors getting into the growth trap.

Index Funds: Index funds are mutual funds, whose portfolio is constructed to track the components of the underlying market index, such as the Sensex or Nifty. An index mutual fund provides broad market exposure, low operating expense, and low portfolio turnover. This form of investing is often referred to as 'Passive Investing.'

Inflation: Inflation is defined as the increase in the general level of prices of goods and services over the corresponding period of the last calendar year. As inflation rises, the availability of goods or services which can be bought by a unit of currency diminishes.

Initial Public Offering: Initial public offering (IPO) is the first sale of stock by a private company to the public. IPOs are often issued by smaller, younger companies seeking capital to expand, but can also be done by large privately owned companies looking forward to become publicly traded.

Intrinsic Value: Intrinsic value of a company is the value of the cash that can be taken out of a business discounted at an appropriate rate. This method of estimating an intrinsic value requires a good understanding of the forces behind the profitability of an enterprise and sustainability of those forces to produce future cash earnings.

Investment Banker: Investment banker is a financial intermediary who performs a variety of services like managing IPOs, underwriting IPOs, advising on mergers and acquisitions, facilitating corporate financing, acting as an intermediary between an issuer of securities and the investing public, etc.

Laggards: Laggards denote stocks, which have under performed in the broader market considerably. They can also be used interchangeably with out-of-favor stocks. Laggards are subjected to all around negative bias toward them.

Law of the Farm: 'Law of the farm' denotes a universal principle saying that you cannot sow a seed today and reap tomorrow. It takes time for a seed to grow in to a tree. It has to go through different seasons. There is no way that we can have a tree yield wonderful results instantly. So is the case with investments. You just cannot hope to make a fast buck by investing. During bubbles, most of the people try to do that in the hope of making fortunes. Look at the successful investors around you. They are successful because they could delay gratification and understood the law of the farm.

Nifty: Nifty comprises of 50 largest market capitalized companies listed on the National Stock Exchange of India representing various sectors of economy.

Paper Gain (or) Loss: The stock prices change everyday. Based on those changes, any day an investor can calculate his paper gain or loss. However, just because today's price makes an investment show a paper gain or loss has nothing to do with the validity of the investment decision made. It only highlights the vagaries of stock market. So if the value remains intact and the recent drop in stock price has only widened the margin of safety, one should not panic at seeing a paper loss but rather should consider whether the investment opportunity has become more attractive. The habit of using stock prices to our advantage rather than becoming a slave to it by letting it influence us is one of the most important requisites for investing wisely.

Price-to-Book Value Ratio: Price-to-book value ratio (P/B) is a financial ratio most commonly used as a quick indicator of the attractiveness of an investment opportunity. Just as a low price-to-earnings ratio is indicative of a potential bargain stock, a low price-to-book value is also indicative of a potential bargain stock. However, as with most other ratios, it must be remembered that this ratio varies across industries based on the return on the capital and equity that the industry has earned in the recent past and is reasonably expected to earn in the near future.

Price-to-Earnings Ratio: Price-to-earnings ratio (P/E) is the most commonly used financial ratio. It is used as a quick indicator of any investment opportunity's attractiveness. It is the price one is paying in relation to its earnings. If the earnings are Rs. 2 per share and the stock is trading at Rs. 20, the P/E is 10.

Public Sector Units: Public sector units are enterprises that are owned by the government. They are a product of socialism. The motive behind setting up public sector units was to ensure that the interest of the customers, i.e., citizens of the country at large, would be put ahead of the motive of earning a profit from the business. A recent example that truly highlights this is the case wherein oil marketing companies had to absorb the sudden and immense price hike in a basic commodity like oil to ensure that end customer does not get adversely affected.

Replacement Cost: Replacement cost is the cost that will have to be incurred to replace an existing asset with a similar asset. In high inflationary conditions, replacement costs play a dominant role in the valuation of equities.

Return on Capital Employed: Return on capital employed is one of the most important financial ratios with important implications for investors and managements alike. It is calculated by dividing the EBIT by total capital employed in the business (market capitalization plus debt minus excess cash). A large return indicates efficient use of capital deployed in the business by the management and a low capital indicates inefficient use of capital invested in the business operations. A business that is capable of earning above 20% return on capital employed is always a much better business than a business earnings 10% return on capital employed. And one of the most important roles of the management is to ensure that the return on capital employed stays handsome. As an investor, however, valuation at which such businesses are available can change the equation drastically. This is where having the ability to combine the qualitative factors with quantitative factors plays a huge role in making wise investment decisions.

Risk–Reward Ratio: Any investment made entails exposure to a risk component. In contrast, it also offers a reward in the form of interest payment or capital appreciation in the future. One must weigh the risk–reward ratio when making investment decisions. The idea is to acquire an asset with a well–balanced risk–reward ratio. In extremely bullish times if one pays 80 times the earnings for a stock, then one is buying more risk rather than reward. The risk-reward ratio is in that case against the investor.

Sensex: Sensex constitutes a group of largest capitalized 30 companies listed on the Bombay Stock Exchange representing the important sectors of the economy.

Technical Analysis: Technical analysis is the act of comparing current price and volume patterns to the price and volume pattern from the past. It deals with the demand–supply of a particular stock and its effect on stock prices.

Tulip Mania: Tulip mania is one of the earliest known market bubbles in the financial history. It dates back to early 1600s when speculation drove the value of Tulip bulbs, a flower famous for its aesthetic values, to extremes in Holland. At the height of the market, the rarest Tulip bulbs traded for as much as six times the average person's annual salary. Like any bubble, it all came to an end in 1637, when prices dropped and panic selling began. Bulbs were soon trading at a fraction of what they once had, leaving many people financially ruined.

Venture Capitalist: Venture capitalists are those who are in the business of investing in the start-up companies. As the name suggests, the very nature of venture capitalism is such that capitalists provide capital to get the venture started and reach a decent size. The risk of the venture failing is high, but so is the reward when the venture works out well.

INDEX

Author's Profile

Parag Parikh, an alumnus of Harvard Business School, has over 25 years of experience in the financial sector. In particular, he is a keen observer, proponent and pioneer in the field of behavioral finance in India. He provides coaching and consulting services to investors, businesses and students.

Parag Parikh is the founder and chairman of Parag Parikh Financial Advisory Services Ltd.(PPFAS) (www.ppfas.com) which is committed to assisting investors in following the time-tested long-term value investing strategies. PPFAS firmly believes that it is in a profession rather than a business and hence treats the interests of the investors to be of paramount importance.

Parag has an insightful knowledge of the workings of the stock market, an analytical eye and an informed outlook. He is a believer in Alvin Toffler's saying: 'Doing the right thing, rather than doing things right.' In an industry where the race is to get bigger and better, his firm's philosophy is clearly that 'slow and steady wins the race.' Parag's abiding passion is to make the financial markets a better and a safer place for investors by helping them direct their focus towards achieving their investing and financial goals, and not be carried away by the noise of the markets.

He is a regular columnist with *The Times of India,* and a guest columnist with *The Economic Times, Business Standard, DNA, Financial*

Express, among other business journals. His views on the financial markets are actively sought by television channels like *Times Now, NDTV Profit, Doordarshan* and *CNBC.*

Parag has also authored a widely acclaimed best seller *Stocks to Riches: Insights on Investor Behaviour* (2005), which is currently in its sixth reprint two years since the first publication.

Parag believes in self-renewal and mental and physical challenges in that he is an avid reader, swimmer, golfer and practitioner of *Vipassana* meditation. He stays in Mumbai with his family, and is fond of travelling, especially to find inspiration for his books and columns.

He can be reached via his blog on www.ppfas.com and email pparikh@ppfas.com.